MEDIA INSTITUTIONS AND AUDIENCES

Also by Nick Lacey

*Image and Representation**

*Narrative and Genre**

Blade Runner

Film as Product in Contemporary Hollywood (with Roy Stafford)

Seven

*Also published by Palgrave

MEDIA INSTITUTIONS AND AUDIENCES

Key Concepts in Media Studies

Nick Lacey

palgrave

First published 2002 by
PALGRAVE
Houndmills, Basingstoke, Hampshire RG21 6XS and
175 Fifth Avenue, New York, N.Y. 10010
Companies and representatives throughout the world

PALGRAVE is the new global academic imprint of
St. Martin's Press LLC Scholarly and Reference Division and
Palgrave Publishers Ltd (formerly Macmillan Press Ltd).

ISBN 0–333–65869–8 hardback
ISBN 0–333–65870–1 paperback

This book is printed on paper suitable for recycling and
made from fully managed and sustained forest sources.

A catalogue record for this book is available
from the British Library.

Library of Congress Cataloging-in-Publication Data
Lacey, Nick, 1961–
    Media institutions and audiences : key concepts in media studies / Nick Lacey.
        p.   cm.
    Includes bibliographical references and index.
    ISBN 0–333–65869–8 (cloth)
    1. Mass media.   2. Mass media—Audiences.   I. Title.

P91.L294 2002
302.23—dc21

                                                    2001053168

10   9   8   7   6   5   4   3   2   1
11   10   09   08   07   06   05   04   03   02

Printed in China

*For my mum
and in memory of my dad*

CONTENTS

ACKNOWLEDGEMENTS

Thanks to Ian Bangay, Kirstie Barnes, Brian Bicât, John Cresswell, J. Digby, Bruce Friedrich, Fiona Gallagher, Catherine Gray, Michael Greenwell, Sue Griffen, Howard Hopkins, John de Mierre, Sue Mitchell, Heidi Morris, Valery Rose, Roy Stafford, Chris Stephens, Jocelyn Stockley, Martin Wainwright and the charismatic Anita Rao-Keech; and to those anonymous individuals who bought the first two books in the series.

The author and publishers would like to thank the following for permission to use copyright material:

The Audit Bureau of Circulations Ltd (ABC) for data appearing in Table 1.2; CIA Media Lab for 'penetration'figures appearing in Table 4.1; Litchfield Morris, Gloucester, for the Motorhome advertisement; Mandy McGarvey at Mixmag for the front cover of *Mixmag*, January 1998; Bruce Friedrich at Peta for the Peta advertisements; Rex Features Limited for the images of Puff Daddy, Xena and ER and Image Select International for researching these; Fiona Gallagher at Sun UK for the Sun Microsystems advertisement.

Every effort has been made to trace all the copyright holders but if any have been inadvertantly overlooked, the publishers will be pleased to make the necessary arrangements at the first opportunity.

SERIES PREFACE

In course planning, 'common sense' often leads to teaching about one medium at a time . . . placing emphasis solely on the characteristics of only one set of practices . . . [which] ignores the fact that all individuals experience media as a set of interrelated and interacting systems.

(Bowker, 1991, p. 5)

The structure of the series of books

The British Film Institute report *Primary Media Education: Curriculum Statement* 'proposed six areas of knowledge and understanding as the basis for . . . curriculum development' (ibid.):

WHO is communicating, and why? WHAT TYPE of text is it? HOW is it produced? HOW do we know what it means? WHO receives it, and what sense do they make of it? HOW does it PRESENT its subject?   (ibid., p. 6)

These 'signpost questions' lead to the following key concepts:

  (i)   media agencies;
 (ii)   media categories;
(iii)   media technologies;
 (iv)   media languages;
  (v)   media audiences;
 (vi)   media representations.

These key concepts inform the structure of this book, and of two others (*Image and Representation*, published in 1998, and *Narrative and Genre*, 2000) on advanced Media Studies. By concentrating on these approaches to the subject I hope to give students the basic skills they require for post-16 education, whether in their final years at school/ college or in the first year of Media Studies degrees at undergraduate level. It is intended that the books be used as a back-up to teacher/ lecturer input.

There is an artificiality in splitting these concepts, for without technology there would be no media; without language we would not understand representation, and so on. However, for pedagogical purposes the categories are very useful.

The adaptation I have made follows the emphasis given by current specifications, but as it is dealing with key concepts of the subject, this book should be relevant to any future media specifications that I can imagine. The adaptation is as follows:

(1) Media Agencies – Media Institutions
(2) Media Categories – Genre
(3) Media Technologies – has a separate chapter in *Image and Representation* but is integrated into other chapters in this volume
(4) Media Languages – Image Analysis and Narrative
(5) Media Audiences – Audiences
(6) Media Representations – Representations

I have paired the adapted concepts to illustrate clearly the interconnectedness of the categories without attempting to encompass the massive intellectual field of the subject in a single book.

The structure of the book

Many students in post-16 education come to Media Studies with little or no previous experience of the subject. Although there is a plethora of books available, most of them are too academic for those who are still at school and some are too complex even for those who are doing a degree course. This book attempts to bridge this gap by offering a comprehensible entry level for those who are just 16, without patronising the undergraduate.

The subject matter of Media Studies is the artefacts that influence us every day of our lives: advertising, movies, videotapes, DVDs, CDs, the Internet and so on. It investigates how the media operate, what are their rules, conventions and ideological purpose, and what are the artefacts' meaning for us in the early years of the twenty-first century.

INTRODUCTION

It is a truism that Media Studies books are out of date before they even get into print; however, what the key concepts describe develops at different rates. Representation is a relatively dynamic concept in that sign systems are constantly evolving in relation to a changing social reality. Media language and genre also change, though a lot more sedately than re-presentations of reality. For example, Todorov's and Propp's narrative theories do not change; narratives evolve basically in the way they are told.

Audiences change slowly, as people grow older; each generation has its own particular way of making meanings in the world. Institutions, however, particularly in the late twentieth and early twenty-first centuries, are moving almost as fast as the electrical impulses that govern the postmodern age. This book, therefore, offers a snapshot of a particular generation (mine – born sometime in the 1960s) at a particular moment, and a freeze frame of where institutions are at, in the first years of the twenty-first century.

Another difficulty in dealing with Media Institutions and Audiences is that they are interdependent. While all the key concepts overlap in some way (genres have typical narratives; media language is necessary to communicate representation), the process of pulling institutions and audiences apart, for theoretical purposes, spills much blood. For example, for Public Service Broadcasting the institutional definition is dealt with in Chapter 2, while how audiences are conceived as being citizens is to be found in Chapter 8. For censorship, Chapter 2 looks at the regulatory framework; Chapter 6 focuses on the 'effects' debate and considers how pro-censorship groups understand audience consumption of media texts. The effect of this closeness of the concepts is that there is some repetition, the function of which is to show how the concepts are directly linked.

Media Institutions is probably the driest of the key concepts. It focuses on the organisations that produce, and the processes used in the production of, media texts; as well as dealing with the regulatory framework within which they operate.

Chapter 1 focuses on how media organisations operate as businesses. The 'bottom line' of profit/loss is the driving force of a capitalist economy and thus has an immense influence on how media texts are presented to audiences. It is crucial that students understand how the business ethic is fundamental to the creation of most texts.

Chapter 2 then considers the regulation and censorship of the media. To an extent these operate in opposition to businesses, as a totally 'free market economy' would have no regulations. However, all businesses operate in a regulatory framework (albeit one that is becoming increasingly loose), hence it is important that these influences upon texts are understood. At the most basic level it can refer to the degree of 'violence' we can expect in a film certified for teenagers; however, it also refers to 'unseen' regulations that can lead to news stories being unofficially censored.

Chapter 3 picks up, to an extent, on the details of Chapter 1. This time it is the texts themselves that are focused on rather than the organisations producing them. The aim is to help students identify the influence the commodification of texts can have. Chapter 4 considers how marketing and public relations are factors in the production of media texts, and looks at advertising itself as media texts.

Chapter 5 attempts to conceptualise different ways of creating texts: the commodification of the mainstream is set in opposition to those alternative texts that try to question the dominant notion of the 'media as business'.

The final three chapters focus on audiences. Chapter 6 offers an in-depth examination of the basic approaches to understanding audiences. This is followed by how media businesses define audiences, who are commodified in order to be sold to advertisers. Chapter 8 looks at the tensions inherent in treating audiences as commodities, to be bought and sold, in a democratic society that is meant to treat its members as citizens.

It is clear from this summary that business dominates this book, but that is true of all western societies. Indeed, this book itself is designed to make money for the author (and potentially improve his career prospects – 'Show me the money!') and the publishers.

Although 'Nick Lacey' is the addresser, he is not a media organisation. Palgrave, the publishers, also 'appear' in the text.

■ Exercise I.1 ■

Analyse Palgrave's logo.

palgrave

Figure I.1   Palgrave's logo

The typeface is elegant with the 'classy' dropping of the upper-case first letter. The word itself is unusual, clearly a name, possibly connoting seriousness, '... grave'. The logo is star-like, reaching out (to the reader?). Your reading may be very different from this but, if you can justify it from the text, is as valid as mine. The designers suggested that:

> The symbol reflects the idea of expanding networks – linking all those in the active pursuit of ideas, learning and scholarship. The corporate typeface Bliss has been chosen to express the modern and forward-looking character of the new company.

The logo is not quite Palgrave's only appearance in this text. All books have a page near the front listing legal details of publication; this is the copyright page. Here Palgrave are asserting their, and my, right over the intellectual property that this book represents. So, unless you are operating within the Copyright Licensing Agency's guidelines, do not photocopy this book! Clearly that is something that is difficult to police, just as is pirating your friends' CDs. Until recently it was illegal to copy anything onto tape (audio or audio-visual), now you are allowed to copy your own albums and from your own television for your own use.

No doubt this is massively abused across the world. Piracy in a number of Far Eastern countries operates on a semi-official basis and few people have much sympathy for the multinational corporations that lose most as a result. The Internet has caused further headaches, particularly the MP3 format, which allows easy exchange of music via the Web. However, it should be made clear that it is not simply the large capitalist corporations who lose out. Artists are usually paid on a royalty basis and so also lose money. I receive between 10% and 12.5% of the revenue the book generates for Palgrave; approximately £1 for each paperback sold in Britain, less for the North American edition.

Such institutional information can be useful though it is doubtful whether the fact that Palgrave published this book persuaded anyone to buy. Certainly publishers do have reputations for having quality book lists but this is probably more important for higher education texts. Much of the publisher's input is not immediately apparent, but before a book appears the following must happen:

- it must be commissioned to be written by someone who apparently knows what they are doing;
- it must fit into the company's portfolio as there is little point in publishing books in a market where they have little presence (or expertise); publishing a number of books in the same sector helps reduce marketing costs;
- once the typescript is delivered, readers are commissioned to comment on it;
- the editor must make a decision about whether it should be published and/or what changes should be made;
- the author gets it back to rework in the light of the comments;
- the copy-editors painstakingly comb the text for spelling and punctuation errors as well as making sure all the references make sense, and also decide how it should be formatted;
- picture researchers try to find images the author requests, and the copyright holders often have to be paid;
- the final typescript must be typeset, and then read again by a proof reader, before it can be printed;
- the marketing department will decide how to promote the text, and will publish flyers or advertisements.

Why does Palgrave do this? Basically for profit though it is important also to have a presence in particular market places in order to maintain, or create, a reputation in certain fields.

■ Exercise I.2 ■

Analyse this book's cover.

We are warned from an early age not to judge books by their covers as a metaphor suggesting we should not take things in life at face value. However, a book's cover does not offer information in isolation: there can be no doubt that this is a Media Studies text-book because it is anchored by the subtitle.

The typeface of the title, and subtitle, is straightforward (sans serif) yet stylish suggesting the book delivers what the titles promise in a no-nonsense fashion and yet with panache. The typeface used for the author's name, however, is more flowery, connoting old-fashioned writing, and suggesting the author is rather flamboyant (particularly the loop on the 'L') and rather traditional. This connotes authority as he is confident in his abilities and has 'been around for a while' (the author wishes it to be noted that he doesn't like the way his name appears on the book but his editor never listens to him; just joking Catherine!).

As this is the third in the series of books, it is no surprise that the design is the same as the others; though the colour and images change. The pinkish tint to the picture gives the image an old-fashioned look, something reinforced by the girl's clothing. Her dad (the most likely relationship between the two) looks a bit like Bill Murray, an impression strengthened by his smile. The framing and focus isolates the pair in an audience and they appear to be sharing a pleasurable moment. The entertainment is likely to have been provided by a 3D film, hence the glasses. This, too, suggests it is old-fashioned, as 3D's cinematic hey-day was in the 1950s. However, in recent years, large format cinema (such as IMAX) has introduced 3D. The era of the photograph is ultimately unclear.

The spectacles help disguise the individuals in the audience; dark glasses are often used to hide identity. This, along with the word 'institutions', suggests a degree of dehumanisation. Institutions can determine an individual's role to a great degree. The spectacles are meant to represent media institutions affecting an audience however, the dad's smile alleviates any sense of threat; it looks like fun.

I hope that when you have read this book from cover to cover, that any blindness you may have, as a member of audiences, regarding the influence of media institutions upon your media texts, has been at least partially lifted. However, in amongst the analysis 'fun' must not be forgotten. Enjoy.

1

THE MEDIA BUSINESS

AIMS OF THE CHAPTER

➤ To see how films have been commodified by Hollywood.

➤ To investigate how synergy is the driving force of many media businesses.

➤ To look at the structure of Viacom as an example of a synergistic company.

➤ To look at how broadcasting and newspapers operate as businesses.

➤ To examine the growth of News Corporation.

➤ To investigate how the Internet has prompted convergence of media.

1.1 Introduction

Media businesses are the organisations that produce media texts. Media businesses are not, in themselves, necessarily institutions; but the way the organisation operates, and the processes by which texts are produced, are probably 'institutionalised' – that is, they work in set ways. For instance, journalists usually structure their reports around a particular series of questions: the 'who?', 'what?', 'when?', 'where?', 'why?' and 'how?' of the event. Similarly, while we can consider the individual businesses that make up Hollywood, Hollywood itself is an institution because it describes the way in which films are made by all these businesses. This chapter focuses on the dynamics of business and assesses how this influences both the way texts are produced and the contents of those texts.

In the last years of the twentieth century old ways of doing business were under threat from rapid changes, mostly motivated by the Internet. Jane Stokes, in the opening chapter of *The Media in Britain* (1999), suggested the key themes of media industries were:

1. concentration of ownership,
2. globalization, and
3. the impact of new technologies.

(Stokes and Reading, 1999, p. 4)

A mere one year later there had been a seismic shift: all the above points were still important, but the impact of new technologies – specifically the growth of the Internet and ways of accessing it – dominated the business landscape. Before considering Net-related issues we shall look at how media businesses operated in the twentieth century, considering, separately, the industries of film, broadcasting and newspapers (music, magazine and book publishing are also important industries but constraints of space mean they cannot be dealt with here). However, there is obviously a great deal of overlap in these industries as many media organisations aim to own a portfolio of companies under the banner of what can loosely be called the entertainment industry. For example, News Corporation owns 20th Century Fox, which produces films and television pro-grammes, as well as owning satellite television broadcasters, book publishers and numerous news organisations. We shall see that, at least since the 1980s, media companies have tended to dispense with non-core businesses in order to focus on the production of media texts.

Media businesses are responsible for an increasing proportion of the Gross National Product in Britain. In 1999 publishing generated £18.5bn of revenue, employed 141,000 people and achieved £1.7bn of exports; TV and radio had £12.1bn of revenue, employed 102,000 and had £440m of exports; and the music industry's figures were £4.6bn, 122,000 and £1.3bn respectively (source: Wells, 2001, p. 7). The entertainment industry is big business.

1.2 Hollywood: a business history

The first new mass medium of the twentieth century was cinema; an industry that began in a rather haphazard way as entrepreneurs exploited what was thought to be merely a 'novelty act'. However, the industry that was to dominate the film world eventually developed in Hollywood during the 1910s.

The 1920s through to the late 1940s is often characterised as the Golden Age of Hollywood, when the major studios generated revenue at every level of the 'cinematic apparatus'. Cinema requires:

1. films to be produced,
2. then to be distributed to
3. cinemas, which exhibit them.

One of the main problems film producers had, and still have, is getting their films distributed to cinemas. It has been estimated that of the 4,000 films produced in North America every year, 3,000 go unreleased in cinemas (Stables, 2000). The best way to guarantee exhibition is to produce, distribute and exhibit your own films; companies that can do this are 'vertically integrated'.

During the 1920s the American film industry consolidated itself with a series of mergers and takeovers that left four vertically integrated companies, which were known as the Majors. These were: Fox (merged with 20th Century in 1935, to be known as 20th Century Fox), MGM (then known as Loews, Inc.), Paramount, and Warner Bros.

Although capitalism is supposedly built upon the idea that competition between companies leads to the availability of the best products at the cheapest prices, the practice of the theory is often somewhat different. The history of American capitalism can best be characterised as companies forming cartels and acting as an oligopoly. In other words, the Majors did not compete with one another to any great degree and each was happy with its market share of the audience. They differentiated their product, so that during the 1930s, Warners was famous for its gangster movies, RKO its musicals and Universal its horror movies. In effect, the major companies were acting like a monopoly but because they were more than one company, they formed an oligopoly (two companies would be a duopoly). When supposedly competing companies act together they are forming a cartel. Cartels are usually outlawed because they are anti-competitive, but it is difficult to prove that companies are acting in such a manner.

Like many other industries, films in North America were made using 'production line' techniques; the Hollywood of the Golden Age was dubbed a 'dream *factory*'. However, filmmakers could still make their own creative mark on production. Indeed, Paul Kerr (1979) has shown how the extremely restrictive constraints of making B-movies during the 1940s had an immensely beneficial influence on the development of *film noir*.

Once an oligopoly has been formed it becomes very expensive for a new company to enter that market; in other words, the barriers to entry are very high. In the late 1920s RKO became the fifth, and smallest, major film company, with the help of capital from RCA (a big radio company).

Despite this industry 'stitch up', cinema was not a very profitable business. An estimated return of 2 per cent on investment is poor (Maltby, 1995, p. 60). However, the Majors were able to generate Wall Street investment capital to pay for the expensive switch to sound at the end of the 1920s by mortgaging their valuable real estate, that is, their cinemas. When the Depression struck in the 1930s, Wall Street called in its loans and basically took over the major studios.

In 1938 the Department of Justice's Antitrust Division filed the Paramount decrees; these led to the major studios being ordered to sell their cinemas because they were operating in a non-competitive fashion. These decrees did not take effect until 1948, and it was not until the 1950s that they were – more or less – fulfilled (Conant, 1976). The effect of this forced divestiture of cinemas, combined with a massive decline in audiences in the post-war period, led to a crisis in Hollywood.

The decline of the film business continued during the 1960s and by the 1970s the Majors were surviving only as part of large conglomerates. Paramount, for example, was part of Gulf + Western Inc., which included the New Jersey Zinc Co., La Romana Sugar Mill and Collyer Insulated Wire as well as media companies such as the publishers Simon & Schuster, and Famous Music Corp.

By the 1980s deregulation was in full swing as the right-wing policies of President Ronald Reagan reduced pro-competition measures and, in effect, reversed the Paramount decrees. Business practices then switched back to vertical integration, except that companies were no longer solely involved in film, they were now part of the 'leisure business'. Douglas Gomery (1998) demonstrated how Steven J. Ross turned Warner Communications into a

> diversified entertainment conglomerate involved in a wide range of 'leisure time' businesses such as film and television, recorded music, book publishing, cable communications, toys and electronic games, and other operations. (Gomery, 1998, p. 62)

The business logic behind this movement was synergy, that is the ability of various parts of an organisation to cross-promote each other as well as generating value that is greater than the sum of its parts;

this is investigated in section 1.4. The next section looks at the current state of Hollywood.

1.3 Contemporary Hollywood: the high concept

Making money from the cinematic release of films is exceptionally difficult. James Shamus (1998) described the breakdown of revenue between the exhibitor, distributor and producer. Exhibitors like to retain their weekly box-office take until they have covered their overheads, or their weekly 'nut'. After that, assuming the film does at least moderately well, a major distributor will receive 50% of the remaining gross; independent distributors, through lack of corporate muscle, will receive only 35–45%, which is known as 'rentals'.

The distributor will retain a 'top-off' fee of around 30% and the print and advertising ('p and a') costs also need to be deducted. What is left remains as profit for the producer – assuming there is anything left. Shamus uses the example of a 'wildly successful' independent film that grossed $10 million but cost only $1 million to make. The producer is left with a 'profit' of *minus* $333,000.

Making a profit is not only difficult for the independent sector, considered in Chapter 5; the Majors themselves rely upon a handful of releases to make film distribution viable. In 1999, 17 films broke the $100 million barrier in North American box-office gross receipts. These accounted for 40% of the total revenue. The other 60% was spread across 327 films at an average of only $14 million each. Given that the average cost of producing and marketing a Hollywood film stood at $76 million that year (including $25 million 'p and a', which was up to $27.3m in 2000), the economics obviously do not add up for most films. Even if we focus upon the major studios, which are likely to be more successful, their 145 releases yielded only an average movie gross of $51 million (source: *Screen International*, January 7, 2000). And this yield does not take into account what the 'middle people' of exhibition and distribution take out, although these are often members of the same organisation that produced the film. (It should be noted that the figures quoted for the purchase of advertising are based on the 'value of the ads bought' (Goodrige and Frater, 2001, p. 1); however, it is unlikely that all – or even the majority of ads – were purchased at full price.)

Making movies for distribution only in the cinema is not, and never has been, a particularly profitable venture. The fact that the major studios do not go bankrupt every year is due to the international box office, the various platforms for distribution and the ancillaries.

In any one year there are up to twenty or so films making $100 million plus (in the North American, including Canadian, market) that make the distribution of films to cinemas at all profitable. These effectively subsidise the vast majority that perform adequately or poorly at the box office. This is not to say that individual movies may not be immensely profitable under the $100 million box-office mark or that those above it will not lose money. However, the major studios have what is, in investment terms, a portfolio of movies and they expect their 'blue chip' blockbuster investments to offset any losses in the medium budget range. These cheaper movies are produced in the hope of a 'surprise' hit that will be very profitable (for example, the phenomenally successful *The Sixth Sense*, 1999, cost approximately $40 million).

In 1975 *Jaws* changed the economic landscape of Hollywood cinema and the high-concept film has dominated much of the world's box office since. Now, the 'main [economic] event' in cinema is the summer box-office season. In 2000, *Screen International* listed 28 potential blockbusters, of which only eleven went on to break $100 million at the North American box office, and most of these movies can be characterised as being high concept.

Justin Wyatt (1994) has offered an excellent definition of the High Concept and this is described below with examples – the headings are derived from Richard Maltby's investigation of Wyatt's ideas (Maltby, 1998, p. 38).

1. A style of 'post-generic' filmmaking based on the simplification of character and narrative

'Post-generic' filmmaking uses numerous genres in one text. For example, *The Faculty* (1999) was a youth picture, horror movie and science fiction. *Narrative and Genre* (chapter 5) considered how action-adventure narratives usually consist of super-genre (another way of describing post-generic) films, movies that draw upon generic conventions but do not articulate the myths associated with that genre. The genres a movie is based on are simply a framework on which to hang special effects and through which to appeal to the widest possible audience. The mixture of genres makes it easier for studios to market the film; we will consider this in Chapter 4.

Similarly, neither character nor narrative complexity is required. The 'event' movie is like a theme-park ride, the sensations physically experienced are more important than any ideas that the film may be articulating. Simple characters and narratives do not demand much thought from audiences and so can be more readily enjoyed.

Paul Verhoeven's (it has his finger prints) casting of *Starship Troopers* (1997) uses actors from US teen TV: Casper van Dien, Dina Meyer and Denise Richards. Their characterisation is so flimsy that 'two-dimensional' overstates the case; Richards, in particular, is unable to summon more than two emotions: one signed by a smile, the other by a frown. This is not simply to denigrate the actors' abilities (Richards was good in *Wild Things*, 1998) as Verhoeven is satirising their 'good' looks (Aryan in van Dien's case) by having the characters live in an authoritarian society. He is suggesting that the emphasis on beauty is fascist in nature. The characters originate from Buenos Aires and go by the names of Rico, Flores and Carmen Ibanez (following Robert Heinlein's source novel), making you wonder what has happened to *Latin* America: has the whole world become WASP? The wonderfully over-the-top newsreel/news broadcasts (a reporter gets 'squidged') set the tone for ironic distanciation from the text.

The movie's end occurs when the Gestapo-like Carl Jenkins uses his psychic powers to save Ibanez. He then proclaims, having read the 'Queen bug's' mind, that 'she is afraid' and the massed troops, who are treated like dispensable 'bugs' by their commanding officers, enthusiastically cheer Jenkins' proclamation. Fear is the foundation of the fascist state and the film is clear in its condemnation of militarism. While such satire is rare in the high-concept film, ironic distanciation is not (see point 10).

2. Extended montages, which are in effect pop videos

These are sequences in high-concept films that are designed to appeal to the young 'MTV' audience but are also easily extractable to be used in music videos. Virtually all Hollywood releases have an associated soundtrack that is used both to generate revenue and to promote the film (which in turn markets the soundtrack album). Although these albums can include music written specifically for the film, they are invariably compilation albums featuring popular artists. A number of these are usually released as singles thereby getting airplay on the radio and their videos shown on television. The latter is an exceptionally useful marketing tool.

The music videos will feature scenes from the film as well as the performing artist. Occasionally the two are brought together as in *Austin Powers: The Spy Who Shagged Me* (1999): Madonna sang 'Beautiful

Stranger' on a stage, gyrating 'sexily' while Mike Myers, as Austin Powers, gurned nerdishly in the audience. Thus any time the music video is played the movie is promoted free of charge. This is particularly useful on the BBC, which does not take advertising.

Occasionally regulators deem this mix of music video and film to have gone too far. Ronan Keating's video for 'You Say Nothing At All' not only featured scenes from *Notting Hill* (1999), but included comments praising the film and a character attempting to buy a video of it. Although the Independent Television Commission criticised this music video it took no action against it.

3. Physical design (look) frequently reflects graphic design and layout of contemporary advertising

This point refers to the overall look of the high-concept film, which can probably be best summarised by the word 'glossy'. The surfaces are lit to have an attractive sheen and any night shooting is likely to be punctuated by spectacular blue light. As in point 5, it is more important that the *mise en scène* looks good rather than that it generates meaning.

Much of this derives from British directors who came to Hollywood from advertising; including the Scott brothers (Ridley and Tony) and Adrian Lyne. There is a scene in Ridley Scott's *Thelma and Louise* (1991) where it is raining very heavily and the sun is shining: it looks fantastic but, when you think about it, bizarre as well.

4. Easily replicated in trailers, TV commercials or publicity stills

The origin of the High Concept was TV movies developed at the end of the 1960s by the ABC network in the USA. Owing to the high cost of buying Hollywood films for transmission, producers at ABC started making TV movies, which were much cheaper to broadcast. However, unlike Hollywood films, TV movies are unfamiliar to the audience as they have never been released. The idea behind these movies therefore had to be easily saleable, hence the simplification of genre, character and narrative mentioned in point 1. They needed a 'high concept', 'a movie that any producer could pitch in thirty seconds and any audience could understand without even thinking' (Fleming, 1998, p. 14).

By the early 1970s the emphasis on the importance of *marketing* of the film over the film itself was becoming felt in Hollywood. The idea that films were primarily saleable commodities certainly was not new; however, the High Concept took this commodification to a new extreme. Writing a screenplay in contemporary Hollywood has been likened to preparing a prospectus for an offering on the stock market (Kent, 1991, p. 121).

For easy replication of marketing material, complexity is eschewed and simplification embraced. Inevitably, the surface attraction of material is more important than any depth it might possess. This tendency is also apparent in the next point.

5. Formal excess which simply 'looks good', be it in the lighting or in the acting of the star

The *mise en scène* is important in the making of meaning in film. However, for the high-concept film, meaning is less important than appealing to an audience. Thus 'looking good' predominates over the 'artistic' agenda of expression. For example, in *Blade* (1998), when Blade (Wesley Snipes) gets into a lift the shot cuts from outside the lift to inside in a high-angle 'over the shoulder' position. Although this serves to make the character appear vulnerable this has no basis in the narrative of the sequence. It simply offers something new to look out for while the character moves from one location to another.

In most action-adventure movies the special effects are designed to be as over-the-top as current technology allows. At the climax of *Blade* our hero decapitates the villain, Frost, only to see him reconstitute himself in an amazing welter of blood. Blade is seen to mouth 'what the fuck?!', just as many in the audience will be doing having witnessed yet another eye-popping special effect. The abundance of special effects is one element of entertainment.

6. Music track interrupts narrative

Possibly as a result of the need to create sequences that can be used in publicity material and/or music videos, many high-concept films include passages that are montages with musical accompaniment. This type of sequence is not limited to high-concept films; for example, the 'independent' *Things to Do in Denver When You're Dead* (1996) includes such a sequence.

In *Armaggedon* (1998) the Liv Tyler and Ben Affleck characters make their farewells against a sunset and a silhouetted tree to the strains of Aerosmith. The shot lingers slightly longer than would be necessary for an establishing shot and the song is foregrounded on the soundtrack, momentarily freezing the action in favour of MTV aesthetics. The fact that the singer is Liv Tyler's dad also acts as a self-conscious allusion.

7. Self-conscious allusion to films and TV

■ Exercise 1.1 ■

Watch *Toy Story 2* and pick out as many references as you can.

Your initial response to the above exercise may well have been
'You've got to be kidding!' or even just 'No.' *Toy Story* 2 referenced,
according to the Internet movie database (www.imdb.com), nearly
50 films. There is no point to the above exercise; most of the references are there for 'fun' and no other reason. Many are meaningless,
in terms of *Toy Story* 2, and are merely an example of postmodern
playfulness (see chapter 2 of *Narrative and Genre*). They spark the
pleasure of recognition in the audience and we can congratulate
ourselves on how clever we are to spot the allusion and how knowl-
edgeable we are to know it.

Films also reference computer games; a whole sequence in *Lost in
Space* (1998) features the youngest member of the family Robinson,
Will, helping to combat the alien spiders by controlling a robot by
remote control. He does this as if he is controlling the robot in a
computer game. The spin-off also works the other way: 1999's *Wing
Commander* was based on a computer game and *Tomb Raider* was
successful in 2001.

8. Detached appearance of stars

Face/Off (1997) was, in part, built around the 'detached appearance'
of both John Travolta and Nicolas Cage. The bizarre, and immensely
entertaining, plot required the central characters – played by the
stars – to swap faces so audiences had the prospect of seeing John
Travolta act like Nicolas Cage and vice versa. They each took on
the mannerisms of the other, mannerisms that were not integral to
the character they were playing but part of the standard reper-
toire of acting possessed by each of the stars: hence their 'detached
appearance'.

9. Hyperbolic physiques of protagonists and hyperbolic action

This was particularly true during the 1980s and was epitomised by
Sylvester Stallone's *Rambo* films and Arnold Schwarzenegger as various Terminators. By the time of *Twins* (1988), the Arnie character
could be seen smirking at Stallone's overblown masculinity in a *Rambo*
poster; this film, and *Kindergarten Cop* two years later, were part of

Schwarzenegger's successful attempt to reinvent himself for the family audience.

Stallone, too, attempted to reinvent his macho persona in *Tango and Cash* (1989) but merely substituted one form of masculinity for another. It was not until *Copland* (1996) that Stallone eventually gained critical plaudits in a non-macho role.

The hyperbolic action refers to the special effects that drive many high-concept movies. Films such as *The Perfect Storm* (2000) are wholly built around the narrative idea of an enormous wave and the invitation to 'feel its fury'.

10. Ironic distanciation: walking-talking brand

This was epitomised by Arnie's 'I'll be back' in *The Terminator*. Macho Arnie never gives in, he always returns. This operates in a similar way to point 8 but here the stars offer the pleasures associated with the way they perform, such as Mel Gibson's eye rolling in the *Lethal Weapon* series and Will Smith's concern for his 'threads'. In this way the stars are brands rather than actors playing a particular role.

Not all Hollywood films are high-concept. The above is simply a typology of most studios' 'tent pole' summer releases – movies they hope will make so much money that they will prop up, financially, the whole industry. Hollywood is often derided for merely producing 'eye candy' but it should not be forgotten that the second biggest hit of 1999 was the thoughtful *The Sixth Sense*, and later that year *Fight Club* was released, one of the decade's most startling movies.

The High Concept was developed to help commodify films. The actual production of a film is barely, if at all, profitable. The most profitable area of the film industry is in exhibition, though cinemas make their profits from concessions (soft drinks and pop corn) rather than the actual film.

In order to offset this difficulty in making money from the actual celluloid (which is now being replaced by digitisation), the studios are now part of large corporations that hope to benefit from the advantages of synergy.

1.4 Synergy

Unlike the 1970s, when it seemed that size was all that mattered, the businesses of the 1980s went for consolidation that focused on one industry. In the 1970s it did not matter that the businesses a corporation owned might have nothing to do with one another, they were simply conglomerated; the 1980s saw the rise of the integrated corporation.

The big idea was that each part of the corporation could help the others. For example, New Line's (a subsidiary of Warners) *Austin Powers: The Spy Who Shagged Me* (1999) had a soundtrack that featured Warner's artists including Green Day, Lenny Kravitz, Madonna and REM. Madonna's specially composed single for the film *Beautiful Stranger* (released on her own Maverick records – part of Warners) was not released as a single in North America (in Britain it reached number two), so Americans had to buy the soundtrack album if they wanted the hit single; the album sold 1.3 million copies. The movie made money; the soundtrack album was a success; Warners artists were promoted: synergistic bliss.

As part of this drive toward synergy in the 1980s two Hollywood studios were the subject of takeovers from Japan, Matsushita and Sony bought MCA (Universal studios) and Columbia respectively. The synergistic logic being that the Japanese companies manufactured the hardware (televisions, VCRs and so on) but also needed to produce software (in this case films) to be shown on their equipment. This may seem like control freakery but Sony had lost out in the 'video format' battle of the late 1970s when their (superior) system, Betamax, foundered as consumers chose VHS. VHS won the battle because there were more films available in that format. Sony thus bought Columbia to guarantee a stream of products for whatever format they would manufacture next.

Sony had already purchased CBS records for $2 billion in 1987 and followed this with the $3.4 billion purchase of the studio two years later. Matsushita spent $6.9 billion on MCA in 1990. Both companies struggled to integrate filmmaking into their businesses, probably because they found the culture of the massively extravagant Hollywood, alien. Matsushita gave up in 1995, selling 80 per cent of the business to Seagram for $5.7 billion, but Sony eventually hit 'pay dirt' with several successes in the late 1990s.

The 1989 merger between Warner Communications and Time Inc., forming what was then the world's biggest media company, set the tone for the 1990s. It was believed, and still is, that only massive companies would be able to compete in the global market. This followed News Corporation's takeover of 20th Century Fox in 1985 and Rupert Murdoch's aggressive expansion policy of attempting to make Fox Broadcasting a fourth major television network (see also section 1.8). Later in the 1990s Disney purchased Capital Cities/ABC for $19 billion and Time-Warner consolidated its position as the world's biggest media corporation by buying Turner Broadcasting (for $7.5 billion). In 2001, AOL and Time-Warner merged to form an even bigger company.

Synergy does not, however, always work. From an organisational point of view:

> The commercial prospects of many media conglomerates have proven to pale in light of the excessive debt connected to mergers, the inability to cut overheads or put efficiency plans in action, and the failure of much of the product placed before an oversaturated public.   (Sanjek, 1998, p. 177)

And although, as we shall see in Chapter 3, media artefacts are commodities, the management of artists as if they were a product, in the same way that baked beans are, is not always a success. George Michael, a massive star in the early 1990s, was unhappy with the way he was treated by Sony (after its purchase of Columbia). He refused to make any more records because he felt he was being treated as a commodity and not an artist. He sued Sony and lost; Dreamworks SKG (in America) and Virgin (in Britain) bought out his contract. Michael did not make any albums for a number of years and Sony did not make any money out of one of their top artists.

The case was also interesting as it revealed financial details normally held secret. Michael received 37p for every CD sold (they were retailing at over £10 in Britain at the time), and:

> Michael's gross world-wide royalties, in a five-year period up to December 1992, amounted to £16.89m. Sony's share was £95.5m. Over the same period, his gross profits were £7.35 m while Sony's were £52.45 m. This disparity is justified, by record companies, by the argument that the music business is high risk and most of their musicians lose money. The big stars, in effect, subsidise the lesser ones.   (Smith, 1994, p. 3)

It is an axiom, of the music business at least, that the bigger the corporation, the further it is from the 'street'. And as the 'street' is where youth culture gets its credibility from, this can be commercially disastrous (see Chapter 5). Despite these difficulties, synergy is still seen as the way forward for media companies.

The benefits of synergy are not necessarily only accrued by a single company. The magazine and radio group EMAP joined forces with Channel 4 to exploit their youth-oriented material on the Internet:

The agreement with Channel 4 [is to] build a website combining content from both companies' youth brands, including Dawsons' Creek, Hollyoaks, Smash Hits, Match and J17. The business will make revenues from advertising and sponsorship, and could lead to joint ventures in other areas – including music – where the two companies overlap.   (Teather, 2000, p. 26)

Although making money out of producing films for theatrical distribution is very difficult, there are now many other platforms of distribution. Instead of simply selling the television rights (a way of making money that Hollywood did not exploit until the late 1950s, fearing competition from television), those new media companies that owned a television network could reap all the profits. In addition, the growth of videocassette recorders, followed by cable (particularly in North America) and satellite television (in Britain), and now DVD videos, offered other platforms to distribute films. One company that has successfully integrated many different media is Viacom.

1.5   Viacom

Viacom boasts a large portfolio of entertainment businesses. The information below, derived from Viacom's website (http://www.viacom.com/July 2001), includes many channels, or brands, that are not available in Britain.

Film
Paramount Pictures – feature-film production and worldwide distribution.
Paramount Home Entertainment – distributor of pre-recorded videos.

Television
CBS Television.
CBS Television Stations Division – 35 local TV stations.
Paramount Television – television programmes for broadcast and syndication, including the *Star Trek* series.
UPN (United Paramount Network).
MTV (Music Television) – mainly music aimed at 12- to 34-year-olds.
MTV2 – alternative music videos.
Nickelodeon – children's channel.
Nick at Nite – 'classic TV' or just 'old' TV depending on your viewpoint.
TV Land – cable 'classic' TV network.

Noggin – 'the first ever thinking network for kids' (website).
VH1 – music videos for 25- to 44-year-olds (note the age range is Viacom's own).
TNN – 'tops in pop culture'.
Comedy Central (jointly owned) – comedy programmes.
Showtime – pay-TV movie cable channel.
The Movie Channel – more movies.
Flix – 'golden oldie' movies.
Sundance Channel (jointly owned) – independent films.
Paramount Stations Group – 'the 6th largest family of TV stations in the US' (website).

Radio and outdoor
Infinity – radio broadcasting and outdoor advertising.

Retail
Blockbuster – video, DVD and games rental.
Paramount Parks – five theme parks.
The Famous Players and United Cinemas – international chain with nearly 1700 screens.

Publishing, Online and More
Simon & Schuster – books.
MTVi Group – 'the world's leading Internet music content company' (website).
CBS.com and CBS News.com – portfolio of Internet interests.
Viacom Consumer Products – deals with the licensing of toys, t-shirts and games for Paramount Pictures and television.
Famous Music – music publishers with a catalogue of over 100,000 pieces.

This way Viacom can exploit its *Beavis and Butthead* animation on MTV, release the film on Paramount and sell the computer games through Viacom Consumer Products.

■ Exercise 1.2 ■

Investigate, using the Internet, any large media corporation to see how it can 're-use' products through different divisions. For example, News Corporation, AOL–Time-Warner, Disney or Sony.

We shall see in Chapter 3 how movies are often used to drive the creation of products in numerous media. Clearly companies that cover all media are in a better position to exploit these properties.

1.6   Broadcasting

Most radio stations and television channels are commercially based and generate the bulk of their revenue either by selling advertising time or by subscription. A few are publicly funded; public service broadcasting is dealt with in the next chapter and advertising is considered in Chapter 4.

At the time of writing, television is undergoing major upheaval in the way it operates as a business although at the end of the 1990s it still seemed very healthy financially. In Britain, Channel 3, the ITV Network (made up of a number of companies – currently ten – excluding breakfast television), generated £1.8 billion from advertising in 1998; Channel 4 snaffled £553 million; S4C Wales, £9 million; Channel 5, £142 million. The 200-plus satellite and cable channels shared £2 billion between them from both advertising and subscriptions.

British airtime is one of the costliest in Europe:

> The estimated cost of buying a 30-second slot in the nation's most popular soap opera, *Coronation Street*, stands at a staggering £100,000. This huge sum will deliver coverage of more than 25% of the UK population – some 14 million people.... UK media agency Zenith Media estimates that the average cost of a 30-second peaktime ad on ITV... is £53,000.   (Darns, 2001, p. 11)

To run an advertisement nationally, airtime will have to be purchased from each of the regions, though the £100,000 refers to the total cost. Obviously the more audience a region delivers, the more it can charge.

In 1999, the arrival of digital TV both expanded the market, as more people subscribed to pay TV, and ate into advertising budgets. If advertisers have more channels at their disposal it means each channel is likely to get a smaller share. The amount companies spend on advertising is also extremely sensitive to the economic conditions of the time: when recession hits, advertising, along with jobs, is cut. When times are good – such as the late 1990s – advertising spend increases; 2000, however, saw a rapid slow-down in this growth. The amount of money raised through the sale of advertising depends upon the size and composition of the audience.

One way of measuring the audiences of television stations is by estimating the audience share each has of television watchers (see Table 1.1). It can be seen that ITV's audience, which had – in effect – a monopoly in selling television advertising until the arrival of Channel 4, had declined considerably from the early 1980s in the face of

Table 1.1 Audience share (percentage of total audience)

Year	BBC1	BBC2	ITV	C4	C5	Satellite and cable TV
1981	39	12	49	–	–	–
1990	37	10	44	9	–	–
1995	32	11	37	12	–	9
1999	28.5	10.8	31.2	10.3	5.4	14.0

Source: Broadcasters' Audience Research Board (BARB).

competition, but it was still commercially dominant. The selective nature of the table's dates conceals some variations but gives an impression of how, inevitably, a multi-channelled environment will erode audience share; though, with its niche audience, BBC2 has bucked the trend.

The market share of many cable and satellite channels is so small that it barely registers. However, these can be successful in delivering niche audiences to advertisers. As the audience fragments, advertising revenue for each channel is likely to decrease, although this has not necessarily happened in the past because advertising inflation has far outstripped the retail price index – advertisers have paid more to reach the same number of people. This expansion cannot continue indefinitely.

Channel 3 has been a cash cow, for the ITV companies, for over 40 years but now it has reached a stage where the channel has to be regarded as a 'question mark'. In other words more will be have to be spent on programmes simply in order to maintain the audience market share and so profitability will decline. Whether this extra spend will be worth it in the long term is questionable. In recent years the numerous ITV companies have sought to defend their position by integrating their scheduling, via a network controller, and consolidating – by buying other TV stations.

In 1993, the fifteen ITV franchises, distributed geographically (in regions determined by transmitter reach) and temporally (GMTV's morning slot and LWT's London weekend slot), all (except Tyne Tees) had different owners. By 2000, Granada Media Group controlled Granada Television, LWT, Yorkshire, Tyne Tees, HTV, Anglia and Meridian (though it was due to sell HTV and Meridian); Carlton held the licences for London weekday, the Midlands and the south-west of England.

This consolidation was based on the assumption that in a world with multiple television channels, only large companies can survive.

The bigger the company the more likely it is to benefit from economies of scale, for example only one advertising sales force is needed no matter how big the company. At the time of writing, further consolidation was very likely and it is probable that the ITV Network will be wholly subsumed under one company (best bet would be Granada).

Another way broadcasters raise revenue is by selling programmes, or formats, abroad. The BBC, through its commercial arm BBC Worldwide, has a deal with cable operator Flextech to provide programming for channels such as UK Horizons and UK Style. Formats (discussed in chapter 4 of *Narrative and Genre*) such as *Who Wants to Be a Millionaire?* have been successfully exported from Britain to North America. *Top of the Pops* is shown in 'local' versions in Germany, Holland and Turkey, with a version also likely to appear in North America. Pearson TV has sold *Family Fortunes* to 26 countries.

1.7 The press

The nationals

In England there are 10 national daily newspapers and 11 Sunday papers servicing, basically, three different markets (see Table 1.2). Although the *Financial Times* is a national daily, it is also classifiable as 'trade press' (that is, those which are aimed at a particular industry) for business and will not be considered in this section.

Table 1.2   The nationals

Market	Owner	Circulation (January 2001)
the 'red tops'		
Sun	News International	3,626,561
Mirror	Trinity Mirror	2,149,422
Daily Star	Northern Star–Express Newspapers	543,807
'middle market' tabloids		
Daily Mail	Daily Mail and General Trust	2,479,768
Express	Northern Star–Express Newspapers	979,042
broadsheets		
Daily Telegraph	Hollingsworth	1,022,263
The Times	News International	734,220
Guardian	Guardian Media Group	410,152
Independent	Independent Newspapers	223,645

Source: Audit Bureau of Circulation.

Geographical and political reasons have meant that Britain has an influential press; Scotland has its own dailies and tailored versions of the 'English' nationals. Geographically Britain is a small, densely populated country, and this allows a clearer sense of nationality than you get in larger, more thinly populated nations. Newspapers, then, can more easily speak to a more or less unified audience:

> Political, economic, legal and social power are highly concentrated in London, in sharp contrast with the much more regionalized societies of the USA and Germany.   (Sparks, 1999, p. 45)

This concentration, and the fact that nearly all the newspapers are based in London, helps cement the press's influence.

Although nine, general, national newspapers suggests a competitive market, the fact that this market is split into three, and News International and Northern Star–Express Newspapers account for nearly half of total circulation, demonstrates that newspapers in Britain form an oligopoly (see section 1.2). The high barriers of entry that result from this have meant that only two general newspapers launched in the last 30 years, the *Daily Star* and the *Independent*, have survived; and both their futures – at the time of writing – are under threat. Other launches, *News on Sunday*, *Today* and the *Sunday Correspondent*, have all failed; the *Sunday Sport* and *Daily Sport* newspapers and the *Sunday Business* have survived by addressing niche audiences: the former focusing on 'tits and bums' fans, the latter addressing business people.

A Scottish newspaper aimed at business people appeared in 2000, the first Scottish national newspaper to be launched in over a century. *Scottish Business* targeted the affluent elite who are attractive to advertisers. This means relatively small circulations can be economically viable – see Chapter 7. *Scottish Business* was published by a Swedish media group, Bonnier, who can be expected to launch a newspaper in England if their foray north of the border is successful.

Despite this new entrant, Sparks concludes that newspapers are a 'slowly declining medium' (Sparks, 1999, p. 55). They are at a mature stage of their product life cycle. A product's life cycle is often characterised as an 'S' curve: that is, sales start off relatively low, rise rapidly (if successful) and then slowly decline. The decline in most British national newspapers' circulation over the past 30 years has almost certainly been engendered by a massive growth in the competition to provide news.

In the 1970s, teletext was introduced and gave rapid updates on events. This probably had little impact on newspapers, as teletext delivers very little detail. It was not until the 1990s when serious news competition appeared with the growth of satellite, cable and digital television (with dedicated news channels), and the appearance – in Britain – of Radio 5 (later re-launched as Radio 5 Live) and, most potently, the Internet.

However, one area that has bucked the trend of slow decline has been the local press.

Local press

At the end of the twentieth century in Britain there were nearly 1400 local newspapers, run by 126 publishing groups, employing about 40,000 people (Peak and Fisher, 1999, p. 36). As an advertising medium, the local press is second only to television in the amount of revenue it generates.

■ Exercise 1.3 ■

List the first 10 advertisers in your local newspaper, determining which are national and which local.

The above exercise is straightforward and the list is almost certainly going to consist mostly of local advertisers. However, some of them may be local retailers advertising national, or international, brands such as Nokia or the Ford motor company. The importance of advertising to newspaper revenue is made obvious with free local newspapers as all the revenue generated is from advertising. When free sheets were first published, over 20 years ago, they had virtually no editorial; now most look like conventional newspapers. In paid-for publications advertising revenue is important because without it the cover price would have to be much higher, so high in fact that people would probably not buy them.

Both free sheets and paid-for local newspapers are in the business of delivering audiences to advertisers. They attract this audience by reporting local news, supporting the local sports teams and campaigning on local issues. For example, the *Wharfedale Observer*, based in Otley, West Yorkshire, had a long-running campaign against Leeds City Council's decision to put 'Welcome to Leeds' all around the metropolitan district; their argument was that the sign should have said 'Welcome to Guiseley' or whatever part of the district it was situated in.

Although the local press usually 'serves the community', it is increasingly likely to be owned by a large media corporation. At the start of 2000 the biggest local press group, in terms of sales, was Trinity Mirror, responsible for 165 titles with sales of over 15 million a week; they also own the Mirror group of national newspapers.

Consider the extract from Regional Independent Media's (RIM) website (June 2000), shown in Figure 1.1. RIM's portfolio of publications ranges from the large regional dailies (for example, the *Yorkshire Evening Post*'s 100,000-plus circulation) to the small *Northallerton, Thirsk & Bedale Times*, circulation 1,057. The portfolio also includes free sheets and specialist publications. Overall, RIM manages to absorb much of the North's local print advertising.

RIM Newspapers
The North's leading publishers

9 publishing centres . . . 75 publications . . . 3.5 million copies per week

Dailies

Yorkshire Post	75,836
Lancashire Evening Post (Preston)	48,831*
Yorkshire Evening Post	100,596*
Evening Gazette (Blackpool)	38,920*
The Star (Sheffield)	84,948*
Wigan Evening Post	11,508*
The Doncaster Star	9,716*

Weeklies

Burnley Express & News (Tuesday)	14,400
Batley News Series	9,013
Burnley Express & News (Friday)	19,437
Dewsbury Reporter Series	13,018
Chorley Guardian	15,129
Harrogate Advertiser	16,449
Clitheroe Advertiser & Times	9,088
Knaresborough Post	3,470

Garstang Courier	4,612
Morley Observer	3,978
Lancaster Guardian Series	18,409
Northallerton, Thirsk & Bedale Times	1,057
Longridge News	2,721
Pateley Bridge & Nidderdale Herald	1,958
Lytham St Anne's Express	9,185
Ripon Gazette	6,009
Nelson Leader Series	15,924
Sheffield Telegraph	20,678
The Visitor (Morecambe) Series	14,926
Spenborough Guardian	8,161
Wigan Series	16,959
Wetherby News	5,489

Frees

Ashton Shopper	24,957 u/c
Champion Shopper	51,166
Blackpool Reporter	102,000 u/c
The Herald (Harrogate)	42,244
Lakeland Echo	19,873
Leeds Weekly News	167,820
Leigh Reporter	66,651
North Yorkshire News	31,426
Preston Reporter	74,165 u/c
Pudsey Times	27,405
St Helens, Prescot & Knowsley Reporter	76,645
Sheffield Journal	83,378
Sheffield Weekly Gazette	122,856
Wigan Reporter	67,475

Specialist Publications

The Weekly Advertiser	53,359
Blackpool Accommodation Guide	
Wharfe Valley Times	47,404

Blackpool Lights Souvenir

Blackpool Community Voice

Angling Star

Lancashire Bride

Biker

Lancashire Jobs & Careers

Farming in the North

Rider

Farming in Yorkshire

Rugby Leaguer

Green 'Un

Steam Railways News

Leather & Footwear

Style in the Fylde

Profile (Leeds & Harrogate)

Style in Preston

Profile (Sheffield)

Style in the Ribble Valley

The Yeller

Style in Red Rose County

Yorkshire Jobs & Careers

Tourist Gazette

Yorkshire Post Business Magazine

Trials & Motorcross News

Yorkshire Sport

Wedding Bells

Yorkshire Farmer

What's On, Blackpool

Source: ABC/VDF, July–Dec. 1998.
u/c uncertified
* Mon–Fri

Figure 1.1   RIM's webpage detailing publications

In recent years, partly because of the sector's success and also contributing to this success, local newspapers, like the ITV companies discussed above, have undergone consolidation. Newsquest, in May 2000, owned 190 regional titles in Britain; it is a subsidiary of

Gannett, which owns 74 newspapers in North America. As long as local editors have control over their product, this foreign ownership is not likely to matter. However, as the respected commentator Roy Greenslade has asked:

> Was it in our interest...for an American company which has attracted opprobrium from journalists in its own country for cost-cutting and squeezing editorial resources to own the...*Bradford Telegraph* and *Argus*. (Greenslade, 2000, p. 6)

At the time of writing, Gannett was looking to buy RIM and any takeover of newspapers had to be referred to the competition commission to make sure the move was not anti-competitive. There were signs that this regulation would be disposed of, allowing even more consolidation of the sector.

1.8 News Corporation

From a newspaper base in Australia, Rupert Murdoch purchased the *Sun* in 1969 and turned it from an ailing, sub-one-million circulation newspaper to one that would sell over four million. The formula was one of (female) 'tits and bums', sensationalist reporting and populism.

In 1981 Murdoch bought Times Newspapers, publishers of, amongst other things, *The Times* and *Sunday Times*. It might seem odd to combine these with the *Sun*, and its Sunday equivalent, the *News of the World*, but Murdoch was interested in the broadsheet newspapers' middle-class audience. The purchase should have been referred to the Monopolies Commission, because of the large proportion of newspapers' total circulation that Murdoch controlled, but this was not done; possibly as a favour to the then Prime Minister Margaret Thatcher in return for Murdoch's newspapers' support.

After the takeover Murdoch owned newspapers that had both a working-class and middle-class readership. In addition, *The Times* newspaper was read by many politicians and 'captains of industry' (that is, business people with a large influence) and so was an ideal mouthpiece for his ideas; ideas that invariably were – and are – about the importance of 'free market' economics. Murdoch has always maintained that editors are able to take their own line on issues; however, Murdoch appoints the editor and one would imagine that the editor knows what Murdoch wants.

For example, for at least the last 20 years Murdoch newspapers have been anti-BBC. In early 2000 his newspapers were railing about whether the BBC should be allowed to spend money on digital television.

> Repeatedly the *Times* and the *Sun* have returned to the subject. In the past three weeks, *Sun* readers alone have been treated to three shrill leaders, as many 'exclusive' articles and a spread of 'big issue' readers' letters (all predictably hostile to the BBC, Greg Dyke, the licence fee and the digital licence fee).   (Elstein, 2000, p. 5)

The reason for Murdoch's antipathy to the BBC is probably related to his company's 40 per cent stake in B-Sky-B, the satellite TV company that competes with the state-run Corporation. Uncharacteristically Murdoch 'missed the boat' regarding cable television in North America. By the early 1980s cable operators were minting money and so, to play catch-up, Murdoch turned his attention to satellite television. Sky Television began in 1981 and Murdoch invested in it in 1983. Satellite TV, however, did not really make much of an impact in Britain until the early 1990s when a cash-strapped News Corporation was battling for market share with British Satellite Broadcasting (BSB), a consortium of broadcasting giants. Start-up costs were immense and it soon become clear that only one satellite company would survive. Sky had started earlier and more successfully than BSB so the companies merged with Murdoch in control.

Free marketeer that he is, Murdoch has a hatred of regulation that prevents businesses from expanding. For example, it was illegal for many years to own both newspapers and a television station, as it was believed the owner would have too much control over the information given to the public. In the USA it was impossible for a non-American to own a newspaper, as it was thought that it was not in the public interest to allow foreign nationals to do so. Thus in order to expand his empire into the States the Australian Murdoch took American citizenship. This lack of 'loyalty' to the country in which News Corporation operates can also be seen in their finances:

> Multinational companies also have the advantage of deciding where they wish to declare their profits for the purposes of taxation. An *Economist* report showed that although Murdoch's company had made £1.4 billion in the past 11 years it had paid no, net, British corporation tax.
>
> (*The Economist*, 1999, p. 83)

News Corporation does not have local loyalties; it operates as a global company. Murdoch's strategy in the early twenty-first century suggests that he has not lost his touch; when announcing an $100 million investment in India he was quoting as saying: 'We are developing 100% Hindi-language programmes over the next six months. We are going to think globally, but act locally' (Lall, 2000, p. 1).

This is a mantra picked up from MTV, as we shall see in Chapter 3, but it can lead to conflicts of interest. When News Corporation's Harper-Collins intended to publish the last Hong Kong Governor's memoirs, the publisher found itself working against its holding company. At the time, News Corporation was attempting to gain access to China, a potential market of billions, and so prevented the book being published because it was unflattering to China's leaders. Many commentators shouted about how this was an affront to 'freedom of speech' because the non-publication of the book was a political, and not a commercial, decision.

That anyone should have been surprised about Murdoch's priorities betrays their naivety; just as the Harper-Collins personnel betrayed their misunderstanding of what it meant to work for Murdoch (unless they were attempting a 'wind up'). Such a high-profile case rarely happens because News Corp. employees know what is required; they know the unwritten rules of the institution in which they work.

The bottom line of Murdoch's actions is invariably the profit figure. This is not to say that he, like many British companies, operates on a short-term basis that worries only about this year's profits; he is a renowned risk taker. However, inevitably in a capitalist society, the decisions he makes are based upon what is good for his company.

1.9 Convergence and the Internet

When, in the late 1990s, the Internet became a mass medium it redrew the boundaries of what constituted the media. The boundaries of the Old Media, of the twentieth century, were more or less distinct: films in the cinema; television programmes and live relays on television; broadcast radio; printed magazines and newspapers. While there was overlap (television broadcast film), each medium played to its strengths. People would not read newspapers on television or listen to them read on the radio; these media had their own set of news conventions. The Internet changed this.

Potentially the Internet can deliver everything. Ignoring for a moment the problem of bandwidth, which meant picture quality for moving image was poor for many years, the Internet can offer magazines and newspapers to be read, or television news to be watched and radio news to listen to. The Internet can deliver films, television programmes and music (via MP3 for example). As a medium, a delivery system, the Internet was the 'killer application'; nothing could compete with it. This did not mean the death of all Old Media, indeed television may eventually supersede computers as the Internet interface, but *all* the Old Media can be delivered through the Net.

Old Media companies realised that without the ability to deliver their product via the Net they risked being marginalized. This theoretical dominance of Net companies was reflected in their initial stock market valuations, some of which were astronomically high despite the companies never having made a profit. Blue chip stock, such as Time-Warner, found itself marginalized despite having massive assets, back catalogues, and the ability to make media products that had mass appeal. This 'dot.com bubble' did burst in the early twenty-first century but that is unlikely to affect the effect the Internet will have upon our consumption of media texts.

The latter part of the twentieth century has been dubbed the 'information age', in contrast to the 'industrial age' that preceded it. In media terms this information refers to any textual content, be it news, documentary, entertainment and so on. So it is ironic that stock markets saw fit to inflate the New Media bubble when, without Old Media content, it would be full of nothing. Not many people watch TV channels that are off the air; we do not sit in cinemas that are not projecting movies, or read blank pieces of paper. In essence that is all the Internet is: a medium that, without content, is empty. Hence the need for Internet companies to have relationships with content-providers and the providers requiring access to the Net to transmit their product. The merger that really grabbed the headlines in early 2000 (though not completed until 2001) was AOL and Time-Warner. This represented a link between New Media (AOL was an Internet service provider) and the Old Media (Time-Warner, a 'traditional' media group from films to publishing). This merger was particularly significant as it represented, at an organisational level, the principle of convergence.

Possibly the Net's primary 'killer application' is its interactivity. Unsurprisingly in a capitalist society, the Net's ability to sell goods and services, by creating a new contact between customer and business, energised the world's biggest corporations to get involved with the new medium. This contact does not require consumers to leave their private space; all the world's products can infiltrate their home.

In May 2000 Sony was restructuring itself in order to benefit from the convergence stimulated by the growth of the Internet:

> In [Sony's] vision of the future, Sony films and Sony music will be distributed through Sony networks, downloaded by Sony PlayStation terminals, edited on Sony computers and screened on Sony televisions. (Watts, 2000, p. 29)

One of the first big name authors to use the Net for publishing purposes was Stephen King. His novella *Riding the Bullet* sold half a million 'copies' in two days; that is, half a million people paid $2.50 to download it onto their computers. This form of distribution was organised by the publishers Simon & Schuster, a company that obviously recognised it was in the publishing business and not simply the book business.

This is not the place to speculate on what effect this might have on the high street, which may well disappear if many stores close down. It is cheaper to buy many products such as DVDs and CDs on the Net because the virtual 'shop' does not have the large overheads (such as lighting, heating, staff) that traditional outlets have to pay for.

One of the most empowering aspects of the Internet is its status as a system of distribution that does not need an organisation to mediate between it and the audience, other than an ISP (Internet Service Provider). The cutting out of the distributor enables media practitioners to speak directly to their audience, assuming the audience can find them.

The Net is famed for 'democracy'; anyone with access to a computer and web page-making software can publish (although clearly there are many people who have no such access). The Net has millions of pages created by people who have never worked in a media business. Although businesses have increasingly used the Net as a new way of reaching consumers, it is likely that we will always be able to produce what we want, within certain legal restraints, and publish it on the World Wide Web. So although the Internet will continue to transform the way businesses operate, it also offers audiences the opportunity to produce media products.

1.10 Conclusion

The driving economic force in western society is capitalism, the pursuit of profit. This means that most media organisations need to commodify their product in order to generate revenue. This has particular consequences for the way in which media business operates, from the high-concept Hollywood blockbuster to the synergy exploited by organisations such as Viacom. As media companies increasingly operate on a global basis this will affect their way of operating as they try to 'act global but think local'. The next development in the media will be the increasing influence of the Internet, a medium in which all other media can converge and be delivered to audiences.

Students need to be aware of the businesses that lie behind most of the media texts they consume and analyse. Knowing that AOL and Time-Warner are the same businesses helps explain the predominance of the latter on the former's websites.

2

REGULATION AND CENSORSHIP

AIMS OF THE CHAPTER

➤ To consider legal regulation and self-regulation of media industries in Britain and how large corporations can pressurise news organisations.

➤ To consider broadcasting regulation in Britain.

➤ To consider public service broadcasting and Channel 4.

➤ To examine the role of censorship.

➤ To explore the role of pressure groups.

➤ To assess how institutional values can affect the production of media texts.

2.1 Introduction

The term 'institution' is derived from sociology and 'refers to the underlying principles and **values** according to which *many* social and cultural practices are organized and coordinated' (O'Sullivan *et al.*, 1994, p. 152). As we saw in Chapter 1, among the dominant social and cultural practices in our society are those associated with business. This chapter focuses on other practices important to Media Studies. These are mostly in the form of regulations that seek to constrain, in either a voluntary or a legal framework, both the content and business practices of media businesses. Public service broadcasting, which has had immense influence on television and radio in Britain, is considered in some detail; formal censorship is examined, as is the role of pressure groups and the effect of institutional values on production practices.

A word of warning: sections 2.2 to 2.6 are not designed to be read in one sitting. These are probably best being dipped into. Although regulations and regulatory bodies are exceptionally dry subjects, Media students do need to know what effect they can have. What follows is not intended to be an exhaustive survey but is, hopefully, one that covers the main areas.

2.2 British legal regulations

Although there is a common belief that the British media operate in an environment that protects 'free speech':

> William Waldegrave's 1992 White Paper, *Open Government*, listed 251 statutory instruments limiting the media's ability to report government business, while there are 50 pieces of legislation that restrict media freedom.   (Petley, 1999, p. 143)

Clearly this idea of 'freedom' of the 'Fourth Estate' is severely limited. The 'Fourth Estate' is a name given to the press and situates their role as being alongside the Church, the Law and Parliament. In other words, news organisations were conceived of as vehicles that monitor the use and abuse of power. However, as the above quotation suggests, this power is severely curtailed both by the judiciary and by Parliament; the power of the Church in a secular society is virtually inconsequential.

Certainly there have been many instances where news organisations have been successful in revealing abuse of power. It is also arguable that news organisations are more likely to defer to the interests of multinational corporations and governments rather than protect readers' interests. For example, financial pressure can be brought to bear on news organisations not to report unfavourable news; this allegedly occurred in the McDonald's libel case in the late 1990s.

McDonald's sued Helen Steel and Dave Morris of London Greenpeace for the allegations in their fact sheet 'What's Wrong with McDonald's'. The leaflet accused the fast food merchants of, amongst other things, damaging the environment, promoting an unhealthy diet and exploiting their staff. The corporation won their case, but because the Judge ruled that the defendants had proved two of their allegations, the defendants only had to pay half of the £60,000 damages awarded.

One of the interesting facets of the case was the lack of reporting in the mainstream media, which was surprising given McDonald's high profile. It is possible that McDonald's propensity to *threaten* legal action might have discouraged reporting, in other words no one would take the risk of being sued. There are other ways in which organisations can escape unwanted press attention:

> It is alleged, for example, that when the *Independent* carried a front-page story about McDonalds' secret attempts to negotiate a settlement after only six weeks of the case, the company withdrew £80,000 of advertising from the *Independent on Sunday*. (Petley, 1998, p. 4)

Such issues are often clouded by terms like 'alleged' as it is rare for anyone to go on record threatening to withdraw advertising unless the media organisation 'toes the line'. However, Ted Graham, British Telecom's (BT) Head of External Communication, did make such a threat to the *Sunday Telegraph* in 1998. Annoyed at an article about tensions at board level within BT, Graham wrote to the newspaper's city editor stating:

> I should also point out that BT spends several million pounds each year advertising in the *Telegraph*; given your apparent vendetta against BT's management, is that advertising spend something we should continue? (Ahmed, 1999, p. 9)

Graham was apparently threatening to withdraw advertising from the newspaper unless the unfavourable reporting stopped. How often this sort of pressure is put on news organisations, and how often it is given in to, is very difficult to find out. The journalist whose articles were called to question was Patrick Weever and the case came to light only because he sued his newspaper for constructive dismissal. His case also revealed the role of public relations companies in the 'planting' of information in Sunday newspapers (see Chapter 4).

In 1999 the People for the Ethical Treatment of Animals (Peta) ran an anti-McDonald's poster campaign (slogan: 'McDonald's. Cruelty to go', or 'McCruelty to go' in some versions – see Figures 7.3–7.5). Because two of Steel's and Morris's accusations against the company were found to be true, Peta could attack McDonald's's record without fear of being sued. However, in the USA many publications would not run Peta's campaign, presumably wary of offending an important advertiser, and in Britain the Committee for Advertising Practices and the Outdoor Advertising Association (both self-regulatory bodies) refused to allow the posters to be displayed. Their argument was that the posters were offensive and were rejected on grounds of taste. This could, of course, also be seen as censorship of a political (animal rights) message:

Conspiracy theorists could question whether a campaign which didn't attack a major advertiser would have elicited such a rapid response.

(Armstrong, 1999, p. 9)

This is an example of 'economic censorship', which is probably more powerful than legal restrictions as there is no formal framework that people can use to make a protest. However, many businesses do also use the courts in their attempts to stifle bad publicity.

SLAPP

Currently finding great favour among multinational corporations are Strategic Lawsuits against Public Participation (SLAPP):

> a SLAPP [is] a civil court action which alleges that injury has been caused by the efforts of non-government individuals or organizations to influence government action on an issue of public interest or concern. (Beder, 1997, p. 64)

These manifest themselves in the media when libel action is threatened if negative articles, or programmes, against the organisation concerned are to be published or broadcast. It may even be unlikely that the libel case would be pursued; the threat alone has meant that many stories have gone uncovered. Robert Maxwell successfully covered his fraudulent tracks for many years using such actions. A SLAPP can also prevent pressure groups from campaigning effectively by taking up their time and money in defending themselves against better-resourced organisations.

In 1998 the entire issue of the September/October *Ecologist* magazine, which investigated the genetically modified food producer Monsanto, was pulped by the printer. The explanation offered was that there was a potentially libellous article in the edition (which the printer would also have been liable for); however, the printer's commercial director was unable to say how he knew what was in the article. *The Ecologist*'s editor believes the printers were 'got at' by Monsanto (Williams, 1998, p. 4).

Prevention of Terrorism and Official Secrets

Possibly among the most far-reaching legal restrictions in Britain are the Prevention of Terrorism Act and the Official Secrets Act. These

38

can be considered as 'catch all' legislation, which means they can be used very widely. For example, Tony Geraghty was charged under the Official Secrets Act in May 1999 for refusing to name his sources in his book *The Irish War*. The book contains allegations that two-thirds of the population of Northern Ireland are under military sur-veillance. If journalists are forced to name their sources then potential 'whistle blowers' are unlikely to inform the press if they know of any illegal actions being perpetrated by government agencies. Hence the confidentiality of sources is crucial to investigative journalists. It has been suggested that Geraghty fell foul of the D-notice (see below) committee for refusing to submit his manuscript for vetting (McCrystal, 1999, p. 8).

Whistle blowers are important to the workings of the Fourth Estate: in 1982, during the Falklands War, the Argentinian warship the *Belgrano* was sunk, killing around 350 people. The destruction was justified in Parliament by the 'fact' that the *Belgrano* was threat-ening British warships. Clive Ponting, then a civil servant, knew this was a lie and made public the fact that the ship was actually steam-ing away from the British taskforce. He was prosecuted under the Official Secrets Act and acquitted by the jury. After this the law was changed so that anybody tried under the Act would not have a jury to judge their innocence or guilt.

D-notices

The Defence, Press and Broadcasting Advisory Committee issues 'D-Notices' to news organisations asking for them to *voluntarily* withhold certain stories from publication. This is a very effective form of censorship because no organisation is being coerced. During the 1990s Gulf War a senior military officer left computers containing battle plans in his car when he went to look in a car showroom. They were stolen but the event was subject to a D-notice and it was not until an Irish newspaper ran the story that the British public found out about this particular piece of incompetence.

Lobby system

The Lobby system allows politicians to brief journalists anonym-ously and say, virtually, anything they want. When the phrases 'sources close to the Prime Minister' or, in relation to the Royal Family,

'Buckingham Palace let it be known' are used they indicate anonymous briefings. These unattributable briefings were used during the Serbian war in 1999 to portray BBC correspondent John Simpson's reports from the Serbian capital, Belgrade, as being somehow traitorous.

2.3 Self-regulation – Press Complaints Commission

Anybody who feels they have been misreported in the press can complain to the Press Complaints Commission (PCC), a self-regulating body set up and funded by the newspaper industry to pre-empt threats of privacy legislation. The PCC was set up in the light of the Calcutt inquiry of 1989 into irresponsible reporting (such as the *Sun's* suggestion that Liverpool fans 'pissed' on the dead after nearly 100 of them died at Hillsborough football ground that year). Calcutt suggested in his report that this should be the last chance the press got to self-regulate. When he assessed their progress, or rather lack of it, in 1993 he stated that legislation was needed as the press could not be trusted to regulate themselves properly.

Political parties, when in power, are reluctant to regulate the press because they like to cultivate positive coverage from newspapers to help them gain re-election. Partly in response to Calcutt's assessment, a White Paper was published on privacy law in 1995 proposing only a tighter code to be administered by the PCC. In the same year the *Daily Mirror* (as it was then) ran front-page pictures of Princess Diana in the gym. These had been taken secretly and therefore broke the PCC code; the *Mirror's* editor said they were in the public interest (and therefore justifiable) as they showed how easy it was to invade Princess Diana's privacy. The situation degenerated into farce when the *Mirror* briefly resigned from the PCC after being censured for publishing the photos.

Lord Wakeham then put a tighter code into place, as the new PCC chairman, and soon afterwards the *Mirror* was again criticised, this time for its anti-German reporting during the Euro '96 football championships held in England. In 1997 the death of Princess Diana put the press in the spotlight for its use of paparazzi to hound 'celebrities' in the hope of candid photographs. Many newspapers vowed never to use paparazzi pictures again; a promise that stuck for a few months. The public's outcry against the tabloid press following Diana's death was somewhat hypocritical since the newspapers that provide numerous 'Royal scoop' pictures sell in their millions.

In 2000 the *Mirror*'s editor was censured again by the PCC for buying shares tipped in his newspaper (he claimed he did not read the column before it was printed). The *Mirror* ran two pages of apology, though whether this sets right the wrong is open to debate. Any success the PCC has had in convincing the public, and government, that self-regulation works is probably due to politically astute chairmanship:

> [Wakeham] has transformed the [PCC] into a highly sophisticated political animal. He has said the things that politicians and the public want to hear, when they want to hear it. (Wells, 2000a, p. 2)

Until politicians grasp the nettle of press intrusion into the privacy of individuals then little is likely to change. However, this privacy has to be balanced by 'freedom of information'.

2.4 Freedom of information

Freedom of information would seem to be a prerequisite for the functioning of a democracy. After all, if the electorate are not allowed to find out what politicians are doing then they cannot make an informed decision when voting. Whilst in opposition the Labour Party, in Britain, promised a Freedom of Information Act to make the workings of government more open. In the USA the Constitution gives citizens a high degree of access to state information. Britain, on the other hand, does not have a written constitution and so it is up to the law to define any rights to information the public have.

In 2000 the Freedom of Information bill was passing through Parliament under the guidance of the Home Secretary, Jack Straw. This bill is almost certainly now law; here it is only possible to comment on how it appeared the bill would work. The *Guardian* was one of the few newspapers that opposed what it saw as the lack of freedom in the bill:

> The freedom of information bill . . . gives fewer rights to official information than those enjoyed by citizens of the US, Canada, Australia, New Zealand and the Irish Republic. (Dyer, 2000, p. 6)

The bill was intended to extend the right of the secret service (MI5) to intercept e-mail as well as letters and telephone calls. For journalists this would mean they would not be able to guarantee the confidentiality of any information held on their computers.

Contrast this with the position in North America where 'freedom of information' is not simply a euphemism for censorship. However, whilst much official information is available in the United States this does not mean controversial information will necessarily get published.

2.5   British broadcasting regulation

The Independent Television Commission (ITC) is charged with the regulation of commercial television. All ITV companies have certain obligations that they have to fulfil as part of the conditions for acceptance of their bid for the franchise. Up until the 1990s this was relatively rigorous, emphasising the public service broadcasting element in British broadcasting (see below). In keeping with the Thatcherite philosophy, the ITC (which replaced the IBA – Independent Broadcasting Authority) was formulated with a 'lighter touch', the weight of which was challenged a number of times during the 1980s.

The new franchises were no longer obliged to schedule certain programmes at set times, such as religion at Sunday teatime, but half an hour of prime-time news was still required. The top-rated news programme, ITN's *News at Ten*, was a source of contention as its position – at 10pm – meant that any programme over an hour long that began after the watershed (9pm – designated as the time after which adult themes and language can be shown on terrestrial television) had to be interrupted by the news. It is likely that millions of people saw the first hour of films only to be too tired to continue watching when they resumed at 10.40pm. As the ITV companies became more commercially orientated during the 1990s, in the face of competition from satellite and cable television, the drop off in audience at 10pm became a source of conflict with the regulator.

ITV's problem was the definition of weekday prime time, 7pm to 10.30pm; it did not want to run news at 7pm, when schedulers were hoping to grab early evening audience share in the hope that audiences would stay with them, so 10pm was the latest it could be broadcast. Prime-time news could only be moved later to make way for live broadcasts (usually sport). When ITV tried to run an edition of *Cracker* that did not finish until 10.15pm they were forced to cancel the broadcast. In 1999, ITV had eventually convinced the regulators that the main *ITV News* should run at 6.30pm (requiring a redefinition of prime time) with the promise that audiences would not be reduced. One year later the move was proving a commercial boon to the ITV companies, with bigger audiences for their prime-time programmes creating bigger advertising rates for advertisers, but had led to a slump in audiences for the news. Regional news was particularly affected, with a 22 per cent drop. In early 2001 a compromise had been reached where ITV ran prime-time news three times a week.

The regulator has powers to impose fines and in 1999 MTV Networks Europe received a £40,000 financial penalty for breaches of its Programme Code and Code of Programme Sponsorship. The adjudication cited:

> the video request programme *Select* transmitted on 30 May which included several scripted references to Alton Towers, the donor of a competition prize, when only one such mention is permissible.   (ITC website)

Most media institutions have compliance officers who make sure that programmes do not break any regulatory rules or, indeed, the law.

In the ITC's 2000 annual review of the ITV network it was particularly scathing of the factual programming that relied upon 'infotainment': documentaries that deal with entertaining subjects (like *Neighbours from Hell*) or serious subjects in a 'tabloid' fashion in its focus on human interest stories. The large numbers of consumer programmes were also criticised. However, the news was praised (if not the time when it was broadcast), as was sport and education.

Broadcasters have a responsibility to be impartial and so cannot promote any particular political party. In 2000, the Radio Authority (which regulates non-BBC radio) fined Virgin Radio a then record £75,000 because the DJ Chris Evans had twice voiced his support for Ken Livingstone in the election for mayor of London.

Regulation can have a profound effect on a medium and this is evident in the way television advertising is broadcast in Europe compared with North America. The first mass broadcast medium, radio, was established as a wholly commercial service in the USA whereas in Britain, for example, it was constituted as a public service.

In the USA, however, the 'market decides' and television programmes are constantly interrupted, with a total of up to 15 minutes in an hour, by advertisements and trailers for other programmes. What is particularly disorientating for the European viewer is that these are not signified in any way: a scene in the middle of a film can be immediately followed by an advertisement or an extract from another film that is to be shown later. In Britain the break is signalled with a title card. It is only relatively recently that commercial television in Britain has started trailing programmes within the 'internal' advertising break (that is, a break in the middle of a programme).

In Britain, advertisement breaks are limited to an average of seven minutes per hour in any one day; advertising is not allowed to interrupt religious or royal ceremonies and is not permissible during schools' programmes. In North America many schools' programmes are made by companies wishing to sell to young people and so are consciously designed with publicity in mind, something that would never have been allowed under a public service broadcasting regime.

In early 2001 the ITC was proposing that the ITV companies should regulate themselves by assessing their performance against a 'rolling annual statement'.

The other main broadcasting regulatory institution is the Broadcasting Standards Commission (BSC), which looks to uphold 'taste and decency' in broadcasting as well 'fairness'. The BSC was set up to represent the consumer, and its three main tasks were set out in the Broadcasting Act of 1996:

- to produce codes of practice in relation to standards and fairness
- to consider and adjudicate on complaints
- to monitor, research and report on standards and fairness in broadcasting

(Peak and Fisher, 1999, p. 263)

Other regulators in the sector include the BBC's governors, who have to make sure the BBC fulfils its obligations, and the Office of Telecommunications (Oftel), which has responsibility for telecommunications. As we saw in Chapter 1, the media are converging toward each other via the Internet. It therefore seems likely that broadcasting regulation will come under one body.

2.6   Public service broadcasting

Public service broadcasting (PSB) began, in Britain, with the nationalisation of the BBC, originally an organisation run by a cartel of radio manufacturers. Owing to the scarcity of airwaves, and the political belief that radio would be a very influential medium, the government has always regulated broadcasting. However, to avoid the charge that the BBC was a government mouthpiece this regulation was kept at 'arm's length'. This did not stop the BBC giving whole-hearted support to the government during the General Strike of 1926.

Under John Reith's leadership, in the 1920s, the BBC saw itself as bringing enlightenment to the masses through 'information, education and entertainment'. It had the elitist purpose of trying to educate the people with 'high culture'. The belief was that once the British had listened to the great composers such as Mozart, they would no longer wish to listen to 'popular music'. This emphasis on high culture, at the expense of the popular, dogged the BBC for many decades and it did not really embrace chart-based pop music until 1967 with the creation of Radio 1. Previously there had been three stations: the Home Service (the talk channel); the Light Programme (popular music, not chart-based, and light entertainment); and the Third Programme (classical music and drama). In 1967 these became, respectively, Radio 4, Radio 2 and Radio 3. PSB was class-based: middle-class values were imposed upon the working classes.

The prejudice against popular and youth culture continued to manifest itself with the relegation of Radio 1 to medium wave until the 1980s and so the most popular channel was broadcast in poor-quality sound, while Radio 3, which had a small listenership, had FM stereo. This idea that the broadcasters know what is good for the audience led Raymond Williams to declare that PSB was a 'paternal system', which he defined as an: 'authoritarian system with a conscience: that is to say, with values and purposes beyond the maintenance of its own power' (Williams, 1976, p. 131). In other words, although PSB is imposed upon audiences (listeners had no choice in this project other than to switch off), it is trying to 'do good'.

Contrast this with a commercially based broadcaster whose only purpose is 'the maintenance of its own power', that is, the ability to stay in business and make profits. 'Free to air' broadcasters (that is, those that can be heard without subscribing via satellite or cable) tend to do this by either offering the audience 'lowest common denominator' material that appeals to the largest group of people, or targeting a niche middle-class audience (defined in Chapter 7). One way of differenciating between PSB and commercial broadcasters is that the former sees the audience as citizens whilst the latter treats them as consumers (also see Chapter 7). So while PSB can be thought of as authoritarian it does offer more than commercial broadcasters:

> public service regulation has secured the survival of a successful broadcasting industry, one which has become more significant economically and which has become an important exporter of programmes while

continuing to discuss and mould national issues.   (Curran and Seaton, 1997, p. 302)

Canadian broadcasting has been held up as an example of what happens when PSB fails to offer alternatives, however authoritarian, to the prevailing commercial offerings. Canada's neighbour, the USA, culturally dominates the nation and Canadian legislators know that they cannot keep American products out of their country:

> Throughout the 1950s, a distinctive physical characteristic of the Canadian landscape within 150 miles of the United States, where 80 per cent of the Canadian population lives, was the proliferation of rooftop aerials for the reception of American TV signals.   (Perlmutter, 1993, p. 17)

Canadian legislators attempted to create a framework where PSBs, which would be culturally Canadian, could co-exist with commercial broadcasters. This failed because although licences were granted to broadcasters if they promised to fulfil certain PSB requirements, such commitments were invariably reneged upon. The companies simply stated that if they were forced to comply they would go out of business. In effect it appears the commercial broadcasters made promises to secure the licence with no intention of fulfilling them, and 'blackmailed' the legislators into letting them get away with it. The effect of this has been the dominance of American cultural products to the detriment of Canadian production; a state of affairs common in many parts of the world – as we shall see in Chapter 3.

PSB as a product of its time

PSB, as all institutional frameworks, developed out of the prevailing social conditions. In the Netherlands, for instance, broadcasters were constrained by a PSB framework; however, unlike that in Britain, it was culturally, not class, based. The principle of 'pillarisation' structured the whole of Dutch society:

> At the heart of the principle of pillarization was the idea that Dutch society was divided into so-called pillars, that is, social groups separated from each other...along the lines of religious or ideological convictions.   (Ang, 1991, p. 121)

Foremost among the pillars were Catholicism and Protestantism, and the system was designed to foment peaceful co-existence. By the late

1960s such an approach to social structure was no longer viable but was still a defining feature of broadcasting institutions.

In Britain, Reith's philosophy was in tune with Matthew Arnold's dictum, as practised by F. R. Leavis and his followers, that high culture could be a civilising influence. It seems churlish to argue with PSB if we agree it is a civilising influence; however, the notion of what is civil is inevitably ideological. Terry Eagleton unveiled Arnold's ideological project:

> literature would rehearse the masses in the habits of pluralistic thought and feeling, persuading them to acknowledge that more than one viewpoint than theirs existed – namely, that of their masters. It would communicate to them the moral riches of bourgeois civilization, impress upon them a reverence for middle-class achievements, and, since reading is an essentially solitary, contemplative activity, curb in them any disruptive tendency to collective political action.   (Eagleton, 1983, p. 25)

Eagleton is arguing that the conception of English Literature as a medium that transcends social and political influences and offers universal truths is simply a ruse that attempts to naturalise bourgeois ideology. There are no universal truths, only ideological truths.

By 2000, the BBC found itself operating, in many ways, as if it was a commercial organisation. The formation of BBC Worldwide was intended to exploit BBC properties commercially by selling its programmes abroad and producing video and audiotapes of BBC material for retail purchase. In the promotion of its own products the BBC was not averse to running what were, in effect, advertisements for its own publications. For example, *BBC Gardening World* and *Top of the Pops* magazine would be plugged after the relevant programme. Other publishers complained that this represented unfair competition, as they could not advertise on the BBC, so such adverts now include the rider, in small print, that other magazines are available.

A similar conflict was seen in the development of BBC Online, the BBC's website. It was amongst the most popular in Europe, and many private companies believed that the BBC's website was stifling competition.

In the late 1990s the BBC received a lot of criticism as it lost the rights to many sporting events and so, in early 2000, the Corporation purchased the rights to the World (football) Club Championship in an attempt to allay such flak. The promotion of this event was a synergist's (see Chapter 1) dream:

> The competition is very important to the BBC. Quite how important has been clear from the coverage on its news shows. On Radio 4's Today programme, most of the sports bulletin this week has been dedicated to updates on David Beckham's underwear or Sir Alex's latest eruption at a press conference. On the Nine O'Clock News Michael Buerk's doom-laden tones make Beckham's sending-off sound like the first toll of impending Armageddon, before he tells us that further coverage is over on BBC Choice.   (White, 2000, p. 5)

Similarly, the BBC's terrestrial news bulletins are usually rounded off with the information that BBC News 24 provides a rolling news service. In cross-promoting its channels, the BBC is using synergy, just like a commercial broadcaster.

Whilst the licence fee funds the BBC it is likely to remain, predominantly, a PSB. However, it is inevitable that the Corporation will be influenced by the ideological conditions of the time. Prime Minister (1979–91) Margaret Thatcher's free-market philosophy manifested itself in the BBC through the introduction of Producer Choice, an internal market place. Producer Choice meant that each BBC department had to compete in order to provide services. This threw up a number of absurdities:

> The record library was turned into its own business unit and so had to make a charge for lending out CDs and vinyl and so on. Unfortunately, in order to break even, they had to charge approximately £10 per item loaned. So producers would pop in to Our Price on the way to work and buy the CD instead!   (BBC sound technician)

The new Director General Greg Dyke, in 2000, set about dismantling the system; the (New) Labour government of the time were not quite so dedicated to the alleged efficiencies of the free market.

Commercial PSB

Up to 1956 the BBC had a monopoly on broadcasting in Britain. When the ITV companies started, broadcasting became a duopoly and it was not until the advent of satellite television in the early 1990s that the medium became competitive. Despite its commercial nature ITV has always had obligations, such as the prime-time news referred to above. By the 1990s these had been massively diluted but ITV was still required to produce 10 hours of children's programmes, 90 minutes a week of current affairs, documentaries and regional programming.

We have already seen, above, how the commercial prerogative led to conflict between ITV and the ITC. In June 2000, however, the moneymakers found an unlikely ally in the regulator. The ITC chairman stated: 'The broadcasting environment is now changing rapidly so we need to reassess and redefine public service broadcasting in the multi-channel digital world' (quoted in Wells, 2000a, p. 3). It is possible, given current trends, that ITV will no longer be a public service broadcaster after the renewal of franchises due in 2003.

Channel 5 had obligations similar to those of Channel 3, though with no regional component as it is a national broadcaster, and smaller quotas of time required for compulsory programming like documentaries.

One of the more explicitly ideological channels to be launched was Britain's Channel 4; explicit because it did not see itself, when it launched, as offering consensus programmes (i.e. programmes reflecting the views of the majority of the general public).

Channel 4 and PSB

By the 1980s, Channel 4 (C4) – bucking the conservative trend of the decade – began broadcasting to a PSB remit. However, this conception of PSB was not based on social class; for C4 PSB was defined as offering, among other things:

> universality of appeal: television programmes [that] should cater for all interests and tastes. Minorities, especially disadvantaged minorities, should receive particular provision. Broadcasters should recognise their relationship to the sense of national identity and community. (Broadcasting Research Unit, 1985)

The idea of C4 was hatched in the 1970s. The economic crises of the early 1970s – induced partly by the 1973 oil crisis – led to a more *laissez faire* approach to managing the economy. Instead of government intervention (in Britain the government ran the utilities of water, electricity, gas and telecommunications), it was deemed that 'free market' economics would best serve the nation. In addition, the old certainties (which were more apparent than real) about popular culture were fading and this put the traditional form of television under threat. During the 1970s half the population of the country would watch the *Morecambe and Wise Christmas Special*, making it a significant cultural event, something that is much rarer now because audiences have many more channels, and so, more programmes, to choose from; 2000's *Big Brother*, and possibly the 'who shot Phil Mitchell' episode of *EastEnders*, in April 2001, are recent examples. Also, the original reason for state regulation of broadcasters, scarce bandwidth, was no longer applicable because of technological developments such as cable and satellite television. However, the Annan Commission, which reported in 1977, recommended that the status quo should only be changed by the introduction of a fourth channel:

> We want the broadcasting industry to grow. But we do not want more of the same.... What is needed now are programmes for the different minorities which add up to make the majority. (Quoted in Watson and Hill, 1993, p. 7b)

Annan was clearly accepting the notion that Britain was becoming, after the immigration of the 1950s and 1960s, a multicultural society; his statement was echoed, as we shall see, 20 years later.

C4 was set up to explicitly address groups who were not catered for by the other three channels (this being a time before a multi-channel environment). Although C4 was set up as a PSB, it was also a commercial broadcaster in that it was funded by advertising; however, it was sheltered from commercial pressures by having its airtime sold by the ITV companies, who had to pay a fixed amount to the newcomer. In the 1980s C4 broadcast programmes never seen on British television before, fulfilling its obligation to be alternative and cater for minorities.

In 1993, C4 began selling its own airtime, very successfully. It, basically, delivered the middle-class audience highly sought after by advertisers. In doing so it also began acting much more like a commercial broadcaster in its pursuit of audiences. This trend had begun a few years earlier with the appointment of Michael Grade as its Controller. Grade – who had been Controller of BBC1 – was recognised as an excellent scheduler of programmes; excellence being defined in terms of numbers of viewers.

That C4 should sell its own airtime was recommended in the Peacock report published in 1986. As mentioned above, C4 was a peculiar mix of PSB, in its remit to cater for minorities, and *laissez faire* economic policy, in that it did not make any of its own programmes and so stimulated the production in the independent sector, and this heightened competition. C4 was therefore a publisher rather than a producer.

After winning her second term of office, in 1983, Prime Minister Thatcher was determined to stamp her own brand of 'free market' ideology onto the broadcasting sector, which she called the 'last

bastion of restrictive practices'. She wished to challenge the dominance of the traditional broadcasters (who had been cosily operating
in a duopoly – a market dominated by two companies – for 25 years)
by stimulating private-sector television through the independent
producers. In addition, the BBC's neutral reporting of the Falklands
War, in 1982, had enraged many Conservatives, so that when the
Peacock Committee investigated broadcasting it was constituted with
an anti-BBC, pro-free market bias:

> Both the background to the committee's establishment and its compos-
> ition, powerfully suggested the government had set it up with the specific
> intention of introducing advertising on the BBC. Such a move would have
> been a considerable blow against one of the central features of the estab-
> lished framework of British public service broadcasting. (Goodwin,
> 1999, p. 136)

Despite this 'free market' bias Peacock rejected the option of introdu-
cing advertising on the BBC, which would have made it subservient
to commercial pressures (as described in Chapter 3), on the basis that
it would reduce viewer choice. This is ironic because *laissez faire* economics suggests that the free market is best at creating choice for the
viewer; the logic of the 'free marketeer's' argument is that if there is
a demand for a product then companies, unrestrained by regulation,
will fulfil this demand. One 'free market' recommendation of Peacock
that did find favour was that the ITV franchises should be auctioned off
to the highest bidder for the right to broadcast for 10 years from 1993.
It was thought that this would maximise the contribution to the Treasury.

This 'free market' approach was watered down slightly with the
introduction of a 'quality threshold' to the applications. It was argued
that, without this, bidders might spend most of their capital on making the bid and have little finance to make decent programmes. The
franchise would then be characterised by cheap imported programmes,
primarily from North America. The 'quality threshold' was sought as
a guarantee that programmes would not deteriorate with the new
franchises. Despite this, the results of this free market experiment
were a disaster.

While some television companies, like Yorkshire Television, bid a
substantial amount of money (£37.7 million per annum), others won
the right to broadcast very cheaply. Central Television (which was
later taken over by Carlton) paid only £2,000. Central TV gambled
that no one else would bid for the franchise. However, it was not
likely to be much of a gamble as much research was required in the

putting together of the bids. It is almost certain that the incumbent broadcaster would have been aware of any other company that was considering a bid. Yorkshire TV knew that two other companies were interested in its franchise and so bid accordingly; one of these companies, Granada Television, eventually gained control of Yorkshire, which was debilitated by the size of its bid. Other companies that got the right to broadcast for 10 years cheaply were Scottish Television (£2,000) and Channel Television (£1,000).

By 1999 Grade's successor, Michael Jackson, was moved to redefine C4's remit:

> 'Channel 4 is no longer a minority channel for minority audiences. Its future lies in being the channel of contemporary culture [which is] ahead of the mainstream.... Think about how different Britain is today from when Channel 4 launched 16 years ago.... Numbers in higher education have doubled. Half the population is now classified as middle class.' And there, in the young middle class (with their appetite for innovation, diversity and originality), is the channel's core audience. (Peak and Fisher, 1999, p. 191)

Peak and Fisher's comment, after the Jackson quote, shows clearly how the station positioned itself to deliver what advertisers want. The weakness of PSB in the early twenty-first century is such that there has been no regulatory inquiry into this autonomous change in the channel's purpose. It is possible that the channel will be privatised in the coming decade, then profits will go to shareholders rather than being invested in programmes.

This is not to say that C4 was no longer innovative, the 1999 series *Queer As Folk* brought 'gay television' into the mainstream, but it was operating on commercial rather than aesthetic criteria. This was also evident when the channel paid £120 million for the right to broadcast *ER* and *Friends*. Operating commercially (prime objective: the pursuit of audiences), rather than aesthetically (prime objective: the making of interesting programmes), changes the rules of the game; as Jackson himself said, *before* he joined C4:

> Am I alone in thinking that the pursuit of demographics – in particular, young lager-drinking, upwardly mobile men – has led to a sapping Channel 4's originality?. (Quoted in Beckett, 2000, p. 2)

Clearly he had changed his mind after becoming Controller but evidence that C4 was failing in its original remit was offered in a

Broadcasting Standards Council report, *Include Me In*, which concluded that, with reference to C4:

> Viewers from minority ethnic groups feel that programmes are guilty of presenting characters from ethnic minorities as two-dimensional and without a role in society as a whole.   (Gibson, 1999, p. 4)

If C4 was not going to acknowledge Annan's belief that broadcasters were essential 'to the sense of national identity and community' then it was unlikely that any other channel would, the BBC being too conservative to be radical and consensus broadcasting had failed to reflect the cultural diversity of Britain.

The ethos of PSB dominated British broadcasting until the 1990s when the so-called 'free market' economic philosophies led to the virtual dismantling of the system in favour of commercial prerogatives.

2.7   Classification or censorship?

In the 1960s the British Board of Film Censorship was renamed as the British Board of Film Classification (BBFC). For many, particularly writer Tom Dewe Mathews, there is no difference between the two. Censorship, it is argued, is necessary to a civilised society as it draws the boundaries between what is deemed good and what is not. In this way censorship tells us much about what is socially acceptable at particular times in a society's history.

The BBFC is a self-regulating body, like the Press Complaints Commission, set up by the industry to pre-empt state censorship. In Britain, after James Ferman's retirement in 1999, the Board seems to have become slightly more liberal in its classification. For example, *The Idiots* (1998), a Danish film that features a male erection, was passed at 18. Any alien viewing mainstream film would have great difficulty in understanding human sexual behaviour: what women do is usually evident; however, men's role has been shrouded in mystery. This is because male erection has been considered synonymous with obscenity, which is illegal in media texts. This has been, at least in part, due to the police's own definition of what will 'deprave and corrupt' and so, indirectly, the police force has been a major influence in the representation of sexuality in Britain. You should make up your own mind whether an erect penis is likely to 'deprave and corrupt' you (it might depend on whose it is).

I Spit on Your Grave (1978) is an infamous example of a film that was banned; it is a rape-revenge movie that many critics have found repulsive because of its explicit portrayal of rape. However, it has been argued that: 'Male spectators are positioned to be disgusted by the rape and to identify with the avenging woman' (Lehman, 1993, p. 104). Audiences are meant to feel sickened by the representation of rape, which is surely a normal response. The question that needs to be asked is whether a film, or any media text, is morally repugnant, in the way that Hitler's *Mein Kampff* is. It is necessary to consider the film's preferred reading (see Chapter 6). If a text portrays rape but 'says' it is wrong then banning it seems to be a strange response. Clearly individuals are at liberty to make their own readings, but that is a liberty we have in a 'free society'. Many texts, it seems, are banned because the censor, or judges if the case is brought to court, cannot decode the text's preferred reading and so the text is misread as depraved.

The certification, uncut, of *The Idiots*, along with that of the infamous Japanese film *Ai No Corrida* (*In the Realm of the Senses*, 1976), featuring hardcore sex and a man being castrated by his lover, indicates the class prejudice evident in the BBFC. Both these foreign-language films had restricted, art-house releases aimed at a middle-class audience. By certifying films that include material deemed obscene in mainstream texts the censor is stating that an educated audience knows how to respond to the explicit representation of sexual activity, unlike a working-class audience. In this case the status of a text is, in part, defined institutionally by the places in which it is consumed:

> Official culture, preserved in art galleries, museums, and university courses, demands cultivated tastes and a formally imparted knowledge. It demands moments of attention that are separated from the run of daily life. Popular culture, meanwhile, mobilizes the tactile, the incidental, the transitory, the expendable, the visceral. It does not involve an abstract aesthetic research amongst privileged objects of attention, but invokes mobile orders of sense, taste and desire.   (Chambers, 1990, p. 12)

The more immediate and sensuous experience of popular culture seems to be more threatening than official, high, culture. In this, popular culture can be seen to be, sometimes, a threat to bourgeois sensibilities. Rock 'n' roll, it was believed, heralded the end of civilisation, as did punk rock in the late 1970s. Indeed, at their moments of inception these new forms of popular culture did threaten the old order of respectable texts. However, as we shall see in Chapter 5, these new forms are often co-opted into official culture through their commodification.

Also in 1999, Abel Ferrara's notorious 'video nasty' *Driller Killer* (1980) was at last passed for video distribution (see below), but only after the distributor had cut the more offending sections. Distributors usually know what is, and is not, acceptable to the Board and so, in order to save time and money, will cut the film before submitting it. This allows the Board to truthfully declare that it did not cut the film in question, although the Board's criteria of censorship have been followed.

In the USA the Motion Pictures Association of America (MPAA) is currently responsible for the administration of ratings. However, unlike in Britain, films do not *have to* be certified and it is an organisation used primarily by the major distributors. For example, independent producer Trimark Pictures, not a signatory of the MPAA, chose not to submit *Romance* (1999) for certification knowing it would have been given the NC-17 rating. This rating rarely does well at the box office and Blockbuster video will not stock films of this certificate, so further reducing a film's exposure. This rating is usually reserved for pornography, and although *Romance* was sexually explicit, it was regarded as an art movie. If it had applied for a certificate Trimark would have been obliged to submit its marketing to the MPAA for approval (de la Fuente, 1999).

In 1999 both *South Park* and *Eyes Wide Shut* were high-profile cases in the USA. Independent filmmaker Palm Pictures, producers of *South Park*, got so irritated with the MPAA's continued insistence on cuts in order to attain an R rating that it posted the offending scene, in both NC-17 and R versions, on the Internet and asked for audience response. *Romance* was also marketed on the Internet: an explicit trailer was placed on a pornographic website. This is more evidence that the Internet causes regulators problems, bypassing the normal routes of communication. NC-17 is not simply commercial death in North America because of its certification, many media organisations refuse to carry advertising for such films and so make it difficult to market the movie in question.

Political influence is also controversial, particularly in democracies that purport to be 'free societies'. It is important for democratic governments to avoid the accusation that they are attempting to censor material. In 1997 the then Conservative Heritage Secretary of State, Virginia Bottomley, in a campaign orchestrated by the *Daily Mail*, suggested that *Crash* (1996) should not be certified by the BBFC for general release and urged local authorities to ban the film. Eventually the BBFC announced that the film would be passed '18' without cuts; this statement was made the day after the General Election was announced. This was astute timing, as the government had more pressing matters than to continue to vilify one film (see Chapter 6). After the success of (New) Labour in the 1997 election, Channel 4, at last, broadcast *Reservoir Dogs* (with its 'stuck in the middle with you' torture scene), probably feeling confident that the new government would not criticise the company for doing so.

'More liberal' the climate may have been in 1999 but *Straw Dogs* (1971) remained uncertified for video because the chief censor, Robin Duval, believed that its depiction of a woman eventually enjoying being raped remained taboo. In isolation, this seems to be a reasonable position as representations of sex and violence together are obviously a potent issue; however, such scenes must be considered in context and many believe *Straw Dogs* to be an important film that is not designed to titillate.

Duval succeeded James Ferman who had been the 'chief censor' for many years. Ferman appeared to fall foul of the then Home Secretary, Jack Straw, in 1998 because he was keen on allowing hardcore (that is the acts are real and not simulated) sexual activity to gain certification. Ferman's motivation was to reduce the number of illicit videos smuggled in from Europe that not only offered hardcore sex but also included scenes of sexual violence. Ferman's logic was that if stronger material was legally available in Britain, as videos with an R-18 certificate that could only be purchased from licensed sex shops, then the more extreme material would no longer be needed. Straw, when alerted by Customs and Excise, stopped Ferman's initiative. However, in May 2000, video distributors of hardcore material won a high court judgement that hardcore sex was not necessarily obscene and so was not necessarily illegal. The BBFC accepted the decision; the Home Secretary will therefore need to change the law if he wants to make hardcore sex illegal; though, as mentioned above, it had already appeared in 'art' cinema.

Video

Every few years, 'moral panics' (dealt with in Chapter 6) gain much media coverage. In the early 1980s the distribution of 'unsuitable' videos caused great controversy. Certifications of films on video are often not the same as those the films received for cinema distribution. The reason for this is connected to the point of sale and the viewing conditions. It is not illegal for a minor to view an 18-certificate film. However, if a cash transaction takes place, in the cinema or video store, allowing a youngster to see a film that is certified older than he or she is, then that transgresses the law. While it will be difficult for, say, a 14-year-old to get into a cinema, that same 14-year-old can easily, legally, see an adult-rated video in the home. So the fact that it is easier for children to see 'inappropriate' material on video is reflected in the fact that certification is more severe for video. For example, 15-certificate films, like *Starship Troopers* (1997), often get an 18-certificate on video.

The other problem censors have with video, and DVD, is the technology's ability to alter the way the text is viewed. Cinema audiences cannot demand stills, immediate replays or frame-by-frame analysis of sequences. This repeated viewing of particular scenes, which may be concerned with sex, violence or both, removes them from their context. In this way, scenes from mainstream films can be viewed solely for their titillation value, divorced from their narrative. Hence it is possible for scenes from *I Spit on Your Grave* to be viewed as exploitative of women despite, arguably, the film's preferred reading, which condemns the men's behaviour.

Issues around censorship

Censorship tells us much about society: it shows what was 'allowed' at a particular time. Watching Hollywood lovers in the 1930s lie diagonally on a bed, because the actors had to have their feet on the floor, is laughable. Indeed, to modern eyes it often appears there is no sex in 'old black and white films', which suggests that the older generations were far more prudish than subsequent ones. In fact many Hollywood films included sex but were forced by censorship to use symbols: see the (phallic) lighthouse in *Casablanca* (1942) or the flapping swing doors and rain in *Out of the Past* (also known as *Build My Gallows High*) (1947).

Although the control of censorship is in less repressed hands now, in Britain, than forty years ago, few would argue there should be *no* censorship at all: only paedophiles and libertarians defend paedophilic texts. Similarly texts that promulgate racial hatred have no role in a civilised society. At the extremes there is little ambiguity; however, if a film deals with a contentious issue, such as paedophilia, in a way that does not condone the paedophile's actions, for example *Lolita* (1997), then it will probably be shown in 'liberal' societies.

When *Lolita*'s distributors asked the Board to certify two extra scenes for the DVD version, no doubt so it could be marketed as the 'uncut' version, they received the following decision:

> The Comic Book and The Lake Point Cottages [scenes] both contain strong depictions of sexual conduct between the adult Humbert Humbert and the 14-year-old Lolita. In the case of the feature version of *Lolita*, the lack of specific sexual detail within the overall context of the film allowed the Board to classify *Lolita* in the adult category. In the case of these two works, however, we are presented with out-of-context sexualised images of an underaged girl. These scenes both contain images of sexual nudity and behaviour which were not present in the feature version. . . .
>
> Our main concern with these highly eroticised scenes is that they might invite feelings of arousal towards a child. We have a particular concern in the context of DVD extras where the scenes in question can be readily accessed and replayed at any speed. The obvious sexualisation of a 14-year-old girl with the use of such provocative detail must raise concerns about the potential misuse of this material by those predisposed to seek illegal sexual encounters. There is, in the Board's view, a serious possibility of 'harm' being caused to some individuals, and potentially through their actions, to society more widely.
>
> The Board has therefore refused certifcates to these two works.
>
> (Source: BBFC website)

The Board's decision explains that the original feature film was passed because it 'lacked specific sexual detail'. However, the additional scenes appear to have been specifically sexual and so were not allowed. Although the film deals with paedophilia there is little, if any, sense that the protagonist is exploiting the underage girl; on the contrary, she appears to seduce him. In other western countries, such as the Netherlands, having sex with minors is not illegal. The Board, as it must, is applying the law of British society and not operating, in this case, on some moral high ground.

The Board's secondary concern, evident in this decision, is the medium through which the film was to be accessed. While there is little doubt that the Board would have asked for the offending scenes to be cut if they had been present in the feature film (their absence suggests the distributor knew the Board would not pass them), the fact that DVD is a home-based, interactive medium is also a factor, as mentioned above.

The easier access to 'inappropriate' material motivated a clause in the Video Recordings Act that states:

classification must have 'special regard to the likelihood of video works ... being viewed in the home'.   (Mathews, 1994, p. 246)

As we shall see in Chapter 6 in relation to the campaign to ban *Crash*, the bourgeois obsession with the dominance of family life is at work here. If the BBFC followed this instruction to the letter, then only Parental Guidance (PG) would be available on video and DVD! The situation looked to be even worse in the early 1990s with the Criminal Justice Bill when, spurred on by the anti-abortion campaigner David Alton, MP, it looked as though the government were going to ban any representation of extreme violence on video. It was pointed out, however, that such classics of cinema as *The Godfather* (1971) and *Raging Bull* (1980) would fall foul of such a 'catch all' legislation.

Indirect censorship

Censorship is not always as open as that of the BBFC, which details its decisions on its website. Most censorship, by definition, is unseen. Some of this is government inspired, particularly in relation to the 'security services', and some of it manifests itself as propaganda.

For example, the 30-odd years of Troubles in Northern Ireland at the end of the twentieth century saw a concerted campaign against the IRA that most British newspapers were happy to go along with. Indeed, such was the ferocity of this stance that any media text (such as the films *The Crying Game* (1992, see Lacey 2000a) and *The Devil's Own* (1997)) that portrayed the IRA as being populated by non-psychopathic human beings was vilified in some parts of the press.

> For decades British newspapers, and particularly the *Sunday Times* and the *Daily Mail*, parroted the black propaganda myth – originally promoted by the British army – that the IRA were 'criminal godfathers', 'psychopaths' and bloodthirsty killers. There was little analysis of the political structure of the IRA, its organisation, or the nature of its support.   (Toolis, 2000, p. 8)

The result of this was that terrorist atrocities on behalf of the Unionist cause (those who wanted Northern Ireland to remain part of the United Kingdom) were underreported and any IRA terrorist acts received blanket coverage. During the late 1980s it became illegal for broadcasters to allow anyone speaking on behalf of the IRA to be heard using their own voice; it was allowable to subtitle or dub the speech. This absurd state of affairs led to even less reporting of the IRA and made explicit that Britain did not really have 'freedom of speech'.

One important aspect of a democracy is the role pressure groups have in attempting to influence governments.

2.8 Pressure groups

Pressure groups are formal organisations that either represent particular interests, such as the National Union of Farmers, or campaign on specific issues. From a Media perspective Anna Reading (1999) has suggested there are three types of pressure group:

1. the moralisers – who campaign on issues of public morality, usually defined as concern about levels of sex and violence in media texts;
2. the sharers – who campaign against a high degree of concentration of media ownership, such as that of News Corporation;
3. the includers – who campaign on issues of equal opportunity of employment in the media and against negative stereotyping of minority groups by the media.

Moralisers – led by the *Daily Mail* – tried to get *Crash* banned and were successful in getting restrictive legislation in place regarding so-called 'video nasties'.

Includers' campaigns have fought against institutional racism within media organisations. For example, a Black Members Council was set up within the National Union of Journalists in order to promote better training and working conditions for black journalists. Such pressure groups are, unfortunately, necessary, otherwise the 'status quo' is likely to remain and this, in journalism, would have meant a continued dearth of black journalists.

▓ Exercise 2.1 ▓

In the late 1990s two British nannies were convicted of killing a toddler in the USA. Name them.

You may well have been able to name Louise Woodward, as her case received blanket coverage in the news. However, the name of Manjit Kaur Basuta is probably less familiar:

Basuta's case has made negligible impact on the nation's consciousness largely because of the media's apathetic attitude. With the exception of her family's local paper in Berkshire, no newspaper or television organisation has taken much interest in her trial, let alone mounted a campaign in support of her.   (Gentleman and Campbell, 1999, p. 4)

Basuta is a Sikh. It is possible that if there were more black journalists working in the press, then her story might have been picked up in the same was as the white Louise Woodward's was. Women also suffer from being underrepresented as media professionals:

New research ... [shows] that the women most likely to feature [in national newspapers] are celebrities and members of the public, rather than politicians, professionals or sportswomen.   (Carter, 1999, p. 6)

One of the pressure groups of most interest to media students is the Campaign for Press and Broadcasting Freedom (CPBF), which was formed in 1979. It believes that:

The contours of the media in the next millennium – what we see, hear and read, how we receive it, who owns and controls it, and how we pay for it – are not minor and marginal policy issues for political parties. Indeed, to the extent that changes in our society make us ever more reliant on the media for information and entertainment, they are becoming more pervasive and powerful in shaping our responses to the actual political, social and cultural changes we are experiencing.
(http://www.cpbf.demon.co.uk/manifesto.htm)

One of the great difficulties that 'sharers' face is that they need to use the media they are often criticising, to get their message across. CPBF's regular call for privacy laws is not likely to get a sympathetic mediation by the press. In an attempt to circumvent this, the CPBF has its own newsletter, *Free Press* (a useful read), and website.

The final section of this chapter attempts, briefly, to give an indication of how the norms and values of media organisations can affect the production of media texts. These are not formal regulations as such, but can be just as influential.

2.9 Institutional practices

All organisations have unwritten rules that employees usually follow; failure to do so may lead to them losing their jobs. In schools these rules are often spelt out and include such things as the school uniform, the need to be polite to others, and what side of the corridor to walk on. In adult institutions, these norms are more likely to be informal and learned through being 'socialised' into the organisation.

When we read most media texts we percieve a product of institutional practices; that is, it has been made in a certain way utilising the medium's conventions. Although these institutional practices evolve, they do represent what an organisation deems to be the correct method of production at any given time. To non-media people, which includes most Media teachers, these practices are invisible, especially as most bourgeois texts attempt to disguise the modes of production used. Only self-reflexive texts reveal, to any extent, how they are made – see section 6.4 in *Image and Representation*. The following paragraphs will consider how the institutional practices of the television industry affect the production of TV programmes.

If we consider Patricia Holland's (1997) list of 'Work areas in the television industry' we immediately get a sense of the collaborative effort involved in the production of most programmes: animation; announcers; archivists/librarians; art and design; costume/wardrobe; direction; engineering; film, video and audiotape editing; graphic design; IT specialists; journalists; laboratories; lighting; make-up and hairdressing; management; marketing and sales; producers; production assistants; production management; production operatives; recording still and moving images; researchers; runners/gofers; set crafts/props; sound; special effects; stage/floor management; support staff; transmission; writers. And this, understandably, does not include secretarial support, cleaners, security and so on. Obviously anyone new to the organisation will have to learn what these practices are. If they try and do things differently then they will probably find that their stay is short lived (or they may be hailed as a genius). A high degree of organisation is required for so many people to work together efficiently and this organisation is the institutional practice, a way of working that changes very rarely.

Technological developments influence the ways in which programmes are made. For instance, the availability of lightweight equipment in the 1960s allowed for location filming. Similarly, the edgy camera style of much of the classic *Boys from the Blackstuff* (1982) was, at least in part, a product of new hand-held cameras.

It is not only the technology of production that influences the way a text is produced, the technology of the medium itself necessitates certain ways of working. For example, the fact that the television image is small, especially when compared with cinema, means that the soundtrack must carry much of the information. This 'fact' about the television medium has an enormous influence on what appears on the screen; the same applies to cinema. There is not space here to consider this in detail but we can consider the way studio-based material is recorded.

▦ Exercise 2.2 ▦

Watch a scene from a soap opera and attempt to work out where the cameras are placed in relation to one another.

You will probably have noticed that the shot/reverse-shot pattern is used and there is a mixture of medium long shots and close-ups (which will be created by the use of a telephoto lens). The producer will edit these at the moment of performance. While it is obvious that this 'editing as you video' is a must for live events, the reason it is used for drama is one of cost: it is quicker, and therefore cheaper. Speed is also a requirement for programmes such as soap operas as they require many hours each week to be made.

Virtually all media texts are the result of institutional practices, which have a profound effect on their production. The high-concept film, described in Chapter 1, is also an institutional practice, as is the production of newspapers and magazines. In some cases, the way in which newspapers work to deadlines for instance, these practices are quite obvious to audiences. However, in other areas, particularly news gathering, they are not immediately obvious (see Chapter 8).

2.10 Conclusion

This chapter has considered how regulations attempt to influence the texts made by media organisations. This can be beneficial for audiences, for example the requirement that broadcast news be balanced, and can be detrimental, particularly in the areas of censorship (again of news). One of the most influential areas of regulation is public service broadcasting, an ideal that is under great threat from commercial pressures.

Another, more obvious, area of regulation is in the censorship, and/or classification, of films. This is determined, to an extent, by the viewing context (in public or in the home). As would be expected in a pluralist society, there are many pressure groups that campaign for more censorship as well as those who are against.

Finally, this chapter examined how the way in which an organisation works, its institutional practices, influence the production of media texts.

3

MEDIA TEXTS AS COMMODITIES

AIMS OF THE CHAPTER

➤ To investigate how film operates as a commodity through merchandising, product placement and previews.

➤ To consider how individuals are commodified as stars, celebrities or personalities.

➤ To assess the effect of advertising on newspapers.

➤ To consider the growth of lifestyle sections in newspapers.

➤ To consider commercial broadcasting.

➤ To consider media imperialism and public subsidy.

➤ To consider music as a commodity with reference to MTV.

➤ To consider news and the developing world.

➤ To acknowledge the Eurocentrism present in this series of books.

3.1   Introduction

A commodity is a product that is harvested, extracted or created in order to be sold for profit. Supermarkets are full of commodities, many of which have been imported and may – like the Windward Islands' bananas – constitute a major part of the source countries' gross national product (GNP).

Most media texts, too, are created in order to generate revenue and, ultimately, profit for the producing organisation. The only exceptions are public sector broadcasters who do not have to generate money from their products (see Chapter 2) and publicly funded texts (see Chapter 5). But media texts are not simply commodities, they are also cultural artefacts. This is also true of other commodities, such as coffee and tea, and we can study why a particular culture freeze-dries its coffee or puts its tea in bags. However, media texts

Art ◄──────────────────────────────► Commodity

Figure 3.1

are much more multifarious: the number of types of freeze-dried coffee is not much more than the number of brands that exist, while *every* media text has a degree of uniqueness.

In addition, many media texts are can also be considered as works of art, and exist on a continuum that has 'art' at one extreme and 'commodity' at the other (see Figure 3.1). Some texts are created *without* the prime intention of generating revenue and these may be defined as art (the determinant of this status being the critical establishment). At the other extreme a text is designed to appeal to a targeted audience *only* in order to make money. This is an over-simplification, even artists usually wish to appeal to a particular audience, and texts created solely as commodities can be considered to be 'works of art', but the continuum helps distinguish between different types of cultural production. Although the 'common sense' assumption that commodities are inherently aesthetically worthless is nonsense, it is useful to distinguish between texts produced as a commodity and those produced to make some kind of artistic statement.

In any case, most texts exist somewhere between the art:commodity extremes. Texts, or artists, that definitely reside at the extremes are rare. We may be secure in thinking of Picasso's paintings as 'art' and such manufactured groups as Milli Vanilli (who did not play or sing their songs) as a commodity; but Picasso became very rich as a painter and we can still analyse Milli Vanilli's product musically.

In Chapter 5 we consider how commerce might compromise artistic integrity but we should avoid the notion that if something is produced solely for profit it is necessarily bad, and the artist who eschews financial gain, necessarily produces anything of worth.

3.2 Films

The commodification of film is most apparent in the way films are marketed (an area considered in Chapter 4), in the merchandise that is 'tied-in' to virtually all 'big' movies, and in the system of previews Hollywood uses before releasing these films. We have already seen, in Chapter 1, how the production of high-concept films is driven by commodification.

Merchandising

Merchandising reached a twentieth-century peak in 1999 with *Star Wars Episode One: The Phantom Menace*, which had nearly 400 different products tied into it. However, it was not the only success of that year: *South Park – the Movie* also spawned profitable spin-off products. Because *South Park* was already pre-sold, through the television serial, the Licensing Agency – which brokered the UK merchandising – found the property so popular with manufacturers that they had a full complement of deals six months before the film was released. The way in which the company's director of entertainment licensing spoke gives a commercial perspective on a cultural product: 'The movie provides another dimension to the merchandising prospects for the property' (Kemp, 1999, p. 11). In mid-September 1999, after only two weeks in the box-office charts, the Licensing Agency was expecting business to reach £150 million by the end of the year. Compare this with the film's box-office take of just around £7 million in Britain and the benefits of merchandising become even more obvious.

Space Jam (1996) 'only' made around $90 million at the North American box office but was reputed to have garnered *billions* of dollars in merchandise. In addition, the Looney Tunes characters were given a new lease of life that Warner Bros could exploit on its children's television channel, Cartoon Network. The chairman of the film's producers, Time-Warner, said, '*Space Jam* isn't a movie. It's a marketing event' (Handy, 1996, p. 78). The film created 200 licensees worldwide; McDonald's, Jell-O and Kraft were partners in promoting the merchandise (Lukk, 1996).

We saw in Chapter 1 how synergy has been the driving economic force since the 1980s; however, it seems that media companies accept that their branch of the entertainment business is very different from toy, or burger, manufacture and so let specialists, in their areas, 'do the business'. The film's producers take a percentage of merchandising revenue; it has been estimated:

> that movie property owners like Disney probably receive at lest ten percent of the wholesale price as their share of the profits.   (Ibid., p. 258).

The major studios do not always get it right; in 1996 the unexpected success of *Toy Story* led to a massive demand for Buzz Lightyear that could not be met.

The phenomenal profits that can be generated from merchandising were first made evident with the original *Star Wars* in 1977. In the late 1990s licensing and merchandising executives were getting involved at the script stage of a film. It is probably not unreasonable to assume that the introduction of Jessie the Cowgirl, in *Toy Story 2* (1999), was motivated, at least partly, by the need to have another toy to sell; as well as addressing the female demographic of the audience at the same time.

Another way products are sold through films is via product placement.

Product placement

Product placement is where a product makes an obvious appearance in a film. So a character ordering a beer may ask for a Budweiser if that company has paid to have this product 'placed'. This device is not new; North American movies have always been produced as commodities and the Hollywood of the 'Golden Era' of the 1920s–1940s was not unaware of the money to be made through product placement. The now almost-forgotten Joan Crawford vehicle *Letty Linton* (1931) helped Macy's sell half a million copies of the dress worn by the star (Mathews, 1998).

Macy's were probably the prime beneficiary of the dress sales; in the twenty-first century – with interactive technology – the possibility of selling clothing through product placement is even more obvious. However, it is also obvious to everyone involved in the production:

> To illustrate the potential complications of high-tech product placement...
> the hypothetical example of a viewer watching an episode of *Ally McBeal* on-line and clicking on star Calista Flockhart's red dress to buy a similar garment. 'Somebody ... has to deal with David E. Kelley, who owns the production, Rox, which airs the show, and Calista Flockhart's agent.
> Everybody wants a piece and how much margin is there in one red dress?' (Hazleton, 2000, p. 16)

It is unlikely that it will be profitable to sell the dress because everyone along the 'chain' will want a cut. The James Bond franchise has been among the forerunners of product placement and the producers are careful to integrate any products (such as BMW) into the storyline rather than have them looking like stuck on advertisements. Indeed, the effectiveness for the companies of placing their product is uncertain: surveys suggest that awareness is raised but purchases do not necessarily follow.

Film studios also benefit from the companies advertising their products in relation to the film within which it has been placed. *Austin Powers: The Spy Who Shagged Me* (1999) had product placement and tie-in deals with Heineken, Philips Electronics, Starbucks and Virgin Atlantic, which brought an 'estimated $60m in advertising support' (ibid., p. 15) from those companies advertising their product in relation to the film. Disney was hoping for $150m worth of promotion from McDonald's in relation to *Dinosaur* (2000).

This joint marketing also occurs with companies that have not placed their product but do have tie-in deals: 'When Burger King invested an estimated $45 million in ads and premiums in its *Toy Story* promotion, they saw a decisive return on their investments' (ibid., p. 262). Burger King was happy (sales of its Kids' Meals doubled) and Disney was happy with the extra promotion.

Previewing

Previewing allows studios to 'road test' their film before releasing it. Bad previews can lead a film to be drastically altered; for example, *Blade Runner* (1982) had a voice-over added and a new ending tacked on. The director's intentions were not seen until the 'director's cut' was released 10 years later, though this version was also a compromise.

The preview audiences consist of people the film is targeting and they fill in a questionnaire supplying information about what they feel is wrong in the film. Peter Howitt (1998) describes how *Sliding Doors* (1998), which he wrote and directed, attained only a 17% 'Excellent' rating (25% is the target) from the preview audience. Parts of the film were then re-shot, it was re-edited and the second version was previewed to an audience, and it was rated 27% 'Excellent'.

Not all reshoots, however, are successful. *Payback* (1999) also received poor preview scores, which reinforced Paramount's view that they did not have the type of Mel Gibson film they had hoped for:

> they didn't like the new macho Mel. He was too hard-boiled, too mean. Maybe his character could he [*sic*] softened up with a few jokes? Then their marketing could lead with the [tagline], 'No More Nr Nice Guy', instead of 'Get Mad. Get Tough. Get Even'.   (Mathews, 1999, p. 12)

Director Brian Helgeland refused to change the film so Mel Gibson's hairdresser directed the reshoots; he didn't really, this was a ruse to avoid falling foul of union rules that do not allow the producer (Gibson in this case) to rehire himself as a director. The reshoot was to no avail as the preview scores of the second version were worse than the first. This did not stop the film doing well at the box office.

This market testing is obviously trying to ensure that the film pleases its intended audience, and so guaranteeing, as far as possible, box-office success. This commodification was made explicit by screenwriter Howard Rodman, who:

> observed that 'When you are writing a screenplay, one of the things you are doing, in a sense, is writing a prospectus for a stock offering', and in the mid-1980s executives at United Artists talked, accurately enough, of high concept as being a fiscally responsible way of making film. (Maltby, 1998, p. 38)

While in Europe this sort of talk can raise the hackles of creative personnel, in North America it is the norm. This is true of both the film and television industries (which are often the same company).

■ Exercise 3.1 ■

When the next 'blockbuster' movie is released, make a note of how many spin-off properties and marketing deals you notice.

3.3 Stars, celebrities and personalities

Stars, celebrities and personalities are a very important aspect of both the content and promotion of media texts. Stars are most evident in film whilst celebrities can come from any walk of life as long as they have achieved something; personalities, on the other hand, are only famous for being famous. All three require the mass media to circulate their images.

Film stars

In early Hollywood, performers were anonymous and often not even actors – the film's technicians would play parts. When stage actors began performing in front of cameras the producers refused to name them, fearing they would demand more money. So performers were known by a studio moniker, the most famous of whom was the

Biograph Girl. In 1910 Carl Laemmle, who was moving from exhibition to distribution, instituted wage inflation by offering the Biograph Girl a pay rise from $25 to $1000; she was tempted, and Florence Lawrence became the first film star.

Laemmle's background in exhibition served him well as he knew the value of promotion. He planted a story in the St Louis press that the Biograph Girl, Florence Lawrence, had died in an accident. The following day his company, IMP,

> took an ad in *The Moving Picture World* to the effect that the story was an invention of IMP's enemies: 'We nail a lie.' And Miss Lawrence visited St Louis with IMP's leading actor, King Baggott: they were mobbed. (Shipman, 1982, p. 38b)

As the above anecdote suggests, the creation of a star requires the mass media. It is insufficient for stars merely to appear in films, or television programmes, where they play characters. In order to create a star persona, details of their own lives need to be circulated within the public domain. These details, as Laemmle appreciated, did not have to be true, simply of interest to the audience. Because of their existence:

> in the world independent of their screen/'fiction' appearances, it is possible to believe ... that as people they are more real than characters in stories. This means that they serve to disguise the fact that they are ... produced images.   (Dyer, 1979, p. 22)

A factual profile of a film star is just as much part of the constructed image as the star's appearance in films. What we know of stars is their persona, 'Will Smith' is a funny guy who is self-deprecating about his masculinity and is careful about what he wears; the real Will Smith may possess some, or all, of these characteristics, but he is different. Human beings are far more complex than star personas can allow. Much of the coverage of stars comes from magazines and film programmes that form part of the publicity circus (see section 4.2).

▄ Exercise 3.2 ▄

List as many different publications as you can that include coverage of film stars.

The reason these publications cover stars is that they will appeal to the target audience and therefore generate sales. If any film or lifestyle magazine actually criticises stars in any way then it is likely to be denied access to them in future. Because stars may be the principal marketing tools of such publications this could be financially disastrous. In recent years stars have even insisted on having the final say on what appears in an article. Though, in late 2000, *Premiere* magazine did run an unflattering profile of Arnold Schwarzenegger, presumably the publication felt Arnie was now a 'has been' and they would not need his cooperation in future.

Celebrities

Whilst movies are virtually always the prime text for film stars, celebrities rely upon the secondary texts for the construction of their persona. Celebrities first come to fame for achieving something of distinction and are most apparent in the field of sport.

In recent years the numbers of sports celebrities have increased, particularly footballers in Britain. Whilst football players do develop personas on the field of play (Vinnie Jones as psycho; Roy Keane's aggression), it is the media coverage that fills this out. This is particularly evident in the celebration of the partnership of David Beckham and Posh Spice and their production of offspring. Such people are covered because this will sell copies, and they sell copies because they are covered.

Magazine and newspaper coverage are the lifeblood of the celebrity, keeping the individual in the public eye. Magazines tend to be kinder in their coverage; newspapers, particularly the 'red tops', are as likely to 'bite' the 'celeb' as eulogise them; for example, the *Mirror*'s coverage of Naomi Campbell in early 2001.

The media coverage of Princess Diana seemed to dominate her life so much that, at times, it seemed she did not feel alive unless she featured in the press (a postmodern life?). The manner of her death, pursued by paparazzi, was, as J. G. Ballard had suggested 25 years earlier in *Crash*, a thoroughly modern way for a celebrity to die. Another apparent victim of her celebrity was newscaster and TV presenter Jill Dando who was murdered in 1999.

Personalities

Personalities are similar to celebrities except they have not done anything worth celebrating. These 'personalities' who inhabit 'gossip' magazines like *Chat* and *Hello!*, and reap coverage in lifestyle magazines and tabloid newspapers, rely upon nothing except the fact they are being celebrated in such publications. They also often appear as guests on television shows. They are postmodern celebrities, famous only for being famous. For example, Caprice Bourret came to 'fame' in 1996 as a 'UK's new Miss Wonderbra' (in itself a publicity stunt) and populated the pages of lad's mags for many years afterwards. By 2001 she was attempting to become a pop star as a way of feeding further coverage and (maybe) a career development.

3.4 The effect of advertising on newspapers

The growth in advertising during the nineteenth century helped newspapers wean themselves off the political parties to which they were tied. Journalists could be better paid, which made them less open to bribery, and more money could be spent on actually gathering the news. Now broadsheet newspapers are particularly dependent upon the advertising they carry to maintain an affordable cover price; tabloid newspapers get a higher proportion of their revenue from sales to the public. However, the benefits of advertising only accrued to certain types of newspapers.

During the late eighteenth and early nineteenth century, Britain had a very healthy radical press who often campaigned on behalf of exploited workers. The government first tried to suppress the radical press through legal means using the libel laws. This was found to be counter-productive: 'When the editor of *The Republican* was prosecuted in 1819, the paper's circulation rose by over 50 per cent' (Curran and Seaton, 1991, p. 12). The government used stamp duty on the newspapers and taxes on paper and advertisements to increase costs, hoping that this would deter the opposition publications. This simply led to a massive growth in unstamped, and therefore illegal, newspapers, which were immensely popular with readers. The government then reduced stamp duty by 75 per cent thus making the smuggling of unstamped newspapers less attractive. This forced the radical newspapers to raise their price four-fold (to 4d), thus making them too expensive for their working-class readership.

In 1853 advertising tax was abolished, leading to a vast increase in advertising volume. The increase in advertising was also helped by new technology that allowed a better quality of reproduction. More revenue from advertising led to a reduction in the cover price of many newspapers, which in turn helped increase circulation. However, because advertisers chose publications according to their political orientation, oppositional newspapers were, comparatively, infrequently used.

> Even non-socialist newspapers found that controversial editorial policies led to the loss of commercial advertising. The *Pall Mall Gazette*'s advertising revenue dropped sharply in response to its 'Maiden Tribute' crusade in 1885 in which the editor 'procured' a 15-year-old girl as part of his paper's campaign to raise the legal age of consent. (Ibid., p. 39)

Advertisers rarely base their decisions on political considerations now, the demographic profile of the publications is far more important, but publications, newspapers or magazines, which propagate non-mainstream values still carry very little, if any, mainstream advertising. So the reliance on advertising to 'subsidise' the cover price in order to sell more copies (as newspapers are a commodity) leads to a narrowing of the viewpoints represented in the news.

In order to generate as much revenue as possible, newspapers have developed lifestyle sections that enable them to provide a suitable environment for lifestyle advertising.

Growth of lifestyle sections

Since the 1980s, the growth of 'lifestyle' advertising has significantly transformed the editorial content of broadsheet and middle-market tabloids. This has led certain types of newspapers to move away from being editorially led, to being publications that serve the lifestyle interests of readers and advertisers. That is, the paper becomes a vehicle whose primary purpose is not to impart news but to deliver audiences to advertisers. Audiences may be happy with this as they get the consumer–lifestyle information they want – from both the editorial and the advertising – at a relatively cheap price. However, this emphasis has, arguably, allowed the advertiser to dominate:

> This concept is known as Total Newsroom, in which editorial, advertising, circulation and promotion are all coordinated around the goal of marketing a product. Instead of worrying about whether this is a good story, editors ask whether the proposed story will connect with the reader's lifestyle. (Fleetwood, 1999, p. 13)

The advertisers dominate the Total Newsroom because lifestyle is defined in consumerist terms: we are what we buy, whether that is products or services. This definition of audiences as consumers ('I shop therefore I am') is obviously capitalist in nature and fundamental to the dominant, bourgeois ideology (that is, the way in which the 'common sense' world view is constructed in the western world – see *Image and Representation*). However, newspapers' *raison d'être* remains *news* and so broadsheet newspapers segment their publication into different sections; take a Saturday edition of the *Guardian*:

Saturday's *Guardian*, 18 September 1999
This newspaper is published in seven sections:

The *Guardian*   (news and comment)
'Sport'
'Saturday review'   (arts)
'Weekend'   (featuring a lifestyle editorial including food, drink and fashion)
'Jobs & Money'
'Travel'
The 'Guide'   (entertainment, including television listings)

▓ Exercise 3.3 ▓

Write down what sort of advertising is likely to be carried within each of the sections of the Saturday *Guardian*.

Predictions for the 'Review', 'Weekend', 'Jobs & Money', 'Travel' and 'Guide' are relatively straightforward. The tabloid 'Jobs & Money', for instance, has approximately 68 pages of advertising out of a total of 88. The 20 pages of editorial function to attract readers to the advertising; the remainder of the section consists of classified advertising (see Chapter 4). In contrast, the 'Review' section is relatively light on advertising as arts-based advertising is limited by small budgets; the biggest advert is for the retailer W. H. Smith.

The 'Sport' section has barely any advertising but gets a section to itself because sport is important in attracting readers. This, along with the 'Review' section, is important for a newspaper's status particularly to ABC1 readers (see Chapter 7). The news section carries 'run of paper' advertising, which may include products or services that 'belong' in the specialist sections ('run of paper' advertising – which can appear anywhere in the paper – is usually cheaper to purchase). On Saturdays there is often a preponderance of electrical retailers, reflecting the fact that weekends are times when men, traditionally, do some shopping.

Once again we may conclude that this, in effect, does no 'harm' as the news section is compartmentalised and, indeed, subsidised by the lifestyle sections, which news junkies can dispense with should they wish. However, once the so-called 'Chinese wall', which reputedly exists between advertising and editorial departments, is breached then audiences can no longer have faith that they are being given news in an unadulterated fashion. As in the nineteenth century, the economic effect of advertisers can be devastating. In 1995 the *San Jose Mercury News* ran an article advising how to negotiate for lower car prices:

> Car dealers, furious, stopped advertising [for four months]. The paper lost more than a million dollars. The publisher got desperate as his automotive section shrank from 24 pages to 12. Publisher Jay Harris met the car dealers and even sent a public letter of apology.   (Fleetwood, 1999, p. 13)

If newspapers are run as commodities, for the revenue they generate, and not to provide their audience with information, then it follows that traumas such as that suffered by the *San Jose Mercury News* are avoided as much as possible:

> Cosmetics are among the most unregulated, and therefore most potentially harmful, consumer products on the market. Consumers fail to realize that what you put on your skin is absorbed into the body. Few publications put effort into investigating the cosmetics industry, which is not surprising since the industry is a major magazine and newspaper advertiser. This is especially true of the women's magazine. Consequently, there is almost no good coverage of the industry.   (Bleifuss, 1998, p. 31)

This is not to suggest that journalists are simply lackeys of the advertising department but evidence suggests that stories that, potentially, will embarrass advertisers are increasingly likely to be compromised. Fleetwood (1999) lists a number of examples, including how an article on poor conditions on Carnival Cruise Ships got 'spiked' when the travel editor learned of it, because of the damage to advertising revenue; how newspapers gave editorial mention to stores that advertised in the newspaper; and the way big advertisers were allowed to see a negative story before it was printed, so they could prepare a defence and, indeed, run the story with their own 'spin' (see Chapter 4).

Even if advertisers applied no pressure to news organisations, the commercial nature of non-PSB businesses would in itself affect news values. For example, the local, commercial radio station Pulse, based in Bradford, lists fourteen items in its news policy. The *top* one is:

> The objective of 'Programmes' is to maximise audience. News is part of 'Programmes'.

It follows from this that what is defined as news is 'what people are talking about in the pub or over the desk at work' (item 3). This is obviously much more likely to be gossip-based rather than hard news. Hard news is usually regarded as dealing with important issues to do with politics and society; soft news is more trivial in nature. Broadsheet newspapers tend to emphasise the former and tabloids the latter.

For many this is an example of 'dumbing down' in the media. While commercial radio and tabloid newspapers have had a populist element for many years, recently a number of previously robust public service broadcasting (PSB) stations have attempted to popularise themselves. For example, BBC Radio 3 has responded to the success of Classic FM (which plays mostly only the 'best bits' of classical music rather than whole pieces) with such programmes as *Brian Kay's Sunday Morning*, and by having a more chat-inflected presenter (or maybe even DJ), Sean Rafferty, in the weekday evening drive-time slot. The 'chattering classes' (that is, middle-class people who make their voices heard) have seen this popularisation (which has been particularly controversial on BBC Radio 4 – see section 7.4) as an attack on their (high) standards. At the root of this argument is the art *v.* entertainment debate that pits middle-class values against those of the working class.

This popularisation in the BBC, however, has not been wholesale; BBC Radio 1, in its evening schedule, has offered a clear alternative to the audience-driven commercial radio (and daytime Radio 1) playlists. However, it would be unfair to simply dismiss the charges of 'dumbing down' as being elitist in nature for, as we have seen, once a media organisation chases audiences then the nature of the texts produced changes.

There seems little doubt that the increasing commodification of the press serves to decrease the news we are able to see and, at worst, suppress stories that it is in the public interest to have aired. The film *The Insider* (1999) showed how corporate pressure on the CBS news division led to an interview with a tobacco industry whistle-blower being censored. Chapter 4 will consider how many newspaper stories actually originate as publicity rather than news.

3.5 Commercial broadcasting

Television

The function of commercial television (as distinct from public service broadcasters) is to generate audiences for advertisers. Indeed, from a television executive's point of view, the medium consists of advertising with programmes inserted around them. Television programmes are therefore produced as commodities whose prime aim is to deliver a particular audience profile. Channel 4, in Britain, produced *Hollyoaks* with the specific intention of generating a young middle-class audience for advertisers.

Unsurprisingly, North America has refined the link between programmes and their commercial prerogative. *Dawson's Creek* was created in partnership with J. Crew clothes:

> Not only did the characters all wear J. Crew clothes, not only did the windswept, nautical set make them look as if they had stepped off the pages of a J. Crew's catalog, and not only did the characters spout dialogue like 'He looks like he stepped out a J. Crew catalog,' but the cast was also featured on the cover of the January J. Crew catalog.   (Klein, 2001, p. 42)

More evidence of the fact that television programmes are more commodities than media texts is in the speed with which those with low ratings are ditched. In the United States programmes are almost immediately taken off the air if they are not reaching the required audience. For example, in June 2000, ABC cancelled *Clerks* after just two episodes; it was replaced by repeats of *Spin City*. In Britain, even unsuccessful programmes are usually allowed their scheduled run; in America they can disappear without ever being fully seen. Only programmes with 'good' audiences are re-commissioned for further series; the most successful, like *Friends* and *ER*, run for many years.

Radio

Commercial radio operates on the same basis as television except that most stations are more recognisably local. In Britain there are four national commercial stations, Talk Radio, Atlantic 252, Virgin 1215 and Classic FM, and over 200 local stations.

Like television, the advent of digital radio broadcasting is likely to increase the number of stations available. Digital radio, however, can blur the differences between the media by offering pictures in addition to sound. It is unlikely that we will be treated to images of the DJ blabbing (though Sky TV did link up with Virgin 1215 so viewers could watch Chris Evans perform his show), and the digital frequency will be primarily used to offer better sound and extra information. For instance, if a single is being played, then the title could be displayed on the radio. In 2000, Radio 3 produced a promotional digital radio CD-ROM featuring jazz saxophonist Evan Parker accompanied by abstract animations.

Radio is flourishing on the Internet, where it is no longer limited by its broadcast area (short wave broadcasts have never been limited but sound quality is poor). It is possible to access radio stations from all over the world. It is this global reach of media texts that has resulted in the phenomenon of media imperialism.

3.6 Media imperialism

American dominance

North American cultural producers have driven the commodification of cultural artefacts. This is not to say that, in the West at least, other nations' media organisations have not also attempted to exploit their product for commercial purposes; however, North American companies do it on a larger scale and, usually, more successfully. This tendency to turn virtually everything into moneymaking – making the United States the capitalist society *par excellence* – was what led the Frankfurt school to assume it would become a fascist state (see Chapter 6).

North America has a large, generally prosperous population of nearly 300 million people, including Canada. This makes it easier for organisations to cover their production costs and make a profit in their home market alone and so any revenue generated from the international market is – after local marketing and distribution costs are taken into account – pure profit. North American media corporations are therefore able to price their product extremely competitively, undercutting local produce, thereby helping North American culture to its hegemonic status in the western world.

This hegemony – an acceptance, by most, of the dominance of North American media texts – is not simply an economic phenomenon. It could be that North American texts are (almost) universally attractive to audiences, with their strong narrative drive and high production values. The production values are a consequence of being able to command a large 'local' audience, so a lot of money can be spent relatively safely. However, the attraction of Hollywood-style films may be a result of their dominance; that is, because they are ubiquitous we have learned to prefer them. Being one of North America's media producers is not exactly a 'licence to print money' but many risk factors are alleviated by their worldwide status.

While Hollywood companies often distribute their own movies abroad, television programmes rely upon 'local' broadcasters to show them. Each year, in May and June, television executives from all over the world descend on Los Angeles to watch the next season's offerings, starting in autumn. In Britain the series that are deemed to have more aesthetic quality tend to be bought by the BBC and Channel 4, while Channel 5 and Sky may pick up the cheaper, 'trashier' products. In 2000 the industry buzz was for a remake of *The Fugitive*; by now you know how successful this was.

The effect of American dominance is not simply economic; it is also cultural. Because Hollywood's films are dominant in most western cinemas (and many non-western), just as US television is ever-present in the schedules, the comparative lack of local products means indigenous cultures are under-represented on their own cinema and television screens. This effect is called 'cultural imperialism'. Instead of physically invading countries, as in the days of empire, the strongest economies 'invade' the economically weaker and this, in terms of the media, often leads to cultural domination.

Cultural imperialism refers to a wider range of influence than we deal with in Media Studies. For example, McDonald's fast-food outlets can be seen as an example of cultural imperialism; from our perspective we deal with media texts and are therefore concerned with the effects of media imperialism.

Cinema

In *Screen International*'s Global Box Office Survey of 1998, the number of non-Hollywood films in each country's top ten was, in Europe, as follows: Italy, 5 (which included two British films); France, 4; and Poland, 3. The remaining countries had no more than two non-Hollywood films in their top ten; Russia, Hungary, Germany and Iceland had none; 75 per cent of European audiences' box-office spend is on Hollywood fare.

The situation for indigenous films was even worse in the rest of the world: Hong Kong and Japan each managed three of their own films in the top ten, and South Korea, two. Australia had only one (a UK–US co-production, *Sliding Doors*), as did South Africa (the UK's *The Full Monty*). Brazil, Canada and Mexico had none (source: *Screen International*, 30 July and 6 August, 1999).

Nations with relatively small populations only have small potential markets and so can only produce low-budget films and television. While spending a large amount of money on a film does not mean it will be successful, it certainly helps in the production of entertainment. When more money is spent on a film this means that the movie's appeal needs to be broadened to sell elsewhere. However, this may in turn make it less appealing to the home market, leaving filmmakers with what may be an impossible dilemma. As a marketing executive at Myung Film said:

> The film industry in Korea is not yet fully viable, especially with such global Hollywood dominance.... Korean films must now become more like Hollywood products and different from them, all at the same time. (Quoted in *Screen International*, 17 September 1999)

This 'same but different' touchstone is one that has dogged the British film industry for most of its existence. In Britain the domination of Hollywood is felt more keenly than in most other nations because of its common language with North America. On the face of it this may seem to be advantageous to British films as non-English-speaking nations' films will be either subtitled or dubbed in North America, a place that resists both. However, British film history is littered with attempts to make big-budget movies that will appeal to Americans but that have made only a 'mid-Atlantic' splash. That is, they have appealed to neither the British nor the Americans.

In 1981, Colin Welland, Oscar-winning scriptwriter for *Chariots of Fire*, famously said, in his acceptance speech, that 'the British are coming'. One year later, when *Gandhi*, like *Chariots*, won the Best Picture Academy Award, he seemed to be correct. The production company, Goldcrest, was certainly convinced and embarked on an ambitious investment programme, which unravelled when, in 1986, three expensive films, *Absolute Beginners*, *The Mission* and *Revolution*, all flopped.

The company went bust because it was under-capitalised: it was too small to sustain such big losses. Hollywood studios, as part of large corporations, can survive bad years; or even several years, as Sony Pictures endured in the early 1990s. It should be noted, however, that not all films that are successful in the USA repeat their box-office performance overseas. In 1999, neither of the $100m+ box-office hits in North America, *The Waterboy* or *Patch Adams*, made much of an impact elsewhere.

The success of Hollywood is not simply down to the fact that the films it produces are popular in many different cultures. As Bernard MacLeod, the chief executive of Channel 4 International, stated:

> [Hollywood is] driven by the concepts of salesmanship and locomotive shows. In Britain there is at times an apologetic approach to selling. (Quoted in *Screen International*, 1 October 1999)

It is not simply the culture of filmmaking that gives Hollywood its dominance, there is the American 'culture of selling'. Film and television are produced as commodities that need to be sold.

North American cultural domination is not, of course, limited to film and television:

> A survey of popular music albums, conducted for CNN in 1998, found similar results; the difference being British pop music was almost as important as North American. Of the Global top ten only Germany's Modern Talking and Denmark's Aqua broke America and Britain's dominance. (Glaister, 1998)

French resistance

France has a long record of resisting cultural imperialism. It almost scuppered the 1993 GATT (General Agreement on Tariffs and Trade) talks and in 1995 vainly pushed the European Union to approve a quota system that would restrict the distribution of Hollywood films in Europe. 'Free' market economics, however, held sway and 'protectionist' moves were rejected; in 1999 the European Commission renewed United International Pictures' (UIP's) licence to operate. UIP, a joint venture between Universal Pictures and MGM, was accused of dominating distribution in Europe, which allowed it to favour Hollywood movies over European. UIP was originally given a five-year exemption from European competition rules in 1989 because there was no other pan-European distributor; in 1999, after it had acquired Europe's PolyGram Filmed Entertainment, this was apparently still the case.

In order to defend its culture France has a quota system that demands 60% of films shown to be French. However, this does not mean that audiences must go and see French films, as the figures quoted above suggest. Even though the home market for French films is relatively robust, the French are only able to produce so many indigenous films because of public subsidy. In 1997 the National Cinematography Centre had a budget of £264 million. Of this, £28 million was put into cinema films, £104 million into TV films and video, £30 million into cinema refurbishment and £5 million into film distribution. This public subsidy was seen as important in order to preserve French culture.

This protectionism is evident in the 1998 Global film chart discussed above. In Europe, France's indigenous output fared best, with three local productions in the top ten, and they only ceded the top spot to that year's box-office phenomenon, *Titanic*. But in 1999 the Hollywood 'summer blockbuster' fever broke out even in France: in one August week North American films accounted for 94% of the total market share; the figure is usually in the fifties (source: *Screen International*, 3 September 1999).

It is not only film that receives state aid in France. The French government acknowledges that not everything can be measured by money alone; for example, the publicly funded *La Maison de la culture* backed the *Label bleu* jazz record label, which has become one of the most important in Europe. And in 1999, filmmaking in Sweden and Denmark was experiencing a renaissance that coincided with an increase in public money for the industry. The French 'cultural umbrella' system has encouraged cross-media alliances and *Label bleu* has also become involved in writing scores for films.

Although Americans are keen to celebrate the joys of the free market, the flow of cultural products is basically one way, with very few non-American media texts (with the exception of some British musicians) making much of a commercial impact in North America. For example, in 1999 European films only had 5.6% of the American market and this was the best proportion for many years. Japan, too, had a good year – 2.1%. Only 3% of this total was non-English-language films. Although these percentages were comparatively high, the bulk of them were made up of three films: *Notting Hill*, *The World is Not Enough* and *Pokemon*. Of these, only the last one can be thought of as being culturally different from Hollywood films in any way.

Why should it matter that North American product dominates the audio-visual industry as well as, along with Britain, the popular music industry? One of the ways in which societies make sense of themselves, and at the same time communicate this information to the members of society, is through media texts. For instance, narratives are usually structured around notions of good and evil, the hero and villain representing these values. In Nazi Germany, Goebbels' propaganda fiction films, such as *Jud Suss* (1934), were influential in demonising Jews, which may help explain why so many 'ordinary' Germans assisted in the mass-extermination of the Holocaust.

A society whose media are dominated by a foreign power may find foreign values gaining precedence over indigenous beliefs. France goes to great lengths to protect its language, through the Académie Française, and it is illegal to advertise in any language other than French. Attempts have been made to ensure that all internet pages based in France are in the French language. However, with increasing globalisation, such measures seem bound to fail; for example, when France won the football World Cup in 1998, the raising of the trophy was accompanied by the theme from *Star Wars*. It is arguable that one consequence of the nation's linguistic conservatism is that the French language has developed very slowly. In contrast, the vibrant adaptation that characterises English may explain why English is a *lingua franca*. Maybe change is coming to France: the prestigious national daily newspaper *Le Monde*, for instance, has no problem in using 'Americanisms'.

Types of financial support

Government intervention can help support national cinemas, through direct subsidy or assistance via the taxation system. The South Korean industry benefited from screen quotas that meant local films had to be shown for 106 days a year, and they took 25% of the box office in 1998. However, in late 1999 the industry's success was creating an inflation of costs that meant it would be harder to break even in the home market.

The Netherlands introduced tax incentives at the end of 1998 with the result that more films, with larger budgets, were being made. The European Union (EU) has a policy of supporting audio-visual culture. In early 2000 it was proposed that a programme dubbed 'MEDIA PLUS' would disperse $386 million (€ 400), of which: '30% of the total ($116m) be devolved to cinema distribution support,

15% ($58m) to development and 2.5% ($9.7m) for on-line distribution' (Davis, 2000, p. 18). This sort of public subsidy is anathema to exponents of 'free market economics', who believe if there is no profitable market for a product, whether it is beans or film, then there is no need for it to be produced. The other side of the argument suggests that national culture, indeed art in general, needs protecting from the reductive market place otherwise we should all be culturally worse off.

In the 1990s an attempt to boost British cinema by diverting National Lottery money to the film industry met with little commercial or, arguably, artistic success. In April 2000, a commercially orientated Film Council was formed, out of the remnants of the British Film Institute's production unit, to plough £150 million of Lottery money into films over a three-year period. The success of this new venture would be judged financially and not aesthetically. This seems to go against the point of public subsidy for art, which has traditionally been to subsidise texts that are not likely to make money, but are artistically worthwhile. Many of the low-budget Lottery-funded British gangster films that followed the success of *Lock, Stock and Two Smoking Barrels* (1998) were of significance neither commercially nor artistically. However, public funding for the arts does offer audiences a wider choice of texts.

Questions about media imperialism

As Richard Maltby (1998) pointed out, the idea of a European national cinema since 1945 is a contradiction in terms, as no national cinema, such as Italy's neo-realism, has actually been popular within its own country. Individual films have been successful, but no body of work, that can be seen to constitute an examination of national identity, has reaped box-office success.

This is not true of the United States of America, where Hollywood's domination is obviously strongest, though it would be wrong to assume that Hollywood is necessarily a National Cinema. Do the bulk of Hollywood productions share a common view of what it means to be American? How do audiences, particularly in such a culturally variegated nation as the USA, read Hollywood films? If US television is anything to go by, there exists a cultural apartheid (separation) between 'black TV' and 'white TV'; no programmes are watched by a 'mass' audience of both races (ignoring for a moment the Hispanics) – see section 6.3.

Does this mean issues surrounding cultural identity are not important? Maltby suggests that the fear of American culture, and the belief that the locals will be 'Americanised', is a manifestation of the 'high culture versus popular culture' debate. The calls for the defence of national culture (whether that be cinematic, televisual, musical and so on) are premised on the fact that American culture is entertainment-based and therefore aesthetically poor. Thus the claims against Americanisation are more to do with the desire to police popular culture than to defend indigenous values; Maltby shows how critics have a crucial policing role in this process.

What is likely is that for many people in the West, American culture is their second culture, important but secondary to that of the place where they grew up. And the immense influence European culture has had on North America must not be forgotten, nor how the roots of today's popular music can be found in Africa.

3.7 Music as commodity – MTV

Since its formation in 1981 MTV's rise to, virtual, global ubiquity has only been matched by CNN. The fact that both organisations are American is obviously a reflection of the dominance of the US culture; however, MTV did not succeed simply because it was American. How, what began as a channel that playlisted videos the way radio played records, became the epitome of youth culture in many countries is an excellent case study of media imperialism.

The American MTV was available on cable and satellite in Europe before the continent got its own version, the imaginatively entitled MTV Europe, in 1987. Brazil followed with its version in 1990; Asia in 1991 (re-launched in 1995); Japan – 1992; Latin America – 1993; MTV Mandarin – 1995; MTV India – 1996; Australia – 1996; MTV Nordic – 1998. In the website of 2000, Viacom (the parent company – see Chapter 1) was boasting about 'MTV: Music Television, the world's most widely distributed television network, reaching over 300 million households in 136 territories . . .'.

That MTV executives were aware of the potential charge of cultural imperialism is evident from their operating maxim, 'Think globally, act locally.' This stresses that the company is sensitive to local culture and is not in the business of steamrolling indigenous musical forms in favour of American musical forms.

This apparent sensitivity is not simply a result of enlightened business practices, it recognises that youth culture is very important to young people's identity. Unlike CNN, and McDonald's, whose product is not directly engaged with lifestyle, MTV has to tread carefully as music plays a central role in youth culture, partly because of its abstract nature:

> while lyrics and song titles may suggest a preferred reading, their abstract nature allows for a mapping of individual experience and meaning that provides a sense of identity and fluidity of engagement. (Whiteley, 1998, p. 158)

If MTV explicitly tried to ride rough shod over music that was subculturally (see Chapter 7) important then they would risk rejection. Instead, MTV has managed, alongside Coca-Cola and Levi-Strauss, to epitomise (western) youth.

> MTV Europe and Levi-Strauss both generate memorable and awardwinning visual identities: blue jeans, youth, rock music and videos are synonymous. Or, as Levi's European marketing director put it, 'MTV Europe represents a youth lifestyle and Levi-Strauss produces the clothing for that lifestyle.' (Frith, 1993, p. 71)

The marketing director makes clear the commodification of cultural product, something that Levi-Strauss excelled in with their series of 1980s commercials featuring classic songs such as 'Wonderful World', 'When a Man Loves a Woman' and 'I Heard it on the Grapevine'. By the 1990s Levis could make songs a hit; Babylon Zoo's 'Spaceman' went to number one, after originally flopping, when used in a Levi advert.

The commodification of youth culture, or the marketing of product so that it becomes part of youth culture, has elements of contradiction. As we shall see in Chapter 5, youth culture is often considered shocking when measured against conventional morality, whether Elvis's rock 'n' roll or the Sex Pistols' punk rock. This shock of the new is something that attracts young people: it helps give them an identity separate from their parents. Commodities, by their very nature (unless it is nuclear waste) tend to be safe and so appeal to consumers. The sleight of hand that a business has to perform, with products aimed at a young audience, is to convince them that it is cutting-edge and rebellious even though it is in the 'adult' business of making money. This contradiction is considered in relation to the 'independents' in Chapter 5.

The numbers that watch the station, and therefore pay subscriptions to have their eyeballs delivered to advertisers, measures whether

MTV is successful in a business sense. In measuring whether the station supports local culture we must assess the degree to which local music is played when compared with North American and British music. One academic analysis concluded:

> For all of the ambiguities and contradictions that appear in implementing a strategy of 'localization,' it appears that MTV Latino serves mainly as a vehicle form promoting US, UK, and western European international rock music and as a one-way vector of transnational advertising campaigns. (Hanke, 1998, p. 232)

Hanke's point about a 'one-way vector' is that we do not see, on MTV in Europe for example, advertisements for products marketed by Latin American companies, though we can be sure that Coke and Levis advertise there. Similarly, Latin American artists are rarely shown on MTV Europe but European artists are shown in Latin America.

That audiences apparently accept US–UK musical cultural dominance is an example of hegemony. A possible chink in this hegemony was evidenced by the splitting of MTV Europe, in 1996, into four zones: UK–Ireland, Central, Southern, and ('the rest' of) Europe; Nordic was added two years later. Presumably the cultural differences across Europe were great enough to demand that 'local' move down from continent-wide to regions in the continent.

American cultural dominance does not necessarily mean that all nations will become clones of the United States. As we shall see in the next chapter, even such completely commercial forms as advertising have to bow to local ways of making meaning. There is, however, one area where media imperialism does have a particularly negative effect and that is in the dissemination of news.

3.8   News and the developing world

While cultural imperialism is likely to threaten cultural diversity, its influence is even more direct in the dissemination of news. 'Whose news?' is one of the central questions of Media Studies: is it the audience's or the news organisation's?

The coverage of the developing world is marginalised by most news organisations – ranging, in Britain, from the virtually non-existent in the tabloid press, through the 'patchy' coverage of television news and radio (though it should be noted that BBC Radio 4 has many features on the developing world in its schedule), to the 'decent' in many broadsheet newspapers. Even at the 'top end', the 'decent' coverage is itself limited by a narrow agenda.

Chapter 5 of *Image and Representation* examined how news values are the structuring influence on new stories. Our concern here is particularly with the values of 'ethnocentricity', 'elite centredness' and 'clarity'.

■ Exercise 3.4 ■

Watch a TV news broadcast and note the number of stories that cover the developing world (that is, non industrialised nations).

The three news values mentioned above could explain the lack of coverage: we are primarily interested in what is happening close to home; developing nations are, by definition, not part of the elite that includes North America and a number of European nations; because of our lack of familiarity with the developing world, events are often puzzling and so lack clarity.

Restrictions of time mean that news must often simplify ('clarify') events. Documentaries, however, have more time to explain complexity. Research has shown that the number of documentaries covering the developing world, with the exception of travel programmes, has declined drastically. Travel programmes will emphasise the picturesque and not the political. In Britain our access to knowledge about the developing world decreased massively during the 1990s. Output fell by 28% on BBC1; 37% on BBC2; 74% on ITV; 56% on C4 (C5's contribution was negligible) (Stone, 2000). These figures give support to those who argue our media are 'dumbing down'; the same is true for the USA, for example:

> Only 5% of [TV's] news output is devoted to news from other countries. In 1987, the American edition of *Time* devoted 11 of its cover stories to international topics. Ten years later there was only one. The selection of news is based on the principle that 'the more blood there is, the better it sells'. (Kapuscinski, 1999, p. 5)

In other words, 'if it bleeds it leads'. Note also that the 5% coverage alluded to refers to international stories and not simply those from the developing world. The USA must be one of the most insular countries in the world.

If you found any developing-world stories in Exercise 3.4 they probably covered war or famine. Africa, in particular, seems to be a particularly unstable place; clearly some countries in that continent are stable but we rarely, if ever, get coverage in the West of stable African nations.

In 1976, 103 developing nations joined to form the Non-Aligned News Agencies Pool (NANP) in an attempt to generate positive coverage for themselves. However, the western agencies, such as Reuters and Associated Press, dominate through their economic power. News agencies are very important as they supply news to all broadcasters and news publications. Although they tend to couch their reporting in neutral terms, as they supply many different clients who have their own agendas, their western bias has helped reinforce Eurocentrism.

3.9 Eurocentrism

In their brilliant book *Unthinking Eurocentrism: Multiculturalism and the Media*, Ella Shohat and Robert Stam show how the West portrays itself ideologically as the dominant civilising force and most advanced society. They posit five main principles that inform western thought:

1. History is seen as linear, deriving from 'classical' Greece through feudalism, capitalism and the industrial revolution. 'Europe, alone and unaided, is seen as the "motor" for progressive historical change' (Shohat and Stam, 1994, p. 2).
2. 'Eurocentrism attributes to the "West" an inherent progress toward democratic institutions' (ibid.).
3. Non-democratic tendencies within European traditions are ignored as is the West's interference in other countries' democratic processes.
4. The West's oppressive practices, such as slavery, colonialism and imperialism, are seen to be accidental and not an expression of the West's disproportionate power.
5. Non-European cultural traditions are appropriated by the West without acknowledgement.

In sum, Eurocentrism sanitises western history, which patronised and even demonised the non-West; it thinks of itself in terms of its noblest achievements – science, progress, humanism – but thinks of the non-West in terms of its deficiencies, real or imagined (ibid., p. 3).

This is not the place to describe their arguments further; the point here is to highlight – assuming you are western – how integral to our world view is the idea that 'the West is best'. One of the best ways of analysing media texts is to use a commutation test (see chapter 1 of

Image and Representation), so it follows that one of the best ways of understanding western media texts is through the study of those from other cultures. However, most Europeans do not bother to consume even texts from other European countries because of the language barrier, with the exception of American popular culture (which is usually dubbed). So it is hardly surprising that the reading of non-western texts is rare.

Anyone who has looked at all three books in this Key Concepts series will realise they are Eurocentric. I hope, however, that this section demonstrates that this Eurocentrism is not 'unthinking' but simply a product of my ignorance.

3.10 Conclusion

This chapter investigated the effect that the business ethic, of extracting profit, has upon media texts. Films are seen to be as much vehicles for the promotion of spin-offs as being something that itself is being sold. The use of stars, one of the ways of promoting films, has been expanded in the creation of celebrities and personalities. While celebrities have, initially at least, some claim to fame, personalities are a palimpsest that only exists in the coverage they are given.

Advertising affects newspapers in a number of ways: it allows the cheaper production of texts but acts as an indirect influence by moving business away from texts that work against the advertiser's interests. It also emphasises the importance of texts reaching particular audiences to be delivered to those advertisers; once again this can have a deleterious effect on texts through what has been called 'dumbing down'.

The commodification of media text has led to the cultural domination, in the West at least, of North American product. This had led to a diminution of local product that, arguably, has a knock-on effect on a culture's ability to make sense of its own world through the media. The worldwide expansion of MTV has made music video a ubiquitous form in virtually every nation in the world. More seriously, the ability for nation states to receive news 'untainted' by the western point of view has been severely compromised by the economic domination of a small number of news agencies. One result of this is the Eurocentric view of the world that dominates in the West, a partial and often inaccurate view.

4

MARKETING AND PUBLIC RELATIONS

AIMS OF THE CHAPTER

➤ To consider the marketing mix.

➤ To look at different types of advertising.

➤ To define branding.

➤ To investigate branding in relation to globalisation.

➤ To look at the relationship between branding and the Internet.

➤ To consider public relations (PR).

➤ To consider how PR affects news.

➤ To explain the 'vortex of publicity'.

➤ To speculate about the future of the Internet in relation to publicity.

4.1   Introduction

In a capitalist society, the purchase of goods defines many people's relationship to the world. One of our prime motivations to work is the desire to earn money to be able to afford consumer goods, either needed or wanted. The most obvious way in which we are urged to spend our income is seen in advertising. This chapter will start by examining the marketing mix, of which advertising is one element. This will be followed by a consideration of branding and, finally, public relations, which can be used to promote both products and ideas.

4.2   Marketing mix

Philip Kotler defines marketing as a:

> human activity directed at satisfying needs and wants through exchange processes.   (Kotler, 1980, p. 13)

This basically means the selling of products and services, an activity that is fundamental to capitalism. Marketing consists of four variables, called the marketing mix, and these are often characterised as the 'Four Ps':

1. price
2. place
3. product
4. promotion.

Unsurprisingly, this framework derives from the discourse of Business Studies and students must be careful, when applying it, to do so from a Media Studies perspective.

If we consider any product (or service), be it soap or beans, then the *price* of the product is usually determined by how much consumers will pay. *Place*, basically, refers to distribution, how the product gets to its target market. *Product* and *promotion* are the two areas of the 'marketing mix' that primarily concern media students: 'product' in terms of branding and 'promotion' in terms of advertising and publicity. The following will use films and newspapers to illustrate the mix.

The marketing mix: movies and the press

1 Price

Pricing of films, whether in the cinema, on video or on pay-per-view television, is relatively uniform. In Britain, cinemas in the West End of London are more expensive than in the rest of the country but, overall, there is little variation.

Ticket prices are not usually related to the length of the film, a factor that can have a considerable effect on an exhibitor's revenues. The 95-minute running time of *Toy Story* 2 (1999) meant it could be shown almost twice as many times per screen than the three-hour-plus *Titanic* (1997). One way in which price could be changed in relation to the running time is the imposition of a supplement to the normal admission price; this occurred in Germany when *Titanic* was screened. Most moviegoers do not base their choice of a film, or cinema, on price though they may take advantage of discounts at particular times of the week.

In other areas of the media, price can have a significant effect on a product. In July 1993 News International embarked upon a 'price war' by reducing the price of its newspapers. This helped increase the circulation of *The Times* but, more significantly, put economic pressure on the company's competition. The *Daily Telegraph*'s Hollinger group could afford the estimated £40 million per annum in lost revenue it cost to compete (McNair, 1999, p. 166) but the *Observer* and the *Independent* did not have the resources and were sold to bigger companies. By 1998, the price war had ended though 'bulk sales' and subscriptions dogged accurate assessment of circulation figures; the *Daily Telegraph*'s circulation, for instance, was being bolstered by a large number of subscriptions.

▨ Exercise 4.1 ▨

Check out the cover prices of publications in the same sector, for example women's magazines, to assess the variation in price.

2 Place

There are two main places to watch films: in the cinema or at home. The distribution of films, however, is more varied. While the cinema holds pre-eminence as the 'shop window', the explosion of platforms that occurred during the 1990s means that films can be seen in a variety of formats at different times. Roughly, in Britain, the 'windows' are:

(a) Cinema release.
(b) **Plus six months**: video and DVD release (may be retail or rental only).
(c) **Plus one year**: pay television (priced the same as video but you do not have to leave your house and you can record for later viewing).
(d) **Plus eighteen months**: subscription-based movie channels.
(e) **Plus two and a half years**: terrestrial 'free to air' television.

These obviously vary; Britain's terrestrial ITV Network (Channel 3) capped their re-run of all the James Bond movies in 1999 with the first television showing of *Tomorrow Never Dies* (1997), which was aired less than two years after its release. ITV Network had purchased the pay-TV window for the film. Terrestrial television, fifth in line for new releases, finds that only the strongest titles will garner big ratings as fans will already have seem most of the films.

The digital distribution of films began on a small scale in 1999. Instead of the expensive creation and supply of prints, the film can be sent to the cinema as a digital stream via a landline or satellite feed. This will obviously save a lot of 'postage' money for distributors; exhibitors, however, will also benefit by being able to offer a better picture quality and the ability to relay live events such as sporting fixtures. In 2000 the haggling was beginning as to who should pay for the expensive conversion of cinemas.

Distribution of the press is through rail and road in Britain. In 2000 the main distributor, W. H. Smith, was threatening to change the way both newspapers and magazines were sent to newsagents in order to make it more profitable. One of the consequences of this may be that remote regions will no longer be able to get newspapers.

Until the 1980s the geographical size of the USA meant that no national newspaper existed. It was not until the advent of satellite technology, which allowed the newspaper to be transmitted to printing presses throughout the nation, that North America had the national newspapers *USA Today* and the *Wall Street Journal*.

3   Product

That poor movies generate poor box office is a tautology because, in commercial terms, the only good movies are the ones that bring in the punters. The summer blockbuster season is the most influential on cinema admissions – see section 1.3 on the High Concept.

In the newspaper market, publications differentiate themselves by their (implicit) political agenda and the social class that they address. In a competitive market it is important that a product possesses a unique selling proposition (USP). This distinguishes it from the competition and offers a reason why this product should be purchased (see Chapter 7).

▩ Exercise 4.2 ▩

How do you think Figure 4.1 communicates its USP?

The Sun Microsystems advertisement suggests that 'The Dot' turns 'information into power'. In the post-industrial age, information is deemed the most precious commodity, particularly so for the 'net economy'. The Dot not only unleashes this power but is also the 'most powerful force in the universe'; while we are used to advertising hype, this is self-consciously over-the-top. The product's USP resides in the power it can offer businesses.

Figure 4.1   Sun Microsystems advertisement

This exaggeration is in keeping with the overall design of the advert, which is a parody of the poster that promoted *Jaws* (1975). Instead of a naked woman, a suited businessman swims; instead of an enormous great white shark, there's a huge dot. The tagline, 'Just when your competition...', derives from the poster for *Jaws 2*

(1978): 'Just when you thought it was safe to go back into the water'. The advert is operating on two levels: obviously it wishes to be taken seriously regarding the product it is selling but it is not really suggesting the product is all-powerful. The jocular tone is continued with the certification (in the bottom left-hand corner): 'LB – Lame business people strongly cautioned'.

The advert is expected to cue recognition, through its association with *Jaws*, and at least make the reader pause rather than flick straight past. It has been suggested that:

> of the 1500 opportunities to see advertisements that people have each day, only between seven and ten are remembered by a consumer. (Brierley, 1995, p. 143)

Therefore it is crucial that the target audience's attention is grabbed. This is partly down to the selection of medium; the Sun advertisement appeared in *Revolution*, an appropriate publication for 'business and marketing in the digital economy'. The *Jaws* reference suggests that Sun expects the target audience – information and communication technology managers – to be at least in their mid-thirties; otherwise they would not remember the film (though *Jaws* has something of a cult status).

4 Promotion

This part of the mix is the most important in determining whether a film is successful or not. For most movies aimed at a mass audience the opening weekend is crucial to its box-office performance: if it does not open well (Friday to Sunday) then it is likely to be a flop. Therefore most film promotion is designed to open a movie big and then hope that positive word of mouth will kick in afterwards.

Trailers, which are much more prevalent in North America than in Britain (the latter sees more adverts in cinemas), are perfect promotion of film as they are very likely to be reaching the target audience, who will, at least, be cinemagoers. Posters and displays also adorn the foyers of cinemas; posters also appear in appropriate magazines. However, those who are only to target occasional cinemagoers it is necessary to reach people in other ways.

Television is the most effective way of advertising films to people who are not regular cinemagoers; and because film is a cultural product, publicity can be generated for virtually nothing; the publicity circus of star interviews can generate much free media coverage. Most stars will be contracted to do interviews with television, radio, newspapers and magazines; they spend a day in a hotel seeing a different interviewer every few minutes and say positive things about the film. A press pack will disseminate information to every relevant publication and will include images and sequences from the film that can be used. Disney's *101 Dalmations* (1996) generated coverage by associating itself with the 'A dog is for life not just for Christmas' campaign.

Premieres are also used to garner coverage, often as a news item. These are often designated 'for charity' to help news editors justify the coverage, and (in Britain) if a royal personage can be persuaded to attend (the Prince of Wales and *SpiceWorld*, 1998) then the 'photo opportunity' is very likely to be taken up.

The release of songs associated with the movie has become *de rigueur* and extracts from the film are likely to be included within the pop video. Any time the song is played on the radio the movie is likely to be mentioned. The Internet, following the phenomenal success of *The Blair Witch Project* (1998), is regarded as an essential medium; the *Lord of the Rings* website was running over 18 months before the first film in the series, *The Fellowship of the Ring* (2001), was released.

These are straightforward ways of promoting a film, but there are a multitude of other ways of getting a film noticed. *The Sixth Sense* (1999), for instance, had heat-sensitive cards distributed in the *Guardian*, these invited readers to previews. Previews, usually starting up to a week before the film's release, are used to generate 'word of mouth'; if your friends tell you a film is good then you're far more likely to see it than in response to official promotion.

Where a film is promoted, and any gimmicks used, is only part of the process. A film must be packaged in such a way as to readily appeal to audiences. As we saw in Chapter 1, high-concept movies are designed as a marketing package from the moment they are conceived. However, non-high-concept movies, such as *East is East* (1999), also need to be sold. Although a movie about an Asian family growing up in the early 1970s in Salford does not sound like it will do big business, FilmFour Distributors managed to make it a mainstream event by positioning it as a comedy about teenagers' problems with their parents. The marketing campaign concentrated on: 'early adopters (heavy cinema-goers) for its first wave of activity, before opening up to a more mainstream audience' (Minns, 1999, p. 7). Using posters and television, and focusing on the film's risqué elements, the film opened well and went on to be very successful in Britain.

Newspapers usually use television to promote themselves, though somewhat sparingly as it is exceptionally expensive, and usually only if they have something specific to promote. This might be a 'be a millionaire type game' in tabloids or a serialisation of a hot, new book. the *Independent* ran a distinctive campaign when it was launched, based around the phrase, '*It* is, are you?' (the 'it' being 'independent'). As we shall see later in the chapter, newspapers use their own front page to promote themselves.

The marketing of products is usually crucial to their financial success. The most obvious aspect of marketing is advertising.

4.3 Advertising

Chapter 7 considers how advertisers define audiences; here we shall concentrate on how businesses use and create advertising. Advertising refers to the space, or time, that is *paid* for in order to promote products or services (unless otherwise specified, the term 'products' includes services).

Different types of advertising

1. Information – ads which, for example, focus simply on the price or availability of products.
2. Classified
   (a) personal – goods; announcements (deaths, weddings); 'lonely hearts' and so on;
   (b) business – business to business; recruitment.
3. Corporate – adverts that promote a company's image rather than its products or services.
4. Lifestyle – often integral to branding (see below), the advert attempts to convince audiences that the product can give the buyer a 'cool' lifestyle.

We can add direct mail to this list, also known as 'junk mail'. Direct mail is 'junk' if the recipient is not interested in the products sold. Companies do not purposely send out sales brochures to people who will not buy, as it obviously wastes their money. Lists of names and addresses can be bought from publishers, so if you subscribe to a computer magazine you probably get direct mail offering you computer products. The Internet may well prove to be a more accurate, and more cost effective, way of directing mail to potential clients.

4.4 Branding

In 1999 the top ten brands in Britain, in terms of the value of sales, were:

1.	Coca-Cola brands	£580m+
2.	Walkers Crisps	£425–30m
3.	Persil	£240–5m
4.	Nescafe standard	£225–30m
5.	Andrex	£220–5m
6.	Stella Artois	£205–10m
7.	Muller yoghurt	£190–5m
8.	Pepsi	£185–90m
9.	Pampers nappies	£185–90m
10.	Ariel	£180–5m

(*Source*: AC Neilsen)

(I must confess to finding the amount of Muller yoghurt consumed quite terrifying; and then there is the amount of nappies!) Lurking just off the top ten was Sunny Delight in twelfth place (£160m), which was the most successful new brand launch of the decade.

Unilever, a company that had over 1,600 household brands at the end of the 1990s, decided in 1999 to drop three-quarters of them and focus only on the most successful – the A brands. Amongst these was the Dove toiletry range, which provided a rare example of proof that advertising can work (marketers now use the term 'personal care products', presumably to avoid any negative vibes associated with toilets). After an advertising campaign in Australia, where its sales had been static, sales rose rapidly; none of the other variables of price, product and packaging, or distribution, were changed.

We will consider Dove below. In order to assess how branding works, Greg Myers (1999) suggested 'four more Ps' (to add to those of the marketing mix): past, position, practices and paradigms. While this is potentially confusing in relation to the marketing mix, his description of each is useful (Myers's 'p's are in parentheses).

1 Heritage (past)

The heritage that brands draw upon is that of the product, assuming it had one. Any new product that Nike produces, for example, can present itself as having the qualities associated with all previous Nike products. Indeed, newer products often try to give a sense of tradition where one does not exist; the Phileas Fogg range of crisps, for example.

In addition, advertising is full of the oxymoron 'modern-traditional', which suggests their product is at the 'cutting edge' of the market while simultaneously evoking the past to give it a sense of permanence.

■ Exercise 4.3 ■

Write down the connotations you associate with 'dove'.

You may have listed such associations as 'peace' and 'white' but Dove's brand name also:

> neatly dovetails into western, Christian iconography as an emblem of the holy spirit which not only cleanses the body but also purifies the soul. (Pandya, 1999, p. 28)

A relatively pleasant association, particularly if it is remembered that the product was originally developed to treat burns victims in the Second World War.

2 Market (position)

Brands do not necessarily attempt to dominate the whole market but try to cultivate niches. Indeed the purpose of branding is to identify the product with its niche market. Dove soap is marketed as a 'beauty bar [that] has extra emollients and does not form residue in hard water' (ibid.). Of course it is still soap, but the branding suggests it is a 'classy' variant of soap and can prevent aging, the 'Holy Grail' of all beauty products. At the other end of the 'soap' spectrum is 'coal tar' soap, which, at face value, seems to suggest that you will get dirty using it, but its appeal is that it connotes a 'no nonsense' old-fashioned product that gets the job done without any fancy emollients.

Sunny Delight positioned itself as a refreshing ('delight') health ('sun') drink that children love to drink. It was heavily advertised on children's television thereby utilising 'pester power' where kids moan so much that their parents buy them the product to shut them up.

Little guilt will be associated with this purchase because parents can console themselves with the thought that the drink is healthy:

> What is Sunny Delight?
> Sunny Delight is a vitamin enriched citrus beverage. Kids love the taste of orange, tangerine and lime juices. Mums love the fact that it's enriched with vitamins A, B1 & 6 and C.   (Sunny Delight website, 1999)

The drink is even placed in fridges, alongside other fruit juices, despite the fact that it is so full of artificial additives that it does not need storing in cool conditions; it is only 5 per cent fruit juice. The Food Commission stated:

> The image comes across as a very healthy fresh fruit juice drink and mums think its [sic] good for their children. In fact it's full of thickeners, colourings and flavourings to make it look like fruit juice when its [sic] basically just a very sugary drink. Basically it's a marketing con.   (Teather, 1999, p. 22)

To reinforce this healthy *image* (for that is what the brand offers), the website also stated that it was a 'proud partner of child health day'. However, by 2001, sales had fallen massively as consumers realised that the product was not all it claimed to be.

It is probably rare for marketing to be so deceitful, but it does serve to illustrate how powerful branding is as a tool. If you compare branded goods with non-branded (an increasingly rare specimen), the only difference is often price. The difference in cost can be attributed to advertising, particularly if television was used; Sunny Delight's campaign cost in the region of £9m in Britain. It has been estimated that it costs each adult, on average, over £400 per annum to pay for ITV's advertising revenue. 'Free to air' commercial television is only free if you do not buy goods advertised on television.

3   Uses (practices)

This refers to how people use brands, something not entirely within the marketer's control. For example, people may purchase Levi jeans to wear as a fashion statement, something the company's marketing suggests. However, they may also buy them to wear as work clothes.

Sub-cultural groups often appropriate brands for their own purposes – see Hip Hop's use of Timberland, in Chapter 6.

4 Social context (paradigms)

It is inevitable that as society changes so should branding. For example, in the last twenty years the importance of eating healthily has become paramount for many. Thus if Sunny Delight had come onto the market thirty years ago it would probably have been marketed simply as 'orange squash'. In the 1990s it needs to convince consumers it is healthy. Conversely, in the future the emphasis on healthy eating may disappear and so the branding of the product will then also change: 'with 50% added fat'!

Types and uses of branding

Both products and services use branding. Indeed, branding is important whatever is being sold to the public. As the number of television channels proliferates they need to brand themselves to stand out from the crowd. While it may seem obvious that it is necessary to brand a niche channel in order to distinguish it from the competition, the traditional mass-audience channels are also developing themselves as a brand. In recent years the disparate companies that make up Channel 3 in Britain have brought themselves together under a controller and have labelled themselves the ITV Network. BBC executives have talked about branding BBC1 as mass entertainment and BBC2 as an arts and documentaries channel.

Celebrities can be used to brand products: Linda McCartney's 'meat free' dishes traded upon her persona of being someone who liked healthy eating. Paul Newman's sauces were aimed at an older audience by invoking nostalgia for a time when Newman was a big star, and sauces, like everything else a generation ago (seen through rose-tinted lenses), were real. The Classic FM brand in Britain is used not only to establish the station's identity but to package music albums and a magazine. The Classic FM audience feels safe in buying these because they know the products' type of music will be similar to that played on the radio station: short and tuneful.

Bizarrely, garden celebrity Alan Titchmarsh 'branded' a classical music compilation 'In a Country Garden' produced by Sony Classical. It seems that audiences who like his gardening show will like music that purports to be recommended by him on an album that has his grinning visage on the cover.

Branding and globalisation

The trend over the final decades of the twentieth century was for companies to expand in order to benefit from economies of scale. With this there has been an increase in the number of brands that have attempted to 'go global'. However, although a large number of brands are recognisable the world over – like Coke, Disney, Fuji, McDonald's and British Airways – Myers's four variables described above suggest there are difficulties inherent in global branding. For example, social contexts vary from country to country, and even region to region, and so the meaning of particular signs can be very different. A Coca-Cola Christmas advert that showed Santa driving lorries laden with Coke coming to Germany could have had negative connotations of invasion, from World War Two – instead of an American army there was an American product. In an attempt to head off this reading, German national monuments lit up as if welcoming the 'invaders'.

A number of familiar brand names have disappeared in the face of globalism as they have been replaced by their multinational version; for example, in Britain the Marathon chocolate bar has become Snickers, while Opal Fruits is now Starburst.

As part of this globalisation we have seen the creation of television networks such as Eurosport and MTV, in its various incarnations throughout the world. Eurosport sends out the same pictures all over Europe with each nation having its own commentator, who watches the pictures from a base in Paris. Each nation, however, still needs its own advertising because of different languages but this does not stop the network's sales teams selling 'Europe' as a whole to companies. That such international television will ever become the norm is unlikely, as we saw in Chapter 3 with reference to MTV, while strong cultural differences exists between nations.

Globalised networks can offer a discordant experience to viewers. For example, a CNN *Europe* broadcast of 'World News', beamed from *Washington* and featuring a *Scottish* anchor, visibly dramatises the ruptures between time and space inherent in global broadcasting. This confusion is characteristic of postmodernism; however, after several viewings audiences probably will not notice anything unusual. It is arguable that if such international broadcasting became the norm then differences between cultures would diminish – see section 3.6 on media imperialism.

Jean Baudrillard has suggested that in the postmodern world there is no difference between reality and images of reality. He characterises the effect of this as being a simulacrum: 'The simulacrum is both the reproduction and the original, both the image and the referent imploded into a single concept' (Fiske, 1996, p. 55). Baudrillard's point is that in a world that is full of media(ted) images there is little point in trying to separate what is real from what is represented for they are essentially the same.

The 'media' are so integral to life in the developed world that we cannot readily conceive of life without them:

> In one hour's television viewing, one of us is likely to experience more images than a member of a non-industrial society would in a lifetime [so] we do not just experience more images... we live with a completely different relationship between the image and other orders of experience. (Ibid., p. 56)

It follows from this that those who live in the developing world are more in contact with reality than those in the industrial, or post-industrial world.

Global branding not only has to think about 'local sign systems', countries have different regulatory networks and morals. For instance the amount of nudity (usually of women) allowed in advertising in France is far more than in Britain, where the Claudia Schiffer ad for Renault was vilified, by many, for its sexism; in France the question would not have arisen.

By the turn of the millennium the number of brands seemed to be reaching saturation point. In 20 years the number of products stocked by a typical supermarket had risen from 5,000 to 40,000 with an astonishing 400 different brands of shampoo. In the 1970s anyone who paid for bottled water would have been regarded as more than eccentric; by the twenty first century a supermarket in Leeds stocked 101 different lines of H_2O. Research carried out by the Future Foundation suggested that:

> an American-style revolution in British consumerism has failed to enrich our lives but has caused confusion and anxiety as people struggle with the mind-boggling array of options available. (Diggines, 2000, p. 7)

How many people can make informed choices from: 180 television channels; 1,600 car models; 250 radio stations; 150 tour operators?

■ Exercise 4.4 ■

If you have access to multiple television channels, list those you watch regularly.

Research has suggested that, on average, homes with multi-channel TV tend to stick to seven channels. Similarly, on the Internet, after the initial burst of surfing indulged in by people when they first use the Net, 'surfers' tend to stick by their bookmarked favourites. Hence it was very important for Net companies to 'get in first'; those who were last would find it harder to be successful.

Branding and the Internet

During the late 1990s the Internet became part of everyday life as access to it became cheaper and easier. The Net, which had begun life as a nuclear failsafe and then a 'free thinker's' medium, soon became the target of companies intending to use it to make money. In fact any company which provided goods and services and ignored the Net's significance could find themselves with problems.

At first, companies tried to make money via subscription: that is, giving access to the public to material in return for money. The only sector that made this pay was pornography; indeed, pornographers were in the forefront of technological development as they tried to improve the quality (if that is the right word) of their product with such innovations as 'streaming video'. Most 'respectable' companies found that Net users would not pay for information on the Net as they were used to getting it for free. Hence, electronic publications – such as magazines and newspapers – could only generate revenue from the Web by selling advertising space. Indeed it has been argued, as we shall see, that the Net could lead to the death of conventional advertising, which, in turn, would have a devastating effect on the media as a whole.

Initially, at least, far from tolling the death knell, the new 'dot com' companies led to a boom in conventional advertising as they strove to create brand awareness in the developing medium, and many new technology magazines were launched. AC Neilsen MMS estimated that dot com companies spent, in Britain, £150m in 1999 on advertising in order to create brand awareness.

▓ Exercise 4.5 ▓

Make a list of the Internet company brands that you know. How many of these do you use and how many are you simply aware of?

Table 4.1

Brand	Spend in 1999	Penetration*
AOL	£7.7m	90%
Yahoo!	£1.2m	90%
Egg	£7.5m	62%
Amazon	£3.4m	75%
Lastminute	£1m	29%
Alta Vista	£0	46%
Smile	£1.8m	31%
Boo	£2.4m	13%

*Penetration was defined as awareness amongst people who have used the Internet in the last month.

Source: AC Neilsen MMS and CIA MediaLab.

There are far too many variables here to be confident about any conclusions drawn regarding the effectiveness of both branding and the money spent on trying to establish it. Amazon, for example, has been in the Net business a comparatively long time while Egg was a newcomer in 1999. Both AOL and Yahoo! are relatively well established players, the first is a service provider, the second a search engine. While it may be that AOL wasted money in its advertising spend, when compared with Yahoo!, it could be that service providers have to spend more than search engines to build awareness.

Another variable is the effectiveness of the campaign in terms of its branding and the schedule chosen. A great idea will fail unless the right people see it; and the right people will not be impressed by a bad idea. It is unlikely that campaigns will suffer from bad scheduling as there is plenty of information about the audience demographics of specific media texts – see Chapter 7.

The above figures may have suggested bad news for Boo, which had the worst penetration for the fourth highest spend. By May 2000 it had gone into liquidation. Boo, a 'sports and streetwear' retailer, had garnered a lot of publicity in the press – partly because of the youth of its proprietors – but this did not prevent it becoming the first high-profile dot com failure in Britain.

Whilst branding was important for Internet companies, the rules of the game for established consumer brands were different. Traditional brands, like Levi's and Nike, did not have enough Net traffic to show up in audience ratings and Net consumers were far more likely to buy on price than on brand (Watney, 2000).

In 1998, Randall Rothenberg suggested that 'The Net's precision accountability will kill not only traditional advertising, but its para-site, Big Media' (Rothenberg, 1998). His argument was that the Net would allow advertisers to know exactly what worked and what did not. It does not matter how well constructed a campaign's schedule is, in terms of addressing the target audience; if that audience pays no attention it will have failed. The Net allows advertisers to know exactly how many hits are made on an advertising banner, and, if the Web is also a point of sale, how many of those turn into actual sales. Indeed, the number of hits usually determines what the advertiser pays the host site for having their advertisement (see also section 4.7).

At last it seemed that the advertiser's Holy Grail (and an advertising agency's nightmare) of totally accountable advertising had arrived. The consequences of this for the media that rely upon advertising revenue – from commercial television to the local freesheet – could be disastrous. Indeed, the ubiquity of the Web means that any company can run its own website and, through being registered with well-used search engines, run its own web promotion thus cutting out the advertising agencies altogether. The agencies may well be reduced to offering web-design work to small companies; larger ones will employ their own designers. Many local newspaper groups in Britain have recognised this possibility by running their own classified advert network on the Web – such as fish4.

If we take an apocalyptic view, the consequences of the Web sucking up the vast majority of advertising would include the end of 'free to air' commercial television; broadsheet newspapers (without advertising their cover price would probably be too high to sustain a viable circulation); special-interest and lifestyle magazines; commercial radio; billboards and so on. Non-publicly-funded television would only exist on a subscription or pay-per-view basis; newspapers would probably continue on the Net, where there are no distribution costs; magazines would probably act as portals on the Net, the cyberspace equivalent of *FHM* would still provide a suitable environment for fashion and alcohol promotion; radio, too, would be Net-based, but not restricted by broadcast 'footprints' as it could be accessed any-where in the world; billboards would probably only be advertising Net portals.

It is ironic then, if Rothenberg's prediction comes to pass, that the Net brands, which will lead to the death of traditional media (Big Media, as Rothenberg terms them), should spend so much money on their victims in order to gain the required brand awareness. One pos-sible restriction on this onslaught, however, is the existence of proxy servers. Internet service providers (ISP) will store the most popular web pages on their own server and so speed up access and reduce web congestion. So any click on a banner advertisement that is stored on a proxy will not register with the holder; a free hit for the advertiser.

By 2000 it was suggested that the Net may be:

> good for tactical campaigns: good, that is, for telling people who are already online about a particular promotion. But they are not so good for building brand awareness, and they are hopeless for reaching out to the mainstream.   (McClellan, 2000, p. 10)

Maybe it won't be the end of the Media world after all (for further information on branding, see Chapter 7).

Clearly advertising and branding are very important in a capitalist society. Both are part of publicising products. Public relations (PR) is another aspect of marketing but has a much wider brief.

4.5   Public relations (PR)

> The aim of PR is to promote positive and favourable images of people or firms in public life, without actually appearing to do so.   (Dyer, 1982, p. 11)

Unlike advertising, where people know they are being sold to, PR disguises its purpose. The latter part of the twentieth century saw an enormous growth in the influence of PR on all areas of life:

> In 1991 the top fifty US-based public relations companies charged over $1,700,000,000 in fees. The industry employs almost 200,000 people in the US; there are more public relations personnel than news reporters. More than 5,400 companies and 500 trade associations have public relations departments, and there are over 5,000 PR agencies in the US alone.   (Beder, 1997, p. 107)

For an industry that does not produce goods, objectively inform, or even specifically entertain the public, these figures are enormous. There is barely an organisation that does not use PR strategies in order to convince the public at large, and their customers in particular, of how indispensable they are. From non-commercial organisations, such as schools (who will try and get photographs of successful pupils into the local press), to the presentation of political policies, PR is involved.

The function of PR is, on the surface at least, to communicate effectively with the public. In reality, however, PR is little different from spin doctoring. Spin doctors are particularly associated with politicians and attempt to portray events in such a way that they show whoever they are representing in the best possible light. Successful politicians themselves often use the 'art' of spin doctoring: the government will say the new economic statistics show their policies are working, while the opposition will describe them as evidence of failure. For example, when a British government minister, David Blunkett, announced that he was considering single-sex classes in the teaching of certain subjects he characterised this as '"ammunition" to tackle poor performance among boys' (Woodward, 2000, p. 5), while the opposition spokesperson 'accused Mr Blunkett of interfering in schools with initiative and "clutching at straws"' (ibid.).

This is not to say that PR is necessarily lies. However, it is essential when dealing with PR to read between the lines, and the media, of course, are not unaware of political parties' attempts to spin news to their own advantage. This has led many news organisations to focus on the spin at the expense of the story:

> The government's increasing expertise in controlling publicity – and the media's growing obsession with 'exposing' the techniques and personalities involved – is displacing genuinely useful information about, and investigation into, real policies.   (Barnett and Gaber, 2001, p. 6)

As we shall see below, PR is the source of much 'news' and is also responsible for a whole range of media texts that are part of the marketing drive surrounding new films or albums. While these may be seen, on one hand, as being relatively trivial, PR can have an immense effect.

During the Gulf War in 1990 a PR company, employed by the Kuwaiti government, set up a witness's testimony to an American Congressional committee. 'Nadia', as she was called to protect her identity, recounted how she had seen Iraqi soldiers throw babies out of incubators. The description of this atrocity was influential in the West joining together to blast the Iraqis out of Kuwait. After the war the truth emerged: Nadia was a Kuwaiti Ambassador's niece and her story false. However, lest we think that PR is all-powerful, it is worth noting the example of Monsanto.

In 1998 Monsanto, a company involved in genetic modification (GM), attempted to convince the public that GM food was beneficial to society. It was an interesting campaign because it seemed to be offering an even-handed argument by publishing the website addresses of pressure groups who opposed the company. A year later however, the company admitted – through its chairman – that:

> We have irritated and antagonised more people than we have persuaded. Our confidence in biotechnology has been widely seen as arrogance. Too often we forgot to listen. (Quoted in Vidal, 1999, p. 11)

This suggests the power of PR is limited, though it should be noted that the chairman's admission was part of a new PR campaign that was attempting to convince the public that Monsanto 'was now committed to engaging in dialogue with society to find solutions' (ibid.).

Whether PR is effective or not is hardly the question, given its ubiquity. The Improperganda exhibition, which opened in London in July 2000, featured the work of Jim Moran, who was one of the first to exploit the photo opportunity. News organisations are far more likely to run a story if pictures accompany it and so a lot of effort is made by PR companies to provide striking images. Moran excelled at producing 'photo opps'; however, after one of his PR stunts was banned, he was quoted as saying: 'It's a sad day for capitalism when a man can't fly a midget on a kite over Central Park' (Armstrong, 2000, p. 8).

When Ken Livingstone was running for election as Mayor of London, 14 different companies had men following him around dressed as animals in order to try and get some of the coverage the candidate was receiving.

In the next section we shall see how influential PR has been in the production and manufacture of news, and then consider how the 'publicity circus' facilitates the marketing of media texts.

PR and the news

Although the news is meant to be free from bias this can never be the case. Even broadcasters, who in Britain are legally obliged to be 'balanced', can be seen to basically reinforce, and reproduce, the views of the dominant ideology (a socially constructed consensus). All newspapers suggest they are telling the truth and if they confess to any agenda then it is one they describe as being 'common sense' and in the interests of their readers. This is the preferred reading offered by news organisations and, as such, is likely to be the one accepted by a majority of the audience (see Chapter 6).

PR, on the other hand, is obviously biased in favour of the organisation producing the information. If audiences are aware of this then they are at liberty to make their own negotiated, or oppositional, readings. PR companies know this and much effort is expended in manufacturing PR as news events so that the information favourable to their, or their client's, organisation can be run as 'factual' news. Jon Bon Jovi once created a news event by alerting news organisations to the fact that he would be busking in Covent Garden. Although he had stage-managed the event he gave his actions further authenticity by complaining that his busking had been turned into a media circus. The fact that he had a full sound system and security was a bit of a giveaway that the busking was not wholly spontaneous, but the news organisations were happy to play along with the ruse and ran it as a light-hearted story of 'a superstar as an ordinary guy' (and an American charmed by a British tradition of busking in Covent Garden) (source: *The Music Biz*). Bon Jovi was described as 'moderately satisfied' with the event.

Although such publicity stunts are not likely to cause too many ethical problems for news organisations, the relationship between news and PR can be a lot more serious. If we ask ourselves the question 'where does news come from?', 'common sense' tells us it comes from what has happened in the world. However, the actual answer is often PR companies.

4.6 Vortex of publicity

Andrew Wernick (1991) suggested the way to consider the advertising and marketing industry as a whole was as consisting of a 'vortex of publicity', of which PR is one element. He offers seven points:

1. *Advertising as a cultural event*

    At the core of the vortex is advertising itself, the status of which is such that it is considered to be significant in a cultural sense: in April 2000, Channel 4 ran a near three-hour programme featuring the 100 greatest television advertisements; advertising is parodied in comedy shows; ads parody each other (for example, the Heineken campaign in 2000 that featured, in 'fast forward', parodies of such staple television advertisements as those for soap powder).

In addition, as a result of well-orchestrated PR campaigns, new advertising campaigns themselves are deemed newsworthy. Research in 1997 found that the British press ran 487 stories about advertising in the first three months of that year. As this was an election year it is unsurprising that the Conservative Party's 'demon eyes' campaign garnered the most – 57 stories. The second biggest story was the switch of actors for BT's new advertising campaign from Bob Hoskins to Hugh Laurie; it was probably worthwhile BT swapping the actors simply for the coverage that the change gained. The importance of celebrities was also evident, with Pamela 'Pizza Hut' Anderson getting eleven (no doubt mostly tabloid) stories, Gary 'Walkers' Lineker having ten, and Jennifer 'L'Oréal' Anniston, five (Archer, 1997).

Other campaigns have generated news coverage by courting controversy. The Wonderbra 'Hello boys!' posters and the Fcuk fashion chain, both emanating from Trevor Beattie's imagination, received much coverage as the former was deemed to be sexist, the latter rude.

2. A medium for advertising

The second ring of Wernick's vortex refers to the fact that some media, such as commercial television, can be conceived wholly as advertising-based, as the only reason the programmes exist is to attract viewers to the adverts – see Chapter 1.

3. Positive world view

The third point follows on from the second. Most advertising creates a positive world view and so it is important that the surrounding text has a similarly upbeat, feel-good, tone. This means that many texts are likely to carry the same pro-consumerist, bourgeois, message as the adverts. When the occasional controversial television programme has been aired, some advertisers have taken their advertisements away; this happens particularly in North America.

On the radio most DJs are positive about the music they play despite the fact that, particularly during the daytime, they are constrained by playlists chosen by somebody else. It is highly unlikely that they like all the tracks but they suggest that everything they play is somehow 'great'.

The influence of advertisers on the tone of a medium can work in a progressive way: when the *Daily Star* tried to stem a falling circulation by transforming itself into a 'tits and bums' newspaper, 'family orientated' advertisers, such as Tesco, took their business away. It was not long before the editor was sacked and the *Star* reverted to its former self.

4. *The influence of advertising*

Advertising has become a particularly influential form whose style has affected many media. Chapter 1 demonstrated its influence on high-concept, Hollywood fare. It is worth noting that, per second, advertising is more expensive than Hollywood blockbuster movies. It has also had a significant influence on the look of pop videos.

5. *The text as a site for promoting itself*

As it is the intention of most media text to attract as many of the target audience as possible, then it too must promote itself. This does not refer to advertising in other media texts but to the fact that many texts are the site of promotion for themselves.

■ Exercise 4.6 ■

Take the front page of any newspaper and list the way it is trying to entice readers to buy the issue.

The very top of a newspaper's front page is usually full of enticements as this is the part usually clearly visible in newsagents' displays. In Britain the 'red top' newspapers often use scantily clad women to entice the male reader; however, it is noteworthy how broadsheet newspapers often use the same technique, albeit more tastefully.

6. *Hooking*

This technique of self-promotion includes: 'hooks' (from the same root as 'hooker' or prostitute); serial promotion; the serial; the series; sequels.

Often magazines tease us on the front page with such lines as 'Locked in a Thai Lunatic Asylum – "How I survived four months of drugs, terror and violence"' (*Later*, issue 14, July 2000). This acts like Barthes's narrative enigmas (see Chapter 1 of *Narrative and Genre*), which will only be resolved if we purchase the magazine to read what is inside. Narrative is often explicitly part of this hook: 'The true *story* of . . .'.

Seriality is itself self-promotion, in that you need to watch the next episode, or purchase the next instalment, to find out what happens. This form teases the audience to spend more; or – if it is 'free to air' television – allow themselves to be sold to advertisers. Seriality comes in four forms: the retake (sequels or prequels); the remake (in cinema: the remake of older movies or adaptations from television); the series (the narrative is stretched over several episodes); the serial (a new narrative – promising the same pleasures – will start again next week) (adapted from Eco, 1985; see also *Narrative and Genre*).

Another way of hooking audiences is the use of well known, and sometimes celebrity, names to sell a text. In recent years directors' names have sometimes featured as part of film titles, such as *John Carpenter's Vampires* (1997). The appearance of stars and television personalities is also used as a selling point.

7. *Promotional transfer across media*

The extreme commodification of western media is made manifest at the final point of Wernick's vortex, which focuses on the promotional transfer within and across the media:

1. A star's appearance sells a text and they themselves, in turn, are sold by the text (assuming it is successful). Hence the Hollywood truism that you are only as successful as your last movie. Film stars have to choose their vehicles carefully, as a bad choice can lead to, at least, a hiatus in their career; for example, John Travolta, one of the biggest stars of the late 1970s, had a bad decade in the 1980s only to be 'resurrected' after *Pulp Fiction* (1994).
2. Any interviews with stars is publicity material for their new movie, or album, or television programme. This promotional aspect of media texts is a crucial component of any media analysis of such interviews where, though we may learn interesting facts about the individual, the primary purpose is to sell the new text.
3. 'The making of ...' featurette is a common way of promoting a film. This programme itself means to entertain while it markets the source text. These promotional tools have found a new lease of life as DVD 'extras'.
4. Any record that plays on the radio is promoting itself. In Britain, getting on Radio 1's playlist is of utmost importance

for artists who wish to have a hit record. In addition to receiving royalty payments, the artists and the record get free publicity.

5. The focus on charts is itself foregrounding the commodification of media texts; the best is the one that sells the most. This can be seen as democratic, the most popular being the winner, or as a utilitarian reduction of art to commerce (see Chapters 3 and 5).

6. Similarly, pop videos have always been used as explicitly promotional vehicles for music and films. Often these are pleasurable short texts; on the other hand, they tend to reduce the song to one particular meaning while the music on its own may have offered a variety of possible readings.

7. Merchandising has become increasingly important to the revenue streams of Hollywood studios (as we saw in Chapter 1).

Much of this final element of the vortex can be characterised by the 'publicity circus'. When was the last time you saw a guest on a chat show that did not have a new film/album/book/show to talk about? The same is true of interviews or profiles in the print media: coverage is given because there is a new product being released.

At the 1996 Brit awards Jarvis Cocker, of Pulp, invaded the stage while Michael Jackson was performing. Cocker waggled his bum at Jackson to demonstrate his contempt, he was promptly arrested though released without charge. As a result both Jackson's and Pulp's record sales rose, probably due to the coverage given to the incident. It was estimated, by CIA Medianetwork, that it would have cost £775,000 to get the amount of media coverage the incident garnered; this included three minutes on *News at 10* and ten minutes on *Channel 4 News*. Whether Cocker meant the whole thing as a publicity stunt or not is irrelevant.

■ Exercise 4.7 ■

Examine a magazine that covers the entertainment industry. List the number of feature articles that are linked to a new product.

There are exceptions to this publicity circus, for example *Sight and Sound* magazine, while not ignoring new releases, does not allow them to dominate its agenda. For example, the May 2000 issue carried articles linked to the new films *Erin Brokovich* and *American Psycho* but also featured Miike Takashi, a Japanese director who was barely known in Britain. Even further from the publicity circus is *The Wire* magazine, which proclaims itself as dealing in 'adventures in modern music'. How many of the top five of its '50 records of the year – 1999' have you heard of: 'Mouse on Mars', 'Sonic Youth', 'Coil', 'Matmos' and 'John Butcher'?

The most recent medium to have come into existence is the Internet. After a degree of hesitation over how to use it, though with an apparent certainty that they would have to engage with it in some way, most media organisations now build the Net into the plans for promoting their products.

The most profitable movie of the twentieth century, *The Blair Witch Project* (1998), used the Internet to build awareness of the film. Artisan Entertainment, an independent distributor, treated the film as a specialised art-house movie that appealed specifically to a young (15–24-year-old) audience. In addition, the ruse of treating the film as if it were a documentary was very successful. In the first nine months of 1999, the 'Blair Witch' website registered 200 million hits and surfers spent an average of 16 minutes per visit at the site (source: Goodrige, 1999, and Kendzior, 1999). The film took around $140m in North America alone; clearly this was not simply due to the website but the Net undoubtedly kick-started the coverage the movie eventually got, which was also fuelled by, and in turn helped generate, the box-office success in its first few weeks of roll-out.

4.7 The Net future?

The head of advertising at Lever Bros – the company which became part of the conglomerate Unilever – famously stated that half of all advertising was wasted, but no one knew which half. There are so many variables involved in advertising that it is very difficult to know what effect a particular campaign has. It might also be suggested that advertising agencies do not *want* to know what effect a campaign had, as the results might not have been good for them. Indeed there has been much criticism of advertising agencies that seem to be merely interested in impressing their rivals with their campaigns rather than selling products. Arty television advertisements, in particular, seem to be engrossed in their cleverness, and sight is often lost of what they are selling. Indeed, this ignorance of how effective advertising is has led, it is argued, to an increase in advertising:

> Hence the Knowability Paradox: The less we have known about how advertising and the media work, the more advertising and media there have been. (Rothenberg, 1998)

As noted in the part of section 4.4 above on 'Branding and the Internet', the new medium could change this:

> The Net is accountable. It is knowable. It is the highway leading marketers to their Holy Grail: single-sourcing technology that can definitively tie the information consumers perceive to the purchases they make.   (Ibid.)

Following on from Rothenberg, Greg Myers offered five ways in which the Internet circumvents the limitations of traditional media:

1. There is no restriction of space; adverts on the net can speak to everyone who is wired and not just limited to the area of distribution.
2. Similarly, there is no time restriction; audiences can access the ad any time they want.
3. Hypertext encourages consumers to follow other connections, so the home page of a company can 'spin' a positive line for the company and include links to any of the products it produces.
4. Webspace is very cheap especially when compared with television.
5. Advertisers can get information about who is accessing their site.

(Myers, 1999, p. 134)

If we ignore, for a moment, the problems of getting consumers to access your particular website, then the consequences of these points are likely to be far-reaching. As we have considered in this chapter, much of the media is sustained by advertising revenue and if this falls, to any great degree, then the costs of newspapers, for example, will rise. However, price elasticity suggests that the higher the price, the less likely a consumer is to purchase products. Circulation will decline, advertising rates are likely to decline with it – because there is an alternative on the Net – and we have a 'vicious' circle, which will see many publications go out of business.

The scenario could be even worse for commercial television, whose mainstay is still 'free to air' broadcasts. These broadcasts are only free because advertising generates revenue – if this diminishes then pay-TV may well become the norm. On average, in Britain and North America, around 24 hours of television is watched by each person each week; how much of this would people pay for?

■ Exercise 4.8 ■

Make a list of television programmes that you watch regularly; how many would you pay for and how much would you pay to see them?

4.8 Conclusion

As Chapters 1 and 3 have already emphasised, the selling of products is crucial in a capitalist society. Marketing is one of the main ways products are sold and is also responsible for a large number of media texts. Of crucial importance to marketing is branding, a way of making a product's image ubiquitous. This ubiquity is linked to globalisation, where multinational corporations transcend national boundaries; the Internet is likely to be very influential in the marketing of global brands but also may have a deleterious effect upon traditional (Old) media.

Public relations (PR) has grown in importance as a way of selling both products and companies' images. In addition it has also started to have a great deal of influence in both politics and the presentation of news. Wernick's vortex of publicity is a useful way of integrating the disparate elements of marketing to see how they can act together.

The selling of products 'infects' the media to such an extent that marketing should, perhaps, be considered the seventh Key Concept of Media Studies.

5

THE INDEPENDENT AND THE ALTERNATIVE

AIMS OF THE CHAPTER

➤ To consider definitions of 'independence' and 'alternative'.

➤ To consider independent film companies in relation to the mainstream.

➤ To consider alternative film forms.

➤ To investigate how alternative texts cross over to the mainstream.

➤ To consider how the music industry mediates the understanding of music genres.

➤ To consider access programmes.

5.1   Introduction

A key issue in the understanding of media organisations is their status in relation to the mainstream: they are either in the mainstream, independent of the mainstream or, rarely, alternative to the mainstream. While the mainstream is relatively easy to define, the concept of independence has many different facets. And although being alternative is often linked to independence it usually refers either to the way media conventions are broken, or to the values represented in the text (which would be in opposition to the dominant ideology). This chapter considers how independently produced texts, which may also be alternative in their make-up, relate to the mainstream and how those which are alternative in nature can cross over to the mainstream.

5.2   Definitions of 'independence' and 'alternative'

There are three broad types of independence:

(a)   independence from the state;

(b)   being independent of political bias; and

(c)   independence from the mainstream.

(a) For example, independent television was set up as an alternative to the state-sponsored BBC in Britain. Despite this independence, ITV still operated as a public service broadcaster for many years and even now retains some elements of PSB (see Chapter 2).

(b) Independence from political bias was the driving factor (or marketing ruse) behind the launch of the *Independent* newspaper in 1986. In order to maintain this independence it was decided that no shareholder should hold more than 10 per cent of the shares. This would greatly decrease the chance of the owners of the newspaper influencing the editorial stance. One effect of this was a rather schizophrenic newspaper where the leading articles were right-wing in nature while the news stories had a definite anti-Conservative (who were in power) slant. However, by the early 1990s, after a disastrous redesign, the newspaper's independence was compromised as Mirror Group newspapers took a controlling interest. Since then an Irish group, also called Independent Newspapers, has bought it.

(c) Mainstream organisations are invariably large and produce conventional texts. Independent organisations, on the other hand, are usually small and often supply texts to mainstream organisations. For example, the independent Hat Trick produces *Have I Got News For You?* for the BBC. Some independents produce non-mainstream texts, such as the record label Mille Plateaux, which distributes Gas.

It is this third type of independence that we are most concerned with in Media Studies. Although it is difficult to define what exactly an independent media organisation is, the issues surrounding notions of 'alternative' are usually clearer in that it refers to texts that offer an alternative to the mainstream.

One way of considering texts produced in either a mainstream or an alternative form is on a continuum, as shown in Figure 5.1. Texts that are completely conventional in their form (such as Spice Girls' songs) or in their ideological agenda are on the extreme right-hand side of the continuum. Texts that are formally completely alternative (for example, Jackson Pollock's abstract paintings) or in opposition to

Alternative ←———————————————————————→ Mainstream

Figure 5.1

the dominant ideology are at the extreme left. Peter Wollen's (1986) conception of 'counter cinema' as an alternative form can be adapted to other media – see section 4.11 in *Image and Representation*. Many texts fall between these two extremes; though wholly mainstream texts are common, totally alternative are rare.

Whilst most mainstream organisations produce only conventional texts, independently produced texts can be either mainstream (such as the first two *Terminator* movies) or alternative. This can be clearly demonstrated with reference to the film industry.

5.3 Independent film

In the film industry the major companies represent the mainstream: Buena Vista (Disney); Sony; Dreamworks SKG; Paramount (Viacom); 20th Century Fox (News Corporation); Vivendi-Universal; Warner Brothers. Most of the films these corporations produce, and/or distribute, are conventional in a formal and ideological sense.

Independent film companies, such as Artisan Entertainment, are far more likely to produce 'off-beat' fare; that is, films that break conventions in some way. The most financially successful company at producing such off-beat films is Miramax. While Miramax acts as an independent, the founders – the Weinstein brothers – have a high degree of autonomy; it is owned by Disney, hence its status is probably best described as quasi-independent.

While off-beat films are not usually aimed at the multiplex audience, they occasionally do generate relatively good box office, such as Lions Gate's *Dogma* (1999). These films' target audience is the 'art-house', repertory cinemas (ones which do not slavishly programme new releases), many of which receive public subsidy (see below). Art-house audiences tend to be more tolerant of difficult fare than those who inhabit multiplexes.

Some films, toward the 'alternative' end of the continuum described above, do not even offer much appeal to art-house audiences; for example, *Institute Benjamenta, or This Dream People Call Human Life* (1995) was a particularly challenging film and did very little business even by art-house standards. Such films usually only exist because they receive public finance and/or money from public service television. Television money, however, is usually attached to more commercial projects.

Major studios rarely, if ever, produce obscure art-house films; these are purely the providence of the independent sector. However, the Majors have been producing 'off-beat' films, usually made by wholly-owned subsidiaries. These are produced in the knowledge that they can be immensely profitable, such as Fox 2000's *The Full Monty* (1997), and are more likely to garner Academy Award nominations than their mainstream fare, for example, *Crouching Tiger, Hidden Dragon* (2000). The Oscars are a very useful way of marketing off-beat films.

To summarise:

- Independent companies produce off-beat and, occasionally, obscure films for the art house.
- The Majors, too, produce off-beat films.
- Independents can produce mainstream films.
- Not all independents are small companies. Miramax is owned by Disney but still acts like an independent.

The relationship between independents and Majors is shown in Figure 5.2.

As we saw in Chapter 1, making profit from producing films for the cinema is a difficult task even for major studios. For independent companies it is even harder. Despite this, independent filmmakers continue to make films, either because they just love to make movies or because they are betting on (a) making a big independent hit, and/or (b) being picked up by a major studio for a big budget project.

The year 1999 was interesting for independent distributors in North America. *The Blair Witch Project* became the most profitable movie of all time (based on box-office revenue alone) after it grossed $141 million, having cost around $80,000 to produce. A glance at the top five independently produced films that year gives a clearer picture:

1. *The Blair Witch Project* (Artisan) $142m
2. *She's All That* (Miramax) $63m
3. *Dogma* (Lions Gate) $29m
4. *Stir of Echoes* (Artisan) $21m
5. *An Ideal Husband* (Miramax) $19m

(Source: *Screen International*, 14 January 2000)

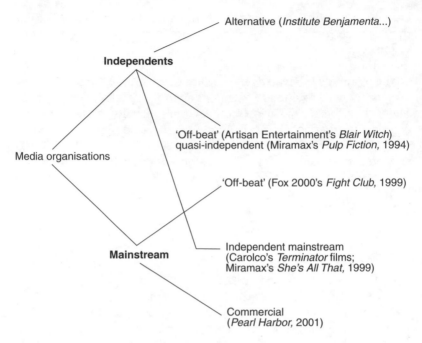

Figure 5.2 The relationship between major and independent film companies

Blair Witch was clearly a phenomenon (it was the 10th biggest grossing movie of the year), taking more money than the next four in the chart, which did little business, *She's All That* excepted, when compared with the top grossing mainstream films.

Veteran independent filmmaker John Sayles offers a non-institutional definition. The independent method

> of making a movie is to have a story in mind and then do everything in your power to get it made without compromising its quality. It doesn't matter what genre it's in, whether the financing of the production is from a studio or not, the driving force is to tell that story as well as is possible. Every decision ... is based on maximising the potential of the story to do its work. (Sayles, 1995, p. 156)

As Sayles is suggesting, most movies are made with the view to making money and so every decision is inflected with the desire to maximise return, and not about maximising the aesthetic quality of the film. The only compromises Sayles makes are economic in the sense that he may not be able to afford to make the film the way he would prefer; however, if he had a higher budget then he would be likely to have less control over his film.

Sayles is able to make a living like this because he is a successful screenwriter. While he has never had a massive box-office hit, to date, as a director he has made many films that are critically respected; *Matewan* (1987), for instance, is a magnificent melodrama–western chronicling a union dispute in a mining community.

We saw in Chapter 2 how public money is sometimes used to sub-sidise non-commercial projects. The premise of such funding is that texts of cultural worth are important to a nation's sense of itself. This worth is usually defined in aesthetic terms, and bodies such as the Arts Council in Britain administer the funds. Up until the late 1990s, the British Film Institute, a publicly funded body, also produced many non-commercial films.

The 1970s was a particularly radical era in Film Studies, and a number of film theorists, such as Laura Mulvey and Peter Wollen, made BFI-funded films such as *Riddles of the Sphinx* (1977) and *Amy!* (1979).

The generation of film-makers applying to the Board for production funds in this recent period have been frequently concerned with nothing less than a *reinvention of the communication process* itself [*my italics*]. (Sainsbury, 1981, p. 10a)

Unsurprisingly much of this product was difficult and seen by rela-tively few people. A number of critics have suggested that because not many people see, or want to see, obscure, polemical films, these should not be publicly funded. It is ironic that many of these films, either explicitly or implicitly, criticised the status quo, or in other words, the state that was providing funds. In the 1970s this criticism was often from a feminist perspective (for example, Sally Potter's *Thriller*, 1979). Although it may appear that these filmmakers were 'biting the hand that fed them', it is surely necessary that a democratic society supports a plurality of views. Many of the advances women have achieved in the last 30 years, such as the right to equal pay, are a result of feminist pressure.

There is little doubt that if these films were not subsidised they would not get made. If the 'market' determined our choice then we would only have mainstream texts available to us.

Many of the radical films of the 1970s were made by 'collec-tives', such as the Berwick Street Collective's *Night Cleaners* (1975).

Collectives often operated in a 'workshop' environment that operated in opposition to conventional industrial practices. The emphasis was on working together, rather than being under the control of a director or producer. Different ways of viewing film were experimented with in an attempt to create spaces where:

> participants, through work-in-progress screenings, could begin to engage not only in the process of exhibition but that of production, or self-representation. (Fountain, 1981, p. 166a)

The collectives not only challenged the conventional way of watching films, they operated equal-opportunity employment policies to make sure non-establishment voices could be heard. The growth of the workshop sector continued in the 1980s. Julian Petley (1989) listed four reasons for this:

(i)   the sector was spurred by the films made in the 1970s;
(ii) the growth of Media courses in higher education stimulated interest;
(iii) the availability of cheaper equipment made film making easier;
(iv) following the lead given by Ken Livingstone's Greater London Council, many local authorities began to take an active interest in minority groups, many of whom had formed workshops to get their point across to a wider audience.

In addition, Channel 4, particularly in its *Eleventh Hour* slot, was broadcasting the collectives' material to a relatively large audience. However, during the 1980s the political climate that fostered public subsidy for the arts was fading, though this did not stop the Black Audio Film Collective forming, in an attempt to give black Britons a voice, and producing the acclaimed *Handsworth Songs* in 1986.

By the 1990s this radicalism was, more or less, spent, though the BFI continued to support non-commercial films such as *Under the Skin* (1997), a fascinating melodrama about grief and sexual insecurity. Some of the collectives, like Amber Films, are still operating, most recently with *Like Father* (2001):

> Amber was established in 1969 with the specific intention of creating a film and photographic practice in relation to the working class communities of the North East of England. A commitment to the continuation and development of that practice is still central to the group to this day. (Amber films website)

This regional emphasis is notable as it acknowledges the importance of having a voice independent of London. London-based practitioners often characterise the rest of the country as regional or provincial, as if, in some way, non-London voices are inherently secondary.

By 2000, public subsidy in Britain for experimental media texts was at its lowest ebb for many years. As we shall see in the next section, the cutting edge, avant garde, is important in the development of mainstream texts.

5.4 Crossing over: the commodification of the oppositional

Conventions of representation are constantly evolving; occasionally, however, there occurs a 'paradigm shift' where there is, apparently, a complete break with previous modes of representation, with the appearance of something new. As we, both audiences and producers of media texts, are all a product of our society, it is probably impossible to offer something that is totally new, though it is feasible to have sudden leaps in development. In *Image and Representation* (Chapter 4) it was suggested that Cubism represented a 'shattering of perspective' in painting. Within a few years, however, the new form had become part of 'establishment' art; just as Impressionism had originally been vilified – before it had joined the mainstream.

In music, Schoenberg, and his disciples, developed an alternative form (based on the 12-note scale rather than the octave). Initially, many critics treated his music with scepticism; by the end of the twentieth century he was considered one of the most important composers of his time and his influence could be heard even in the mainstream – the musical soundtrack to many horror movies is atonally based.

While not all formal innovations join the mainstream, it is possible to characterise the history of art – in any medium – as a series of innovations that at first offers the 'shock of the new', and then, as artists, critics and audiences get used to the changes, becomes established as the (new) mainstream.

The part played by critics is often crucial in this. Their role is to mediate between the media producers (whether an organisation or artist, and usually both) and the audience. Critics are not a homogeneous bunch: some are progressive in welcoming innovation and offer ways to come to terms with change; others are conservative in outlook (such as Christopher Tookey, the *Daily Mail*'s film critic, as we shall see, in Chapter 6). Critics' acceptance of new innovations helps legitimise them in a commercial context. Critics offer, in a sense, consumer guidance: is the new show or film worth seeing? If they are favourable to something new, then audiences may follow their advice; the text may then become (commercially) successful, which will inevitably be followed by imitations or other texts that take their lead from what is new. In this way, innovation becomes established; the commercial aspect of this, as we shall see, is crucial.

The birth of rock 'n' roll

In simplistic terms, 'rock 'n' roll was born' with Elvis Presley's Sun sessions recorded in 1954, with an 'intense fusion of black and white Southern musics – gospel, R & B and country' (Hardy and Laing, 1990, p. 638b). The songs Presley sang were not, in themselves, innovative. The fact that he was white, and therefore imbued with white 'country' culture, meant he sang what were essentially black R & B songs in a new way:

> he evolved a personal version of this style, singing high and clear, breath-less and impatient, varying his rhythmic emphasis with a confidence and inventiveness that were exceptional for a white singer. The sound sug-gested a young white man celebrating freedom, ready to do anything, go anywhere ... (Gillett, 1983, p. 28)

Also, owing to the institutional racism prevalent at the time, the fact that a white man was singing these songs gave them a legitimacy they previously did not have. The racism was institutional because it formed part of the organisation's norms and values. In North America the fact a white man was singing 'black' songs was immensely shock-ing to some. However, Elvis was in tune with the time's *zeitgeist*, which 'encouraged' youthful rebellion, and he became, like Marlon Brando and James Dean, a teen icon.

Sun was a small label based in Memphis, run by Sam Phillips, who was instrumental in bringing Elvis to the songs that ultimately made him famous. Elvis's five Sun singles were successful, but only in the South and a major record company, RCA-Victor, bought out his contract. At RCA, Elvis became a superstar but not without cost to his art:

> Presley's voice became much more theatrical and self-conscious as he sought to contrive excitement and emotion which he had seemed to achieve on his Sun records without any evident forethought. (Ibid., p. 29)

This pattern of moving from a small, independent record company to a major, often accompanied by a diminution in artistic level, is a paradigm that describes the relationship between small independents of many media and their mainstream (major) counterparts. Enthusiasts often run small independents for artistic reasons; the major corporations exist for commercial gain. Therefore independents are more likely to take risks; the major company executives tend to be risk-aversive in order to protect their jobs.

Whenever a small company introduces an innovation that appears to be popular with audiences, then major companies, who have greater resources for marketing and making the artist rich, often step in to reap the economic rewards. Elvis, along with rock 'n' roll in general, represented a threat to middle-class values, particularly with the blatant sexual references of both the songs and his hip-wiggling performances. In true corporate fashion, under RCA-Victor's stewardship, aided by Elvis's manager Colonel Tom Parker, Presley's performance style was toned down to the (almost) anodyne. Similarly, Fred Goodman's *The Mansion on the Hill* (1997) compares the artistic credibility of Bob Dylan and Neil Young with what he describes as Bruce Springsteen's sell-out.

Punk rock

In the late 1990s the iconic British punk rock group of the late seventies, the Sex Pistols, re-formed for their 'Filthy Lucre' tour. However, the irony of the tour's title could not disguise the fact that the Sex Pistols in their earlier incarnation would have spat at themselves for re-forming in order to make money (as John Lydon said, before the dirty deed was done, 'you can't reform [the dead] Sid').

Punk rock, at its best, did not allow the major corporations to have their way. EMI were forced to drop the Sex Pistols after shareholder complaints about the band's behaviour. The 1970s Pistols did not succumb to the corporate 'suits'.

In Britain, punk rock has probably been the most recent musical genre to attack bourgeois values head on. In 1977, when many in the country were celebrating the Queen's 25 years on the throne, the Pistols released 'God Save the Queen'. This may sound respectful; however, sung in Johnny Rotten's distinctive sneer with the drum-driven wall of guitar sound it was anything but. The first two lines ran:

God save the Queen,
And her fascist regime.

Added to the refrain, 'There's no future for you', the establishment was shocked:

Reactions to the record [were] predictably hostile.
'If pop music is going to be used to destroy our established institutions then it should be destroyed first,' pontificated Labour MP Marcus Lipton. All the major high street stores refuse to stock the single. The BBC ban it. The BPI, the record industry's ruling body, secretly manipulate that week's [Jubilee] chart so that – in a pathetic attempt to pretend that it's business-as-usual – Rod Stewart's 'I Don't Want to talk About It' can keep 'God Save the Queen' from the top spot.   (Martin, 2000, p. 63)

The philosophy of punk rock was strictly non-commercial: anyone can make a record but then they must disband. Music was made as a statement, not necessarily *for* anything, but definitely against the mainstream 'glam rock' (and hippies). Followed to the letter, this philosophy would mean it was very difficult to commoditise punk music.

Just as it is arguable that 'alternative' and 'mainstream' are at the opposite ends of the continuum, the same could be said for 'art' and 'commodities'. Popular-culture theorists have taken polar viewpoints on this: Theodore Adorno, for instance, believed that any cultural artefact that was produced as a commodity would necessarily be degraded and therefore not art. Walter Benjamin, on the other hand, believed the mass production of artefacts to be a progressive force. Such extremes of view, it has been suggested, are 'moribund' (Sanjek, 1998). Take hip-hop, for example: it offers a dazzling mix of the 'street' and the 'corporate' and blurs the distinction between artistic statement and commercial product.

Hip-hop

Hip-hop is, arguably, the most vibrant musical form of the last 20 years. This vibrancy is a result of its ability to renew itself so that, at its cutting edge, it is never old-fashioned, or retro. It has succeeded in remaining at the avant garde of popular music because of its relationship with the 'street' and the authenticity this engenders.

Writing at the beginning of the twenty-first century, from Britain, it appears ironic that hip-hop is now the biggest selling musical genre in North America. Ironic because the America we see through

Hollywood and on television (in shows and on the news) remains predominantly WASP (white, Anglo-Saxon, Protestant). Hip-hop is a quintessentially African-American musical form that has come to represent youthful rebellion and expression for any race. The title of Nelson George's essential history of the form, *Hip Hop America* (1999), suggests as much. Inevitably hip-hop is now a commodity but it started as an expression of a subordinate sub-cultural group. As we saw above, this movement from the 'street' (or the 'underground', as it is not seen or heard by mainstream media) to being the product of multinational corporations is a common one. Possibly uniquely, hip-hop has made this journey without losing its artistic credibility. If we focus on one aspect of hip-hop we can see how this line between art form and commodity has been trodden.

Black Americans are, as ethnic minority people are in Britain, a subordinate grouping. This can be measured statistically in terms of average earnings, educational achievement and criminal records. The fact that non-whites earn less, achieve less and are incarcerated more has led a number of commentators to suggest that black people are less intelligent than whites. *The Bell Curve* (Herrnstein and Murray, 1996) became a best-seller by promulgating such a claim. From a liberal Media Studies perspective such claims are viewed as ridiculous (and vile, as they promote racial hatred). The reason for differences between social groups is ideological: institutional racism means that, on average, black people are paid less or have less opportunity for promotion; similarly, education favours the white mainstream, just as law enforcement agencies inculcate into their officers the idea that black people are more likely to be criminal.

Despite the subordination of many black people in economic terms, materialism, along with rebellion and aggression, has always been part of the hip-hop genre. Hip-hop, at street level, in common with most sub-cultural groups, used 'found' materials as a badge of identity (see Chapter 7). When Adidas sponsored Run DMC to the tune of $1.5 million it was not seen as a 'sell-out' but rather as a seal of approval of African-American culture by big business. The cry of 'sell-out' is a dangerous one for the 'street' artist, for it suggests that they are selling their heritage, their rebellion, to the highest bidder and, in doing so, become what they are rebelling against. Musical genres associated with sub-cultural groups are particularly potent as they are used by the groups to define themselves against the dominant group; consider, for example, Public Enemy's political hip-hop. Anyone who goes 'overground' joins the repressive order and so is a traitor to their group.

One of the reasons that hip-hop seems to avoid this charge is because it has always been, in itself, materialist in outlook. So any financial success gained through the music was to be celebrated and not seen as a sell-out; unless it was a particularly puerile version of the genre practised by early crossover artists such as MC Hammer. Run DMC's 'My Adidas' started as a sub-cultural expression; they got the sponsorship deal with Adidas afterwards. Similarly, Tommy Hilfiger's career took off after he was name-checked by the respected Grand Puba (George, 1999, pp. 161–2).

Not all of Corporate America appreciates being tagged by hip-hop. Timberland boots found that their reputed dislike of being associated with the music (middle-class product meets crack-dealer couture) led to their disappearance as a hip-hop accessory.

Although hip-hop is now mainstream it has remained connected to the street:

> [Hip-hop] culture's connection to the African-American working and underclass, people usually without a media voice, enables it to communicate dreams and emotions that make outsiders uncomfortable. (George, 1999, p. 155)

It is hip-hop's ability to make outsiders uncomfortable that has kept it ('real') in the forefront of youthful expression. As a genre it has developed massively from the first mainstream hit (listen to the Sugar Hill Gang now, it sounds tame), through the extreme misogyny of gangsta rap, to the present where the hip-hop sound world is ubiquitous. This discomfort has not always been easy for capitalist corporations to swallow: Time-Warner dropped Interscope Records in response to white middle-class horror of gangsta rap; 2 Live Crew successfully used the Supreme Court in 1989 to overturn the ban of their *Nasty As We Wanna Be* album, making certain that rap was protected under the Constitution. However, as recently as 1998, C-Bo (Shawn Thomas) was jailed for breaking his parole. The terms of his parole were a direct attack on hip-hop:

> Thomas had been released on parole...with the undertaking that he 'not engage in any behaviour which promotes the gang lifestyle, criminal behaviour and/or violence towards law enforcement'. (Lewis, 1998, p. 29)

The police were apparently confused about the differences between art (hip-hop) and the realities of gang life:

C-Bo's parole officer read the lyrics to his first major label release 'Til My Casket Drops.' To say the least, the parole officer was not amused. The song 'Deadly Game' contained lyrics criticizing California's 'three strikes and you're out' law. 'You better swing, batter, swing 'cause once you get your third felony, yeah, 50 years you gotta bring.... Fuck my P.O., I'm going A.W.O.L....bound for another state, me and my crew.... California and Pete Wilson can suck my dick.' Within days of the album's release, Thomas was arrested and charged with parole violation. (Nuzum, 1998)

As Lewis points out, today's action film stars do not get arrested for any 'criminal behaviour' they live out on the screen so it is not hard to conclude that Thomas was a victim of a police vendetta. This establishment attack on hip-hop is, of course, useful in defining it as being against the establishment and so helping retain its street credibility so attractive to young people. In 2001, Eminem was keeping hip-hop at the forefront of rebellion against middle-class values (expressed primarily through the misogyny and homophobia of Eminem's characters, such as Slim Shady) and at the top of the charts. Frederic Jameson suggests the commodification of rebellion is a characteristic of postmodern culture:

The most offensive forms of...art – punk rock, say, or what is called sexually explicit material – are all taken in stride by society, and they are commercially successful. (Jameson, 1993, p. 204)

Whereas in the past the 'weird and repulsive' (ibid.) belonged to the realm of 'high art', now it can immediately find a place in the mainstream as a commodity. In 2001, *The Marshall Mathers LP*, by Eminem, was the first hip-hop album to be nominated in the Grammys' 'best album' category, which was another 'establishment' seal of approval; however:

Some of us...wonder whether the Academy feels more comfortable nominating a white rapper when Black artists like Snoop, Jay-Z, Pac, Biggies and OutKast were passed over time and time again. (Frosch, 2001, p. 43)

One way in which music is commodified is through being packaged by record labels and labelled by music critics. This tension between musical development, and the industry and critics' need to give music a label in order to sell it, can be seen in drum 'n' bass music.

5.5 Music, mediation and industry

Martin James defines Jungle, an early variant of drum 'n' bass, as:

> The generic term for all versions of the sound. A combination of timestretched breakbeats playing at approximately 160 beats per minute (bpm). With bass lines lifted from Reggae, running at 80 bpm and the metronomic 4/4 bass drum removed. (James, 1997, p. xi)

And he identifies 15 versions, or sub-genres, of Jungle:

- ambient drum 'n' bass;
- balearic;
- dark;
- drum 'n' bass;
- hardstep;
- hardcore;
- hip house;
- jazz step;
- jazzy jungle;
- jump up;
- jungle;
- ragga;
- ragga-jungle;
- sleng teng;
- techstep.

His definition of Jungle offers a clue to why it can be so difficult to categorise music generically, since, as well as having numerous sub-genres, Jungle is clearly influenced by Reggae. More than any medium, music can be an eclectic mix of – potentially – anything that is going. BBC Radio 3's music programmes *Mixing It* and *Late Junction* are based upon the premise that distinctions between, for instance, classical, folk and world music are completely debilitating and so Coldcut can feature happily with Nusrat Fateh Ali Khan and Arvo Pärt.

One of the reasons why there is such a plethora of genres, or styles, in music which might be loosely categorised as 'dance', is because it has an alternative, 'cutting edge', status. The record industry, however, likes genres, as they make it easier to classify and package the artists. Similarly, genre gives critics labels by which to communicate with their readers. While many artists are happy to work within generic confines, many resent the labelling.

Many artists, and audiences, resent the commodification of the expression of their sub-cultural group and so, in vibrant musical cultures, when a particular variant of dance music 'crosses over' into the mainstream a mutant strain appears behind in the 'underground'. Some strains of dance music are associated with particular (independent) labels, reflecting the tastes of the label's controller, who is also, usually, the founder. For example, Skint was the driving force behind Big Beat, featuring such acts as Bentley Rhythm Ace, Fatboy Slim and the Lo-Fidelity All Stars. Big Beat is characterised by an irreverent humour: think of Bentley Rhythm Ace's initials.

Jungle first appeared in the clubs during 1991, but it was not until three or four years later that the mainstream press took notice. The non-club audience requires the music press, or music pages of the broadsheet newspapers (the tabloids rarely touch anything other than pop unless scandal is involved), to inform them of new developments, and this may lead to a wider market for the music. Once an 'underground' music starts to enter mainstream publications its sub-cultural status alters. David Sandall, in the *Sunday Times*, concluded an article written at the end of 1994 with the following:

> A music which started out, like rave, priding itself on the anonymity and invisibility of its artists now carries its own hierarchy of stars, many of whom seem to be in two minds as to how famous they want to be – jealously guarding their cool cult status on the one hand, talking to big labels on the other. If jungle does move overground to become *the* sound of 1995, it's a fair bet that with the success will come the inevitable chorus of complaints about a sell out.   (Sandall, 1995, p. 20)

At some point Jungle mutated into 'drum 'n' bass'; a response, in all probability, to the racist overtones of the term 'jungle', though some argued that it was a label embraced by black artists as a way of subverting the association of 'jungle bunnies', just as Niggers With Attitude co-opted a racist term for their group. If Sandall was slightly premature in his prediction of Jungle being '*the* sound of 1995', then in 1997 it certainly gained mainstream acceptability when Roni Size and Reprazent's album *New Forms* (what great Media Studies names) won the Mercury Prize.

The Mercury Prize is slightly different from many prizes, such as the Brits and the Oscars, which are essentially industry-devised promotions, because it is sponsored by Cable & Wireless, a telecommunications company. Its remit is to 'reflect the diverse qualities of current

British music from contemporary classical through to pop and rock'. The 1997 nominees were:

- Suede
- Chemical Brothers
- Radiohead
- Primal Scream
- Beth Orton
- John Taverner and Steven Isserlis
- Roni Size
- The Prodigy
- The Spice Girls
- Mark-Anthony Turnage

This is an impressively eclectic list. Of course whether they constitute the best albums of the year clearly depends upon your opinion (and the list of judges does look suspiciously like it leans toward the middle-aged). The appearance of Roni Size in the list did offer a stamp of establishment approval for drum 'n' bass. While many in the dance/club scene eschew this respectability, it is clearly important for commercial success. Roni Size was featured on the January 1998 'Heroes of '97' *Mixmag* cover (see Figure 5.3); *DJ* (which calls itself 'the world's best underground dance magazine') eulogised Size, and fellow Reprazent member, DJ Krust, as 'two of the most successful pioneers of 1997'; Pete Tong (he of BBC Radio 1's Essential Selection) praised the album, suggesting that the 'scene' was happy with this cross-over.

> Four years ago people would be shouting sell out but d&b as a community has since learnt, through the efforts of Goldie, Bukem and Photek, that success in itself isn't a sell out, moreover staying underground for the sake of it is selling the music short. In today's climate, this music should be heard and Reprazent have manoeuvred into a position where they can accomplish this, without suffering any compromise.   (Marshall, 1997)

However, the eulogies were not unanimous:

> The soft tracks on *New Forms*, taking up about half of the two-CD set, sound like drum 'n' bass by committee – not a cohesive, well-oiled groove collective, but a suited-up boardroom meeting of corporate suits analyzing focus-group results. Roni Size's attitude, spiced up by his obvious credentials as a DJ and an aficionado of all forms of music from dub to soul, can't

Figure 5.3 *Mixmag* cover

save the album from descending to the depths of cynical exploitation of a vital genre.   (Tweney, 1997)

Tweney's metaphor, 'suited-up . . . corporate suits', reveals disdain of what he perceives as a commercial sell-out by Size and 'his' collective.

The increasingly mainstream acceptance of dance is not restricted to Britain. In May 1997, the National Academy of Recording Arts and Sciences (NARAS) recognised dance music as an important musical genre by establishing the categories of 'Best Dance Recording' and 'Remixer of the Year'. In addition, and almost certainly not unconnected, DJ/producer Frankie Knuckles – who helped pioneer House music – became a member of the New York Chapter of NARAS.

Despite this growing respectability there does not seem to be any lessening on the alternative edge of drum 'n' bass at least. For instance, the language Reprazent use to describe their music:

> They name-check funk as their gelling influence and describe their sound in the kind of way a futuristic gang in a William Gibson novel might speak. During the interview, they answer collectively. Each member speaks in short sentences, which, all added together, create the big picture of what they are about:
> 'We're trying to do something new ... It's the use of sounds and not treating them in a conventional way ... A fresh angle ... Morphing things together ... Everyone is into sonics, the way a sound works, the space it occupies, as opposed to whether it's a good sale ... It's not important if it's A minor or E sharp, fuck all that ... '.   (Chernin, 1998, p. 167)

This echoes James's description of Jungle, 'it is a magpie genre taking from the entire spectrum of music as it sees fit' (James, 1997, p. 5). The rejection of conventional musical form, and therefore conventional ways of perceiving, is linked to the drug culture out of which dance music sprang. This is despite the fact that the acid in 'acid house', from where dance music emerged in 1987, originally meant something different:

> When British youth first encountered the term 'acid house' they misconstrued it. In Chicago, the word 'acid' derived from 'acid burn', slang for ripping off someone's idea (i.e. by sampling it). In Britain, it was instantly assumed that 'acid' mean [sic] psychedelics.   (Reynolds, 1995, p. 730)

The dance sub-culture is now indelibly associated with Ecstasy, which helps induce a feeling of euphoria that epitomises the hedonism of Friday and Saturday night for the clubbing public:

> The subculture's metabolism has been chemically altered, till the beats-per-minute ... soar in sync with pulse rates and blood pressure levels. (Ibid.)

It has been argued that this sort of music cannot be appreciated unless the listener is 'high'. However, while drugs 'certainly help hype the metabolism to the necessary frenetic pitch' (ibid., p. 731), they are not necessary. To appreciate the music, audiences must learn to listen to the new form and so the suggestion of many, often from older generations, that Jungle, or any of its variants or antecedents, is not 'real music' indicates that they are not listening to it correctly.

Although no genre springs from nothing, it is arguable that dance does represent a quantum leap away from rock, which has been the staple form of popular music since the late 1950s. 'Rock 'n' roll', however, was about having sex in dance music:

> sex as the central metaphor of dancing seems more remote than ever. Rave dancing doesn't bump and grind from the hip; it's abandoned the mode of genital sexuality altogether for a kind of amoebal frenzy. It's a dance of tics and twitches, jerks and spasms, the agitation of a body broken down into individual components, then re-integrated at the level of the entire dancefloor. (Ibid., p. 732)

In addition to this different emphasis, drum 'n' bass is dependent upon the digital technology developed in the 1980s. The use of sampling, for instance, allows the DJ to steal/recycle/recreate other material, both musical and non-musical. This postmodernist borrowing manifests itself as 'bricolage' – see Chapter 9. Although, when dance recycles other music, the potential for the subversion of conventional signifying systems is limited, when rappers Run DMC sampled, and then re-recorded with, rock band Aerosmith in 1986 for 'Walk This Way' they encountered some resistance from what were, presumably, white rock enthusiasts in Boston. In this instance the *bricoleurs* were Run DMC and their producers, who appropriated the 'white rock' sound; this, however, was only menacing to racists who could not cope with the mix of black (rap) and white.

A genre is usually defined by the texts that constitute it, but in music this may not always be the case as genres are an ideal way of commodifying the medium. In late 1997 the latest 'dance-floor' sensation was 'Speed Garage':

> In essence speed garage is funky four-four music. The concentration is on drum loops and bass-lines, although it also has a strong association with jazz house and disco-diva vocals... alternatively, speed garage is simply a huge cauldron of bubbling London sounds, bringing together drum 'n' bass, ragga MCs, house, acid jazz and garage. (Osborne, 1997, p. 16)

Speed Garage's breakthrough to the mainstream was probably the Armand van Helden remix of Tori Amos's *Professional Widow* that topped the British charts in 1997. Osborne concluded that Speed Garage 'probably owes more to media hype than musical origins' (Osborne, 1997, p. 16). His article was hooked onto a review of a Virgin compilation of Speed Garage, *Maximum Speed*.

Media institutions use genre as a way of packaging diverse products and the press has a pivotal role in mediating between the texts (and the institutions producing the texts) and the audience. By 2000, Speed Garage had (unsurprisingly) mutated and was now called UK garage. Referring to its early days in 1997:

> the public at large dismissed it as just another fad, a fictitious scene concocted by some desperate music journos ... (Hall, 2000, p. 28a)

So in this case it appears that Osborne was wrong, as the genre had evolved:

> 1999 saw the underground make its first serious inroads into the overground. ... Basement Jaxx's awe-inspiring 'Remedy'. One of the biggest crossover acts of last year ... paid enormous homage to a sound which was beginning to become known as UK garage. (Ibid., p. 28b)

Music journalists work under the constraints of deadlines and have to fill a certain amount of space. They also do not have the luxury of distance that the historian has. This distance helps to give a perspective on events and it is easier to see patterns and progression. The use of labels, valid or otherwise, is a good way to get a handle on what is going on. Often musicians resent being categorised (Tricky reputedly hated the description of his music as 'trip hop'), but it does help audiences understand what is being described. These labels, in turn, help record companies sell the product, just as Hollywood uses genre to sell its films.

A very rare example of a mainstream band going back into the 'underground' occurred in 2000. Radiohead's *Kid A*, and follow-up *Amnesiac*, repudiated their 'greatest rock band' status with explorations in electronica.

Clearly one of the major institutional factors is the media organisation distributing the text. The producers are likely to emphasise a text's genre in both the marketing and the credit sequence. We have seen, in Chapter 1, how Hollywood often eschews traditional generic categories in order to appeal to as wide an audience as possible. The credit sequence is used to cue the audience into a particular generic framework by using iconography and to create an atmosphere and a sense of anticipation. In addition to the producers, there are other institutional variables including: exhibition; critics and arbiters; classification; political considerations; *zeitgeist*.

1. Any film that plays at a multiplex, or a programme that runs during prime-time on a mainstream television channel, creates an expectation that the text will be conventional in character. Similarly if, say, blockbuster films appear in a repertory cinema, the art-house audience may assume that the film is something more than 'just entertainment'. Many will not countenance watching a subtitled movie as they assume it will be difficult.

2. As we saw in section 4.5 of *Narrative and Genre*, critics can create a genre. In this case, French critics originally categorised, and even acted as curators of, *film noir*. Some critics achieve the status of being arbiters of popular taste: for film, Barry Norman in Britain and *Leonard Maltin's Movie & Video Guide* in the USA. Hence if Norman states that *Se7en*, for example, is a thriller then it is likely that many in the audience will have this expectation of the film.

3. Many people choose films by their certificate. For example, PG (Parental Guidance) movies are anathema to many teenagers, while if an 18, or NC-17 in the USA, is slapped on the film it becomes immediately enticing. In this way the certification triggers expectations. Indeed, many film producers make certain they include enough nudity and/or 'bad' language in order to guarantee an R rating in North America and a 15 in Britain.

4. As we shall see in the next chapter, the campaign to ban films that offended bourgeois society resulted in the creation of 'video nasties', a hitherto unknown generic classification.

5. *Zeitgeist* is slightly harder to define (and is not, strictly speaking, an institutional factor as it exists outside organisations) in relation to genre definition. As society changes, the way texts are read will inevitably alter: 'Films featuring close friends of the same sex have been produced for decades, but not until the era of gay liberation did the *buddy film* come out as a genre' (Altman, 1999, p. 93). Before the 1970s the buddy film could not have existed; from this time any movie made featuring close friends could be said to belong to the genre.

The above may give the impression of consumer powerlessness in the face of corporate capital. However, some media texts are devoted to giving the 'ordinary' punter a voice.

5.6   Access programmes

Access programmes give the non-elite a voice in the media. The elite consists of media professionals who put together the programmes, and those who regularly appear in the media, be they stars, politicians or simply VIPs. This access is essential because, to take TV as an example:

> Television creates cultural capital; if we are misrepresented or under-represented our stake in the culture is devalued.   (Dovey, 1993, p. 163)

As Dovey suggests, television has such an important role because it is the prime mediator of how we understand our society. Nearly everyone watches television and average viewing per week is over 20 hours, a considerable portion of our leisure time. One of the functions of public service broadcasting (see Chapter 2) has been to create institutional mechanisms whereby under-represented people, and groups, can gain access to mainstream television.

For many years access television flourished, relatively, in Britain with the BBC's *Open Door* programmes and Channel 4's *Right of Reply* (which was axed in April 2001). *Open Door* was produced by the BBC's Community Programme Unit, which was established in 1972. During the 1970s it was broadcast on BBC2 with an early evening prime-time slot. The programme allowed social-action groups, such as campaigners for better housing, a national voice; crucially they had a high degree of control over the programme's construction.

In the 1980s this mutated into *Open Space*, which had a more professional look facilitated by greater professional intervention by the BBC. At this time there was a switch to individuals telling their own stories rather than groups speaking together, which reached its apotheosis with video diaries in the 1990s.

'Access' includes 'phone in' programmes, ubiquitous on the radio, where members of the general public can air their views and/or ask prominent people questions; in Britain, BBC Radio 5 Live offers numerous opportunities for listeners to join in programmes. Children's television often has phone-ins for viewers to ask questions or take part in competitions. E-mail has allowed listeners and viewers to get involved: during the Euro 2000 football championships, panellists would answer questions sent by e-mail regarding the evening's game. In some texts, Jo Public is centre-stage, particularly in 'Confession TV' – see Jerry Springer – where people are invited to share their traumas. The public here, however, are characterised as freaks rather than ordinary human beings.

Whilst these programmes do offer a platform for people outside the broadcasting industry to get national coverage, 'access' programmes are most effective when the 'outsiders' have control over the means of production of the programmes. In the current market-orientated environment such opportunities are getting fewer.

5.7 Conclusion

This chapter has attempted to look beyond the mainstream (mainly commercial) production of media texts through an investigation of the problematic notion of independence and the, ironically, more straightforward conception of alternative texts. Non-conventional ways of working were described, as were groups that attempted to make statements in opposition to the mainstream. However, there is a discernible pattern, particularly in music, suggesting that when oppositional forms are successfully created – that is, they find an audience – they are soon commodified and so cross over into the mainstream. Genre is a powerful tool in this commodification, as it helps the categorisation (packaging) of texts.

There is the possibility of 'ordinary people' making themselves heard within the media 'monolith'. Access programmes, particularly associated with public service broadcasting, allow members of the public to get their voices heard.

6

APPROACHES TO
AUDIENCES

AIMS OF THE CHAPTER

➤ To consider the 'effects' debate.

➤ To investigate moral panics.

➤ To consider the campaign against *Crash*.

➤ To consider the 'uses and gratifications' theory with reference to women's lifestyle magazines.

➤ To examine the nature of entertainment with reference to *ER*.

➤ To consider criticisms of the 'uses and gratifications' theory.

➤ To look at Hall's encoding–decoding model.

➤ To consider ethnography.

➤ To briefly touch on a dialectical-audience model.

6.1   Introduction

There is little doubt that media texts affect audiences; what that effect is, and how it happens, is open to considerable doubt. The debate is clouded with, on the one hand, emotion, and on the other, the vagaries of social science. The emotion is often a result of 'moral panics' and the science has been so agenda-driven that conclusions cannot safely be drawn from research. Despite this, audiences must be considered as a key concept of Media Studies and therefore we need theories to conceptualise them.

The main theories of audience research have been the 'effects debate', the 'uses and gratifications' model, the 'encoding/decoding' model, and ethnography.

6.2 The 'effects' debate (the hypodermic model)

Research based on the 'effects' debate works on the premise that audiences uncritically absorb media messages and act upon them. In this theory, if we watch a party-political broadcast we will then desire to vote for that party; we will want to buy every product that we have seen advertised; we would want to perpetrate violence if we saw violence represented in the media. It is often termed the 'hypodermic model' because it assumes that consuming the media is the same as injecting a drug, as it has a direct effect upon audiences.

The 'debate' would be laughable, as it is ridiculous, if it was not for the fact that much censorship is 'justified' because of the alleged effect the material would have on (certain) audiences. David Gauntlett has surveyed the effects-debate literature and one conclusion he has drawn is:

> that if, after over sixty years of a considerable amount of research effect, direct effects of media upon behaviour have not been clearly identified, then we should conclude that they are simply *not there to be found*.   (Gauntlett, 1998, p. 120)

Despite this, the *belief* that the media can have a direct effect on audiences has a great influence on our lives.

Origins of the 'effects' debate

The 'hypodermic model' grew out of the Frankfurt school of the 1920s and 1930s, which consisted of Marxist theorists who attempted to explain the rise of fascism with reference to the growth of the mass media. Although the mass production of media texts had been possible since Gutenberg's printing press in the fifteenth century, it was not until the twentieth century that the media reached a critical mass that made it endemic in the West. While newspapers in the nineteenth century were influential they were limited by their relatively narrow range of distribution and the poor levels of literacy in the populace as a whole.

The Frankfurt school believed that popular culture, because it was a commodity (see Chapter 3), was essentially trash. For example, Theodore Adorno, a respected musical theorist and member of the school, believed popular music to be inherently corrupting:

In Adorno's view, the pleasure derived from popular music is superficial and false. Thus the listener may be what Adorno calls 'rhythmically obedient'. He or she is a 'slave to the rhythm', following the standardized beat of the song and becoming over-powered by it. For Adorno, individuals who enjoy these pleasures are corrupted by immersion and are open to the domination of the industrialized, capitalist system. (Abercrombie and Longhurst, 1998, p. 19)

Beneath this nonsense is a traditional view that sets art in opposition to mass culture. This 'High Culture versus Low Culture' has consequences, as we shall see, for the 'uses and gratifications' theory.

The Frankfurt school's theory faltered after the Second World War because it posited that the United States would become a fascist state, as it was saturated by popular culture. Ironically, the baton of the 'hypodermic' theory has passed to the conservatives (Adorno and his colleagues were Marxists), who assume that all 'vulnerable' people will unquestioningly be adversely affected by any 'distasteful' text. The right-wing fear of popular culture has manifested itself in 'moral panics'.

Moral panics

Many, possibly all, media have at some time been the focus of a moral panic. During the late 1990s the Internet was the centre of concerns about pornography and children's access to it. A *Time International* magazine cover (July 3, 1995) was illustrated with a zombie-like boy staring at the reader with a look of horror and shock. The story, 'On a Screen Near You: Cyberporn', quoted 'facts' in support of its argument including:

- In an 18-month study, the team surveyed 917,410 [items of] sexually explicit [material].
- It is immensely popular.
- It is ubiquitous.

(Elmer-Dewitt, 1995, p. 34)

In terms of the World Wide Web, under one million pages is not a large amount; even taking into account that the number of web pages has grown exponentially since 1995. The other two 'arguments' illustrate the roots of all moral panics: the fact that the medium is both popular and 'everywhere'. As we shall see, as each new medium during the latter part of the nineteenth century and the twentieth century became popular, it was characterised as a threat.

Hollywood was in the dock in 1999, in the wake of a series of shootings in North American schools, for its portrayal of violence. A few years earlier the 'first lady', Hillary Clinton, accused it of encouraging young people to smoke cigarettes. In the early 1990s Michael Medved's diatribe *Hollywood vs America: Popular Culture and the War on Traditional Values* (1992) suggested that Hollywood was guilty of nihilism. Also, early in the 1990s, it was computer games that were corrupting the youth of the western world. In the early 1980s, films on videocassettes, the so-called 'video nasties', were accused of corrupting children and therefore endangering civilisation. Comics were guilty of the same in the 1970s (and in the 1950s) and rock 'n' roll was considered to be an insidious influence on its fans in the 1950s. Hollywood was again guilty of being a corrupting influence with Universal's cycle of horror films in the 1930s and 'penny dreadfuls' – pulp fiction – were thought to 'soil' the minds of young, working-class women in the late nineteenth century. If we 'rewind' a little faster, Plato – in ancient Greece – suggested that poets would not be allowed in his republic.

Moral panics are engendered by social anxiety, which may be a manifestation of a fear of change. Anyone who focuses on the media as the *cause* of society's ills is doing little more than scapegoating. The judge who suggested that the murderers of two-year-old Jamie Bulger, in Liverpool in 1993, were influenced by the horror film *Child's Play 3* (1991) did so with no evidence that the perpetrators had even seen the film. It is easier to blame a media artefact than confront the problems within society that could have led to Bulger's death.

Hollywood films are routinely blamed for the massacres that have plagued the USA in recent years. From a British perspective it seems obvious that the easy access to guns in North America is the major factor contributing to the violence; however, after the shooting of several young people in a church in Texas in September 1999, local people blamed a lack of religion and not the lax gun laws. This explanation seemed even more bizarre when it was reported that the murderer – who killed himself – came from a deeply religious family. Indeed, much of the world's violence is a result of religious conflict and hatred. The most common media text cited by serial killers is the Bible. Maybe, then, we should ban religion. Although this is an absurd suggestion it is no more absurd than the attempt to ban films that portray violence.

The assumption behind the call for greater censorship of representations of violence, and often also representations of sex, is that the media have a direct affect on certain people in the audience. Note that the censors, who often spend every day watching 'debauched' material, do not believe they have been corrupted by their experience. Their belief is that 'vulnerable' people can be 'forced' to alter their behaviour on the basis of consuming certain media texts.

'Vulnerable' people

As we saw in Chapter 2 on censorship, the working class are often categorised as a group who are easily influenced by media texts. It is only a short step from this to the racist characterisation of black people as simple and childlike and therefore in need of (white) 'protection'. Children, also, are thought to be in need of protection or they will go astray. As is so often the case, when an ideological position is being expressed, this characterisation of children's vulnerability is contradictory:

> From this perspective, children are at once innocent and potentially monstrous: the veneer of civilization is only skin deep and can be easily penetrated by the essentially irrational appeals of the visual media. (Buckingham, 1998, p. 133)

Like everything else, the construction of the idea of childhood is ideological.

■ Exercise 6.1 ■

Write down a list of connotations of the concept of childhood.

Possibly among the first things in your list is the idea that children are 'innocent'. We have to ask where this idea of innocence came from.

> The concept of childhood as a time of blissful ignorance . . . has its roots in the late seventeenth and early eighteenth centuries. This was expanded upon by the Romantics who picked up notions of 'original innocence', of the child as *tabula rasa*, of the child as having innate and intimate connections to the natural world and to the realms of imagination and fantasy . . . (Watt, 1994, p. 12)

Children are in no more contact with nature than adults but this myth (that is, an ideological construction) of childhood is used to justify their protection from what are defined as corrupting influences; usually defined as 'sex and violence'.

Children are not the only group who are defined as being 'vulnerable'; people who have not had much formal education are also thought to require protection. In other words, there is a class-based prejudice to censorship, as working-class people usually have less formal education than the middle class. Robin Duval, the current chairman of the British Board of Film Classification, stated as much, at the 1999 British Film Institute post-16 Media Studies conference, when he said the Board used different criteria when censoring films destined for the multiplex (which includes the working class) from those for films that would be seen on the (middle-class) art-house circuit. In that year, two exceptionally sexually explicit (for Britain) films – *The Idiots* (1998) and *Romance* (1999) – attained their '18' certification because they were not likely to be seen by a mass audience. When FilmFour first aired the former on its movie channel it had to blur the scene showing an erect penis; however, they negated the censorship, to an extent, by webcasting the most controversial scenes uncut.

This patrician view of the working classes has been more explicitly shown in the past. A BBC *Yearbook* from the 1930s described a 'programme of interviews with "peasants from remote northern districts"' (Frith, 1988, p. 35). The districts in question were Lancashire and Yorkshire, which, even with the advent of high-speed trains, still appear to be remote to some in London.

One of the highest-profile pro-censorship campaigns at the end of the 1990s in Britain surrounded *Crash*.

The campaign against *Crash*

David Cronenberg's adaptation of J. G. Ballard's 1973 novel *Crash* caused much heated debate in 1996. The controversy was sparked by Alexander Walker's review in the *Evening Standard* (London's daily newapaper), which appeared under the heading 'A movie beyond the bounds of depravity'. Walker had seen the film at the Cannes film festival and it was not submitted to the British Board of Film Classification (BBFC) until later in the year.

The film has numerous sex scenes and deals with characters who are obsessed with car crashes. Although it is a non-mainstream film it did relatively good business in France and in the director's home country, Canada. In Britain the *Daily Mail* led the campaign to have the film banned. The *Daily Mail* film critic, Christopher Tookey, summarised his view as follows:

> Whatever [Cronenberg's] intention, the effect is to make us share in the characters' emotions or lack of them. In short, his movie condones many practices which the vast majority of people would find disgusting and degrading. (Tookey, 1996)

The 'effects' model is implicit in Tookey's argument: 'the effect is to *make* us share'. Films cannot make audiences do anything, but he uses the assertion that they can to conclude that the film should be banned: '*Crash* is the point at which even a liberal society should draw the line' (ibid.).

The rhetoric of Tookey's piece is interesting as he states that even a 'liberal society', that is one that is relatively lax in terms of censorship, should ban the film. So if the film were banned, liberals could feel comfortable about the fact because the film was 'depraved'.

The logic of the complaint is that if people went to see *Crash*, a film about having sex and crashing cars, then the audience would want to have sex and crash cars. The human sexual drive does not need films to stimulate it and the idea that people, having seen the film, would wish to crash cars is self-evidently absurd.

This absurdity did not, however, prevent the *Daily Mail* launching a full-scale campaign, well summarised in Kermode and Petley (1997), to get the film banned in Britain. The question for Media students is: why, assuming the editor of the *Daily Mail* is not completely demented, did the newspaper embark on such a ridiculous campaign? A brief analysis follows.

(a) Consider the following, from the *Daily Mail*'s campaign:

> As evidence of [the film's] perverted morality, the reader's attention is drawn to the fact that 'the initially heterosexual characters lose their inhibitions [and] they experiment pleasurably with gay sex, lesbian sex, and sex with cripples.' (Petley and Kermode, 1997, p. 16)

Commentary

The *Mail* is suggesting here that gay and lesbian sex is perverted, as is a non-crippled person having sex with a crippled person.

150

(b) Two weeks later the *Mail* attacked the managing director of the film's distributors, Columbia Tristar, emphasising that she was single and childless. Later, the non-family nature of a number of the BBFC's examiners was called into question.

Commentary

The *Mail* is suggesting that any adult who lives outside the nuclear family is suspect in some way.

(c) The *Mail*'s sister paper (both owned by Associated Newspapers), the *Evening Standard*, continued its campaign against the film by listing a number of other controversial films and stating:

All have aroused successive waves of public protest, Parliamentary questions, editorial disquiet, even rank bad reviews. (Quoted in ibid., p. 17)

Commentary

It sounds from this that a major social upheaval is about to take place. The emotive language in, 'aroused successive waves of public protest' makes it seem that complaints about the possible certification of the film were legion. In May 2000 an actual (that is one that existed) wave of public protest, the Reclaim the Streets campaign, was vilified in many newspapers.

It is a common tactic of newspapers to ring up MPs whose views they know are similar to their own, to get a quote. This gives the newspaper's viewpoint an apparent legitimacy; any quotes that oppose the newspaper's agenda are far less likely to feature. The 'editorial disquiet' was limited to newspapers of a similar political persuasion, just as the 'bad reviews' were much more likely to appear within these publications. Besides, if films that received bad reviews were banned then we would lose many of Hollywood's summer blockbusters. The newspapers also campaigned for the BBFC to be disbanded and censorship to come under the remit of the Home Office.

Conclusion

The reason the *Daily Mail* attacked the film was ideological. Associated Newpapers' emphasis on 'family values', belief in government involvement in censorship, and disgust at anything other than heterosexual sexuality demonstrates their conservative agenda. It is arguable that the newspapers campaigned against the film not because they believed people would become 'depraved and corrupted' (the legal test of obscenity) by the film but because they were disturbed by the film's non-bourgeois nature.

Crash offers no sense of conventional characterisation, we are not sure why the characters are behaving the way they do. The representation of sexual activity is arguably neither pornographic (because it is not shot primarily to stimulate sexual arousal) nor situated in a loving context; it falls outside easy categorisation. The lack of clear narrative resolution – the main characters seem to be pursuing a sado-masochistic relationship, to their deaths – offers no certain moral stance.

The film portrays modern alienation and our relationship with the motorcar; as Cronenberg said: 'Our attachment to [the car], as discussed in the movie, is very primitive indeed. It has become the quintessential human appendage' (Rodley, 1996, p. 9).

Basically what the *Mail* and *Standard* objected to was the *difference* represented in the film. They saw the non-judgemental presentation of non-bourgeois values as an attack upon the *status quo*. This is usually the agenda behind any pro-censorship position. Prominent during the 1970s and 1980s was the Mary Whitehouse-fronted National Viewers and Listeners Association (NVLA). The Association believed:

> that Christian values are basic to the health and wellbeing of our nation and therefore calls on the broadcasting authorities to reverse the current humanist approach to social, religious and personal issues.   (NVLA leaflet)

Clearly they were attacking not only secular society but other religions too. They stated:

> That violence on television contributes significantly to the increase of violence in society and should be curtailed.   (Ibid.)

In a pluralistic society such views are, of course, allowable. They are problematic when they have a disproportionate influence on our legislators. In the representation of sexual acts, Britain has the most censored cinema in the West. However, *Crash* was passed uncut in May 1997 and greeted by universal indifference by British audiences. There were no reported increases in sex, car crashes, or sex in car crashes. The British film institute included the film in its Modern Classics series where Iain Sinclair declared 'the surreal translation "a masterpiece"' (Sinclair, 1999, p. 122).

Of course, you should make your own mind up about whether the film is depraved or not. It was released on both video and DVD, no doubt trading upon the notoriety generated by the *Mail*'s diatribes. If the censorship campaigners had been successful then British audiences would have been unable to make their own judgement on the film; just as British audiences have not seen the uncut version of *Basic Instinct* (1992), the four seconds cut from *Fight Club* (1999), or *Straw Dogs* (1971) on video.

David Gauntlett (1998) has suggested 'Ten things wrong with the "effects model"':

1. The effects model tackles social problems 'backwards'.
2. The effects model treats children as inadequate.
3. Assumptions within the effects model are characterised by barely-concealed conservative ideology.
4. The effects model inadequately defines its own objects of study.
5. The effects model is often based on artificial studies.
6. The effects model is often based on studies with misapplied methodology.
7. The effects model is selective in its criticisms of media depictions of violence.
8. The effects model assumes superiority to the masses.
9. The effects model makes no attempt to understand meanings of the media.
10. The effects model is not grounded in theory.

One of the large numbers of spurious arguments used by the 'effects' lobby is that if media texts had no effect on people then no company would ever advertise, as they would be wasting their money. This argument reduces all texts to, just that, texts; that is, it does not distinguish between the different purposes of texts. As anyone who has studied discursive writing knows, there are many different types of writing, including argumentative and persuasive. Advertising texts intend to persuade their target audience to purchase a product or service. Films, however, rarely attempt to persuade audiences to behave in, what might be called in consensus terms, an immoral manner. For example, the 'stuck in the middle with you' torture sequence in *Reservoir Dogs* (1991) is intended to portray the psychopathic nature of Mr Blonde, and not to make the audiences psychopathic.

The hypodermic model, if it were the correct way of understanding audiences' relationship with media texts, suggests that:

horrible things will make us horrible – not horrified. Terrifying things will make us terrifying – not terrified. To see something aggressive makes us feel aggressive – not aggressed against . . . (Barker, 1997, p. 23)

We enjoy watching horror films, for example, for the visceral effect they have upon us and not because it will turn us into something monstrous.

Advertisers create positive scenarios in the hope of convincing us that we too could enjoy the positive feelings experienced by the characters in the advertisement if we purchased the product or service. The only time a negative scenario is produced is when the intention is to *dissuade* audiences from a particular product (in the case of illegal drugs), or behaviour (in the case of drinking and driving). It therefore follows that persuasive scenarios, including violence, could reduce the likelihood of aggression occurring. Research has suggested that the biggest factor in the 17 per cent drop in road deaths between 1987 and 1991 in Britain, was the advertising campaign. This fall continued throughout the 1990s.

The kinds of film which the campaigners attack are, on this principle, the *least likely to be influential*, since they depend on the construction of feelings of negativity: fear, anxiety, shock, horror, and so on. (Barker, 1997, pp. 23–4)

However, this does not stop media texts being blamed by members of the judiciary in Britain, and by people seeking financial damages in North America. Two students who dismembered a friend were sentenced to be 'detained at Her Majesty's pleasure' by the judge, who summed up:

Videos – not recognisably extreme and designed to be seen for entertainment – have, I have very little doubt from the synopses, served to fuel your fantasies and isolated you from conventional counter-balancing. They carried a potency that could not be readily predicted, and served to desensitise you and remove you from the enormity of killing another person by stabbing them. (Quoted in Gentleman, 1999, p. 8)

You would have thought the judge would have bothered to watch the films (*Scream* and *The Evil Dead*) if he intended to make such a pronouncement. Once again the class basis for censorship is evident (though the judge did not call for the films to be banned he was providing material for those who think they should be): judges, on the whole, have no interest in horror films. In fact, they have no understanding of the generic conventions involved and cannot read the texts in the way they were intended.

It is not only films that are implicated in negatively influencing audiences. In 1999 a 15-year-old boy claimed that he got the idea of sexually abusing his eight-year-old half-sister from an episode of *The Jerry Springer Show*. Some serial killers use a similar technique, 'God made me do it'. That is, I am not responsible.

Most in the audience, however, tend to have a more sophisticated way of reading texts. Research by the Independent Television Commission (ITC) suggested that audiences accepted extreme violence – such as when Vince accidentally blows Marvin's head off in *Pulp Fiction* (1994) – if it is justified in terms of plot or distanced from reality by humour. The gruesomeness of Peter Jackson's *Bad Taste* (1987) is extreme but, as the title suggests, also totally ironic. Interestingly the ITC survey did find viewers disturbed by a scene of domestic violence in Ken Loach's *Ladybird, Ladybird* (1994). Loach has a reputation of being an *auteur*, a director who is considered to create art; that is, he works outside the commercial arena and outside easy generic classification. Loach is also a realist in his representations and no doubt intended that audiences should be disturbed by domestic violence.

An Austrian director, Peter Haneke, made *Funny Games* (1997) as a critique of the way Hollywood represents violence. Violence in many big-budget movies is portrayed in a 'comic book' fashion, and usually draws attention to itself as unreal. *Funny Games*, which concerns the torture of a middle-class family by two bourgeois psychopaths, eschews this form of representation by focusing on the psychological state of the victim. Watching the film is an uncomfortable experience, there is no pleasure available (except for the pathological), only a convincing portrayal of what it might be like to be tortured. Most of the violence occurs (just) off screen.

Comparing *Funny Games* with, say, *Face/Off* (1997) directed by John Woo, is an interesting exercise. The film that did not show the violence had a stronger effect on me as a viewer; I was glad when *Funny Games* was over. I watched *Face/Off* twice to enjoy the action sequences, where extreme violence is aestheticised by slow-motion and soft-focus cinematography. Neither, of course, made me feel violent: *Face/Off* taught me nothing about violence (and it was not meant to); *Funny Games* gave me an (apparent) insight into psychological torture. I could imagine the psychopaths of *Funny Games* 'getting off' on both types of film. But most of us 'don't get' off on real violence (boxing fans may be an exception), though we might be entertained by violence.

ypodermic' theory is deeply problematic; what can we use?

6.3 The 'uses and gratifications' theory

The 'uses and gratifications' model, though not without its critics as we shall see, proposes a more dynamic audience than the passive consumer of the 'hypodermic' model. It suggests that audiences *use* the media rather than being used *by* the media. This use may help give a sense of *personal identity* or help gather *information*; alternatively it could gratify the desire for *entertainment* or assist *social interaction*.

Personal identity: we can get a sense of ourselves and our peer group from media representations. This is probably particularly important for adolescents. Lifestyle magazines, as we shall see, have an important role in this.

Information: the media are full of information which we are at liberty to use; even the weather forecast is sometimes correct.

Entertainment (dealt with in detail in the next section).

Social interaction: the news, films or last night's television programmes are common topics of discussion; we use the media to feed this social interaction. The media may also 'keep us company': radio, in particular, addresses its audience on a personal basis. We may feel we know characters in, say, soap operas, better than we do our own friends and thus engage in parasocial interaction when 'interacting' with them.

It is important that students are able to apply this approach to all media texts, though it should be noted that most texts do not provide all four uses or gratifications (a useful mnemonic is 'PIES').

■ Exercise 6.2 ■

Look at an issue of a lifestyle magazine and consider what uses and gratifications audiences might get from the publication?

The following analysis considers the main articles in the January 1998 issues of *B*, a 'brilliant new women's mag' (so says the tagline) launched in 1997, and *Cosmopolitan*, 'the world's No.1 magazine for young women'. The articles have been categorised under headings that are typical of lifestyle magazines with the associated 'uses and gratification'.

'True life stories' (social interaction/entertainment/personal identity)

Cosmo:
- '"My brother is the father of my child"'
- 'Where Women Learn to be Ladies'
- 'The Arrival of the Male Golddigger'
- 'Confessions of a Sex Surrogate'
- '"My father never hit me, but…"'
- '"Why I'm staying in on December 31st"'

B
- '"I thought suicide was my only way out"'
- '"We killed our personal demons"'
- '"Trading places" – where women of very different backgrounds "swap lives"'
- 'Get on the Line' – what chatlines are like
- 'Penny' – a mother's story
- '"If only I'd picked Number 3…"' (a story about a *Blind Date* contestant)

Most 'true life' stories detail lives, or events in lives, which are different from the norm, thus giving plenty of material for conversation ('social interaction'). These narratives can give a vicarious pleasure ('entertainment') though many of the tales are tragic. If the emphasis is on the tragic then how can this be deemed to be entertainment unless the audience are engaged in prurience?

This illustrates the difficulty in all audience theories; it is impossible to know how individuals in a mass audience are reading the texts. It could be that part of the audience reads the tragedy to laugh at the victims; however, it is more likely their entertainment is derived from getting a sense of relief that their situation is better.

Health (information)

Cosmo:
- 'Positive News on AIDS'
- 'The Secret Life of the Women Who Drink' – alcoholism

B
Nothing. *B* appears to be aimed at a younger age group than *Cosmopolitan*, possibly 'twenty-somethings'. Health usually becomes an issue more as the individual gets older.

Relationships (personal identity)

Cosmo:
- 'Love & Hate in '98' – certainly about sex but also religion, children, cooking, holidaying...
- 'In Pursuit of Safety' – why some 'smart, modern' women want a man to look after them
- 'You've Made your Relationship Resolutions'
- 'Why Men are Crazy about Sport'
- 'Winter *flirt*!' – How do you go out with three men at once?
- 'Warning! You may be allergic to your emotions'

B
- 'Spot the Bastard by His Star Sign'

Pin-ups (entertainment)

B
- 'Get Some Emergency Servicing' – A B portfolio of TV's Sexiest 999 Men

Both magazines offer reams of 'fashion and beauty', material probably, in the main, used for 'personal identity'; *Cosmo* also has some minimal coverage of the arts.

The uses and gratifications theory gives us a much more dynamic picture of audiences' interactions with magazines. Probably one of the most important uses we have for media texts is entertainment.

Entertainment

Richard Dyer offers an institutional definition of entertainment, which emphasises how it is almost always produced by businesses such as film studios, broadcasters, publishers and so on:

> [Entertainment] is a type of performance produced for profit, performed before a generalized audience (the 'public'), by a trained, paid group who do nothing else but produce performances which have the sole (conscious) aim of providing pleasure. (Dyer, 1992, p. 17)

A key word in Dyer's definition is 'pleasure'; most of us conceive of entertainment as texts that provide pleasure. This pleasure is often

characterised as 'escapism'; however, while it is obvious what we a
escaping *from*, day-to-day life, what we are escaping *to* is more prob
lematic. Audiences can hardly escape into the text; though people
often, metaphorically, talk about the pleasure of being 'lost in a book'.
One of the attractions of 'cult' texts, for instance, is the opportunity
to 'join' the narrative world through: merchandise (which may enable
fans to 'dress up' as their favourite characters); fan conventions, where
they can meet like-minded people and sometimes see the actors who
appear in the cult programme; discussion groups on the Internet;
fanzines, which provide information about the cult text. However,
this is a rather literal form of escapism; most entertainment texts
offer a more abstract place to escape toward.

> Two of the taken-for-granted descriptions of entertainment, as 'escape'
> and as 'wish-fulfilment', point to its central thrust, namely utopianism.
> Entertainment offers the image of 'something better' to escape into, or
> something we want deeply that our day-to-day lives don't provide.   (Ibid.,
> p. 18)

The utopia audiences are offered is not of the sort that resides in
some science fiction novels, 'rather the utopianism is contained in
the feelings it embodies' (ibid.). Dyer offers another dichotomy to
help characterise this world we figuratively escape to; inevitably this
utopia is contrasted with day-to-day reality, as shown in Table 6.1.

As in any dichotomy, the definitions are offered as 'ideal types';
that is, they are an extreme description of a tendency. So when Dyer
characterises 'reality' as 'exhaustion' (defined as 'work as a grind,
alienated labour, pressures of urban life', ibid., p. 24) he is not stating
that reality is *always* like this (though it may be for some). Those of
you who are seriously studying for advanced level examinations,
particularly if you also have a job, will have some inkling about what

Table 6.1

Reality	Utopia
Exhaustion	Energy
Scarcity	Abundance
Dreariness	Intensity
Manipulation	Transparency
Fragmentation	Community

Source: Adapted from Dyer (1992) p. 12.

'exhaustion' means. The suggestion is that reality, at one extreme, *can* be like this; similarly, at the other extreme there is 'energy'. Entertainment texts offer energy, the 'capacity to act vigorously; human power, activity, potential to counteract this exhaustion' (ibid., p. 20), which is also defined as 'work and play synonymous' (ibid.). This energy is not transferred to the audience but refers to characters in the text.

Scarcity is all too real as it describes the 'actual poverty in the society; poverty observable in the surrounding societies, e.g. Third World; unequal distribution of wealth' (ibid., p. 24). This is 'anti-doted' by 'abundance': 'conquest of scarcity; having enough to spare without sense of poverty of others; enjoyment of sensuous material reality' (ibid.).

Dreariness ('monotony, predictability, instrumentality of the daily round', ibid., p. 24.) is counteracted by intensity ('experiencing of emotion directly, fully, unambiguously, "authentically", without holding back', ibid., p. 21).

Manipulation is slightly less straightforward, it is defined with examples ('advertising, bourgeois democracy, sex roles', ibid., p. 24). The idea here is that life in the western world is characterised by a constant bombardment of advertising messages which attempt to part us from our money; democracy, it can be argued, is hardly an expression of the People's will because the choice offered is often between two very similar ideologies; sex roles determine, to a great degree, the way we behave, so any freedom we may feel we have is more apparent than real.

Entertainment nullifies this manipulation by offering transparency ('a quality of relationships – between represented characters (e.g. true love), between performer and audience ("sincerity")', ibid., p. 21). Narrative and genre facilitate much of this transparency between the performer and audience as they offer familiar frameworks within which to experience the text. It is of no surprise that alternative texts, which are non-generic and have an unconventional narrative structure, do not, for most people, offer entertainment.

The final nail in the 'coffin' of our reality is fragmentation ('job mobility, rehousing and development, high-rise flats, legislation against collective action', ibid., p. 24), which, by entertainment, is 'papered over' with a sense of community ('togetherness, sense of belonging, network of phatic relationships (i.e. those in which communication is for its own sake rather than for its message', ibid., p. 21).

The categories of entertainment function 'as temporary answers to the inadequacies of the society which is being escaped from' (ibid., p. 23); this is similar to Aristotle's definition of art 'as catharsis'. It is ironic that both art and entertainment, despite being conceived as being opposites, can serve the same function.

Dyer's categories are summarised in Table 6.2.

■ Exercise 6.3 ■

Choose a text that you find to be entertaining and apply Dyer's theory to it.

Entertainment and *ER*

ER (standing for Emergency Room) is one of the most popular programmes currently broadcast (see Figure 6.1); it was so popular that NBC reportedly agreed to pay £7.8 million per *episode* for two

Table 6.2

Reality	Utopia
Exhaustion 'work as a grind, alienated labour, pressures of urban life'	**Energy** 'capacity to act vigorously; human power, activity, potential to counteract this exhaustion'
Scarcity 'actual poverty in the society; poverty observable in the surrounding societies, unequal distribution of wealth'	**Abundance** 'conquest of scarcity; having enough to spare without sense of poverty of others; enjoyment of sensuous material reality'
Dreariness 'monotony, predictability, instrumentality of the daily round'	**Intensity** 'experiencing of emotion directly, fully, unambiguously, "authentically", without holding back'
Manipulation 'advertising, bourgeois democracy, sex roles'	**Transparency** 'a quality of relationships – between repre-sented characters (e.g. true love), between performer and audience ("sincerity")'
Fragmentation 'job mobility, rehousing and development, high-rise flats, legislation against collective action'	**Community** 'togetherness, sense of belonging, network of phatic relationships'

Source: Adapted from Dyer (1992) p. 24.

Figure 6.1 *ER* – emphasises community

seasons, a total of nearly £515 million for 66 episodes. Institutionally it is certainly entertainment (see definition above) but how does it evoke a utopia? As in all genre texts, it is highly likely that the same sort of events will occur in most episodes; I have chosen the first ever episode of the hospital drama to characterise *ER*'s utopian project.

Energy

The episode begins, and ends, with Dr Greene grabbing what sleep he can. However, he is constantly disturbed and he is obviously exhausted. Despite this he has the 'capacity to act vigorously': he manages to assist a drunk Dr Ross and is able to state, without a moment's hesitation, the dosage of an injection. Although the conditions he works in are difficult, particularly when contrasted with the private hospital he visits when he's offered a job, he stays in the ER because it is 'real medicine'. While his work is certainly not play, it is an immensely important part of his life. His wife wants him to join the private practice, which would increase his salary five-fold, but he obviously will not.

Abundance

As has already been suggested, the conditions of work are far from ideal. In fact they are characterised by scarcity; on a number of occasions the doctors and nurses are scouting for beds. Much of the narrative conflict of the hospital-drama genre is generated by the lack of adequate facilities; this 'lack' is therefore the Proppian villain. *ER* does not offer an abundant utopia and this is part of its liberal agenda. The answer, of course, is more money to buy more resources.

Intensity

As in all soap operas, of which hospital dramas are a sub-genre, there is never any lack of intensity. The melodramatic exaggeration of soap reaches a fever pitch in hospitals because life and death are a constant issue. In this episode Dr Peter Benton decides to operate on a man in a serious condition despite not being fully qualified to do so. Benton's fear, resolve and intense relief (he is successful) are all presented directly to the audience; his private turmoil is presented 'publicly'. As in traditional melodrama, music is used to sign particular emotions, often starting just before the narrative enigma (will the patient live or die?) is resolved.

Transparency

Dr Greene's actions in assisting a drunk Dr Ross, despite his own exhaustion, show the sincerity of their friendship. When a patient asks Dr Weaver what the shadow on his lung means she prevaricates, not wishing to tell him bad news, until the patient begs her to be candid and so she does. This is transparent because we *know* Ross and Greene are friends and that Weaver is telling the truth. Once again, the hospital drama is an ideal vehicle for this, for not to be honest in such a situation (the man is going to die of cancer) would suggest a very sick comedy.

Community

When Nurse Hathaway attempts to commit suicide she is brought into the ER. Most of the staff are so stunned that they can do little more than stand and watch as she is attended to. Although Greene berates them for their voyeurism, they are obviously only watching because they care for her, knowing her suicide attempt has been caused by Doctor Ross ending their relationship. Despite, or more likely because of, their unit's difficult working conditions the staff operate, professionally, as a team, and emotionally, as a community.

To adapt Fiske's work on *Miami Vice* to *ER*:

> The 'success' of the [ER community] at the end of each episode is only temporary and in no way offers a permanent resolution of the conflict. It is only the hero figures of [for example, Edwards and Ross] who demonstrate that society has ways of living with and coping with [issues of life and death]. (Fiske, 1987, p. 133)

Of course if the success were anything other than temporary, the narrative closure would signal the end of the series.

Audiences use entertainment to help them escape from reality. If we want to be entertained rather than, say, be educated, we choose texts that we believe will be pleasurable. Berger has produced a useful table demonstrating which genres are appropriate to particular 'uses and gratifications'.

In Table 6.3 I have added a few 'appropriate genres' to Berger's original list.

Berger has clearly used the term 'genre' in a very loose sense: 'advertising' is not a genre. However, his table is useful in demonstrating how audiences can use particular genres. We may ask the question *why* we need to use genres in this way. *Why* do we need to escape? Why is 'reality' so bad?

Dyer's theory brings us back to the Frankfurt school that believed that capitalist society was based on the exploitation of the masses by those who 'owned the means of production'. This exploitation leads to feelings of exhaustion, a scarcity of resources, a dreary existence, a sense of being manipulated, and living a fragmented life. From this perspective we can see that entertainment acts as an antidote, a bromide, to our feelings of being exploited. We can, their view suggests,

Table 6.3

Selected uses and gratifications	Appropriate genres
1 Be amused	Sitcoms, comedies
2 See authority figures exalted, deflated	News, comedies
3 Experience the beautiful	Travel, love stories
4 Obtain a common frame of reference	Media events (defined as 'Academy Awards, visits by the pope, the Super Bowl, etc.')
5 Satisfy curiosity, be informed	Science (documentary), soap operas
6 Identify with deity, divine powers	Science fiction, religious programmes
7 Find distraction and diversion	Sports, soaps, melodrama
8 Experience empathy	Soaps, melodrama
9 Have strong, guilt-free emotions	Soaps, melodrama, cops
10 Find models to imitate	Soaps, melodrama, sports
11 Gain an identity	Commercials (advertising), soaps, melodrama
12 Reinforce belief in justice	Cops, mysteries
13 Experience romantic love	Soaps, romance, melodrama
14 See magic, marvels, the miraculous	Science fiction, 'bizarre tales'
15 See others make mistakes	Sports, news
16 See order imposed on the world	Science, news
17 Participate in history	Media events [I would question this 'genre'; 'news' might be more appropriate, such as coverage of the 'fall of the Berlin Wall']
18 Be purged of powerful emotions	Soaps, melodrama, cops
19 Find vicarious outlet for sexual drives	Soaps, melodrama, pornography
20 Explore taboo subjects with impunity	Soaps, melodrama
21 Experience the ugly, grotesque	Science fiction, horror
22 See moral, cultural values upheld	Sports
23 See villains in action	Spy, crime, mysteries

Source: Berger (1992) p. 70.

only bear our lives because of the existence of entertainment. (Preston Sturges's classic film *Sullivan's Travels* (1941) deals directly with this idea.)

Karl Marx suggested that 'religion was the opium' of the people and so the Christian formulation that 'the meek shall inherit the earth' was merely a device to keep the people passive and stop them rebelling against their exploitative masters. In a secular society, however, other means of social control are required and one of these means is entertainment that 'provides alternatives *to* capitalism which will be provided *by* capitalism' (Dyer, 1992, p. 25). So capitalism creates the need for entertainment *and* provides entertainment, for a price.

Even if this is the case, entertainment does not take us away from all the problems of reality. For example, as Dyer himself points out, in the left-hand column of his defining dichotomy there is 'no mention of class, race, or patriarchy' (ibid.). So:

> While entertainment is responding to needs that are real, at the same time it is also defining and delimiting what constitute the legitimate needs of people in this society. (Ibid.)

In other words, because entertainment defines what utopia is, there is no room in this 'ideal world' for a classless society or for equality between races and sexes. In addition, capitalism not only defines the utopia, it provides the economic means to attain a place in this 'bourgeois heaven':

> With the exception perhaps of community (the most directly working-class in source), the ideals of entertainment imply wants that capitalism itself promised to meet. Thus abundance becomes consumerism, energy and intensity personal freedom and individualism, and transparency freedom of speech. (ibid.)

Arguably the sense of community helps legitimise our subordinate position. We see many other people in positions like ours, the 'community', and therefore accept this position as normal.

The emphasis of conventional narrative is on closure, where everything is wrapped up satisfactorily with the success of the hero and what bourgeois society holds to be good triumphant. Nevertheless, the tensions of gender, race and class are obviously real and if entertainment continues *not* to offer a utopia where these tensions are eradicated, then there is a potential for dissatisfaction. However, viewing patterns in the USA suggest that racial tensions are in fact alleviated by an 'apartheid' in television viewing:

> Put bluntly, white Americans over the age of 21 just don't watch black American shows. And the converse is also true. Fourteen of the 20 most popular shows among African American viewers don't even rank among the top 100 shows white people watch.... In fact, not a single show is both in the Top 10 for blacks and the Top 10 for whites. (Wittstock, 1998)

You do not have to accept this left-wing critique of capitalism to find Dyer's categories useful in the analysis of texts. However, this ideological analysis of entertainment also relates to the institutional battles in which many media producers, or artists, find themselves embroiled. Even though most mass entertainment is produced by capitalist institutions this does not mean the dominant ideology will be simply reproduced, as there is often conflict between, in Marxist terms, 'capital (the backers) and labour (the performers) over control of the product' (Dyer, 1992, p. 18).

166

The 'backers' may be the institution funding the text, such as Warner's funding of *Se7en* (1995). The bleak conclusion to this film only survived because Brad Pitt insisted upon it (the producers wanted a dog's head in the box). In 1942 RKO butchered the original ending of Orson Welles's *The Magnificent Ambersons*, replacing bleakness with schmaltz.

The reason there is such conflict in the entertainment business is because the cultural industry is:

> unusual in that: (1) it is in the business of producing forms not things, and (2) the workforce (the performers themselves) is in a better position to determine the form of its product than are, say, secretaries or car workers. (Ibid., p. 18)

Hollywood is a classic example of such conflict, particularly during the Golden Age (1920s–1940s) where the sheer volume of films produced necessitated a production-line system. However, and this brings us back to the false, and endemic, distinction between art and entertainment, simply because texts are produced primarily for profit in a formulaic fashion this does not mean they cannot be more than entertainment.

Entertainment, it should be remembered, is not limited to fictional texts. Dyer suggested ways in which television news can be considered as entertainment:

Energy: speed of series of sharp, short items; the 'latest' news; handheld camera.

Abundance: technology of news-gathering – satellites, etc.; doings of rich; spectacles of pageantry and destruction.

Intensity: emphasis on violence, dramatic incident; selection of visuals with eye to climactic moments.

Transparency: 'man of the people' manner of some newscasters, celebrities and politicians; ... simplification of events to allow easy comprehension.

Community: the world rendered as global village; assumptions of consensus.

(Dyer, 1992, pp. 20–1)

■ Exercise 6.4 ■

Using news values (see chapter 5 of *Image and Representation*), suggest which apply to Dyer's categories of entertainment (see Table 6.4).

Table 6.4

News values		Entertainment	v.	Reality
1	Magnitude	abundance; intensity		
2	Clarity	transparency		manipulation
3	Ethnocentricity	community		
4	Consonance	community		manipulation
5	Surprise	intensity		
6	Elite centredness	abundance		fragmentation
7	Negativity			scarcity; exhaustion; fragmentation; manipulation; dreariness
8	Human interest	community		
9	Composition or balance	abundance		
10	Location reporting	transparency		manipulation
11	Actuality reporting	transparency; energy		
12	Inheritance factor			
13	Framework	community		manipulation
14	Frequency	intensity		
15	Impartiality	transparency; community		manipulation

A textbook is not the medium with which to engage in too much contentious analysis. However, it does seem that the application of Dyer's categories to television news is a fruitful exercise. At first glance, the news value of 'negativity' suggests that news represents reality exactly as Dyer's ideal type describes it; but most of the other news values offer the 'utopia' promised by entertainment. To paraphrase T. S. Eliot: it could be that humankind cannot bear much reality; so even *the* media form that signs itself as being about reality, the news, is entertainment based. Television news in the USA has been criticised for many years for its 'tabloid' emphasis and paucity of serious news, so even the 'counterbalancing' news value of negativity may be absent there.

It is also interesting to note that many of the news values can be described as being manipulative. For instance, many news stories that are presented with 'clarity' are in fact quite complex; the implicit consensus offered by the news is likely to be a reflection of dominant ideological values rather than an actual consensus. Clearly there is much analysis that can be done in this area.

Christine Geraghty has applied Dyer's notion to soap operas, even using the categories to distinguish between British and US soaps, as shown in Table 6.5. It is interesting to note the lack of 'abundance' in British soaps compared with those of the USA. Note, also, how the expression of 'community' is achieved in Britain, but in North America

Table 6.5

	British soaps	US soaps
Energy	Strong women characters, quick repartee, pace of plot	Strong male characters, business activity, pace of plot
Abundance		Glamorous settings, clothes, luxurious objects, food, etc.
Intensity	Emotions strongly expressed at key moments	Emotions strongly expressed at key moments
Transparency	Sincerity of key characters	Sincerity of key characters
Community	Characters offer support, friendship, gossip outside programme	Asserted within family, rarely achieved, relationship with audience

Source: Geraghty (1991), p. 119.

it is only aspired to. These differences are probably due to the working-class milieu of British soaps, which, by definition, does not possess 'abundance' but, probably increasingly mythically, does have communal roots. The community is essential to British soaps in that the generic setting is always a clearly defined, and local, area, be it a Square or Street.

As a postscript to the section, it is worth noting that one of the ways Peter Wollen characterised 'counter cinema' (see Chapter 3 of *Narrative and Genre*) was:

> pleasure v. unpleasure. (Entertainment, aiming to satisfy the spectator v. provocation, aiming to dissatisfy and hence change the spectator.) (Wollen, 1986, p. 506)

Although it is arguable that entertainment sets out to satisfy the audience in an unsatisfactory world, this does not mean that entertainment cannot offer subversive pleasures. Wollen, at least at the time of his essay on counter cinema (1972), belonged to a critical 'clique' that distrusted pleasure. However, other critics have shown how entertainment texts can be subversive. Many Hollywood films, which are virtually all made in order to create profit for the studio and are therefore entertainment, offer a subversive take on their subject matter.

In *Mercury Rising* (1998), Bruce Willis is pitted against a self-seeking, high-ranking secret service official (Alec Baldwin). At a climactic point the American flag is looked down upon from an extreme high-angle shot, suggesting we are seeing a very negative portrayal of America. As in *Enemy of the State* (1998) the narrative resolution, the death of the 'bad apples', is not sufficient to deny the sense of injustice being perpetrated on behalf of the state; the last words of *Enemy of the State* are spoken by Larry King, who says 'You've no right to come into my home.'

This critique of the state is couched in left-of-centre terms; that is, the government has too much power to intervene in people's lives. However, right-wing groups in America share this view, so *Mercury Rising* establishes a distance between militia 'survivalist' groups and itself in the opening sequence, where one such group is represented as being demented (the father) and misguided (the son). The Bruce Willis character's humanity is emphasised in this scene and he carries the moral weight of the film.

Those who dismiss all Hollywood, and all entertainment, as politically irredeemable, are missing the point. Even one of the meatiest meathead movie stars, Steven Seagal, has in *On Deadly Ground* (1994) made a political statement. After he has wrought mayhem, and saved the day, the film's coda is a quite astonishing pro-green and anti-industrial documentary.

Other films, of recent years, that offer subversive representations wrapped as entertainment include: *Falling Down* (1992), *Gattaca* (1997), *The Truman Show* (1998), *Pleasantville* (1999) and *Fight Club* (1999).

Criticisms of the 'uses and gratifications' approach

While the 'effects' approach focuses too much on the text and models the audience on a sponge, the 'uses and gratifications' approach goes in completely the opposite direction by assuming that individuals have *complete* autonomy from the media. This is an unrealistic perspective.

The media can create a panic where none should be. For example, in the United States in 1938, an Orson Welles and Howard Koch adaptation of H. G. Wells's *The War of the Worlds* terrified many people because it sounded like a news report. It is easy to scoff at such naivety; however, the world was on the brink of a war at the time, Percy Lowell had declared he had found canals on Mars, and the radio was a trusted mass medium. If CNN declared that aliens had attacked the USA then most people would probably believe them now.

Abercrombie and Longhurst (1998) list a number of problems with the approach (as described by Elliott, 1974), two of which are:

- it focuses on the mental states of individuals; something – in the absence of mind reading – we can never know about anyone else (and often do not know about ourselves);
- it focuses on individuals while audiences are usually made up of groups; our behaviour and understanding of texts is different when we are part of a group.

James Watson summarises the situation:

> As ['effects'] theorists became aware that they were studying texts without readers, gratifications researchers came to realise that they were studying readers without texts. (Watson, 1998, p. 65)

That said, at advanced level Media Studies the 'uses and gratifications' approach is basic to our understanding of how audiences engage with texts. The next 'paradigm' to gain widespread credence was developed in the 1970s: encoding/decoding.

6.4 Encoding/decoding

Stuart Hall in the 1970s, at the Centre for Contemporary Cultural Studies, Birmingham University, offered what can be considered as a 'halfway house' between the 'audience as victim' and 'audience as completely autonomous being' approaches. The premise of his encoding–decoding approach was that most media texts had specific meanings encoded within them but the audience receiving the text determined how they were read.

Hall was trying to conceptualise the complexity involved both in the production of media text and its 'meaningful discourse', and in the reading of this discourse (see Figure 6.2). Involved in the creation of a media text are (Hall uses television as an example):

> the institutional structures of broadcasting, with their practices and networks of production, their organized relations and technical infrastructures, [which] are required to produce a programme. (Hall, 1992, p. 129)

Hall stresses that 'meaning structure 2' may not be the same as 'meaning structure 1'; audiences must understand the codes used in 'meaning structure 1' in order to access the intended meaning. However, even if the audiences do understand the codes this does not mean they must necessarily agree with the suggested reading.

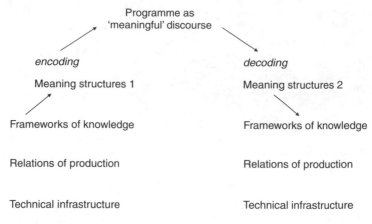

Figure 6.2   Meaningful discourse
Source: Adapted from Hall (1992) p. 130

Politicians, for example, often explain their unpopularity by saying that they are not 'getting their message across'. The implication being that if they were communicating effectively then everyone would agree with them. The audience, however, can read this as 'No, I hear you loud and clear; that's why I won't vote for you.'

Hall suggested that three types of reading were open to audiences: the preferred, where the dominant meaning encoded within the text is accepted; the negotiated, where the dominant reading is accepted but the individual decides it is not applicable to them; and the oppositional, where the dominant reading is rejected in favour of another not intended by the producer. He stresses that although we can make different readings of the same text this does not mean that 'anything goes'. We cannot, with any sanity, watch *Se7en* and decide it is about flower arrangement. Texts are not anarchic, they are polysemic. Society: 'impose[s] its classifications of the social and cultural and political world. These constitute a *dominant cultural order...*' (ibid.).

An individual's understanding of the 'dominant cultural order' will vary; children, in particular, tend to have a partial knowledge of conventional meanings. This is one of the reasons why different generations can have very different experiences of the same texts. For example, consider the opening of *Saving Private Ryan* (1998) and imagine the different readings likely to be made by the following groups:

(a)   Allied veterans of the D-Day landing;
(b)   German veterans;

(c)   war veterans in general;
(d)   people born before 1940;
(e)   people born between 1940 and 1960;
(f)   the rest of us.

While speculation about the first three readings may be relatively straightforward, an explanation may be helpful for (d) to (f). People born before 1940 are more likely to have memories of the Second World War and so remember the emotions of the time. Seeing such a convincing representation of the D-Day landing may bring back their memories of the era. (e) refers to those too young to remember wartime life but who did grow up in the post-war era. At this time the conclusion of the war had an immense impact on national identity: in Britain the Allies' triumph gave a strong sense of worth despite the nation being diminished as a world power, whilst many Germans felt guilt about the Nazi atrocities. For 'the rest of us' the war is history and we probably cannot appreciate the sacrifices made to defeat fascism.

Bourdieu (1984) has suggested that social space is constructed of a number of distinct fields; in this context we are interested in the field of cultural production. Each member of a society possesses 'cultural capital', that is an area of culture in which they have a degree of expertise, or 'cultural competence'. These competences can be influenced by our social status, ethnicity and gender; for example, an appreciation of heavy metal music is associated with working-class, white males. While it is not true to say that this is the only type of person who appreciates this music, their social position has made it more likely that they have the competence to understand the genre.

Age is also an important element, particularly in regard to youth culture. It is often the case that people of an older generation do not have the competences to understand youth culture and so dismiss it as 'trash'. This is useful in the creation of youth culture because it allows young people to possess a particular 'cultural area' for themselves.

Considering the social context of the audience leads us into ethnography, the most recent area of audience studies to find favour.

6.5   Ethnography

After Media theorists began to realise that audiences were real people and therefore needed to be treated like human beings rather than statistics or abstract models, the ethnographic approach was developed. Sociologists had much earlier realised that to understand human behaviour the social scientist had to observe groups as closely as possible. This meant actually joining the groups and observing their behaviour at first hand; what was termed 'participant observation'. It was also recognised that this approach was problematic as it was likely to sacrifice any objectivity – difficult enough to achieve anyway – the sociologist may have been able to claim.

The premise of ethnographic study is that the researcher should become part of the audience he or she is studying. At its weakest, this might involve the use of questionnaires to find out what an audience thought about a text; at the other extreme we have academics who write about texts, self-consciously, as fans:

> Jenkins discovered the *Star Trek* in syndicated reruns in the early 1970s, mastered the arcane lore in *The Making of Star Trek* and treasured the James Blish novelizations.... He learned of fandom through *Star Trek Lives!*... He ventured to his first convention as a reporter for his college newspaper ripe with many of the 'Trekkie' stereotypes he now critiques. (Tulloch and Jenkins, 1995, p. 20)

Questionnaires are a weak weapon in research as they impose upon the audience what is being investigated, and the questions asked might not be appropriate. The 'fan' approach may suffer from a lack of objectivity as the academic is too involved within the audience.

The main benefit of the ethnographic approach is that it looks beyond a text to understand what readings audiences make. Whilst we can make our own reading by simply analysing the texts, and speculate about others' readings, if we ignore the social context of an audience our understanding can never be more than partial.

As the quote from Tulloch and Jenkins above suggests, sub-cultural groups are particularly adept at forming their own 'en masse' reading of texts. Trekkies, or rather – as I believe they now prefer to be labelled – Trekkers, have their own language and attend conventions where they can recycle their enthusiasms. Alternative narratives have been created, and disseminated in fanzines and on the Internet, where Captain Kirk and Mr Spock (from the original series) are lovers. In addition, the series has been used to critique mainstream television. The producer Gene Roddenberry's vision was of a utopian future where the human race lived in harmony. However, according to his vision there will be no homosexuality in the twenty-fourth century. His utopia, it seems, is wholly heterosexual. Apparently Roddenberry acknowledged his mistake and publicly committed himself to the introduction of gay characters but he died before he could fulfil his promise (ibid., p. 238).

Fanzines, cheaply produced amateur publications, were once the main mode of communication amongst fans. Cheaper desktop publishing has allowed a higher standard of publication but the Internet has superseded the medium. A quick trawl of the Net finds numerous examples of how audiences can co-opt mainstream texts (which rarely have overt representations of homosexual characters) for their own fantasies that express their, and potentially their sub-culture's, identity. Fantasy TV seems to offer a rich vein for this form of appropriation, for example, *Xena: Warrior Princess* and *Buffy the Vampire Slayer* offer many women a strong role model (see Figure 6.3). One website, 'Eranese's Temple', begins:

> My name is Eranese and I am but the humble keeper of this temple, dedicated to Xena.

Eranese explains why she idolises Xena:

- She kicks major butt
- She is a strong female hero/role model
- She has loyal and super cool friends
- She has sinfully evil enemies
- She wears leather without chaffing
- She never seems to have a bad hair day
- She has that really cool round killing thingy, oh, yeah, her Chakram!
- Her horse, Argo, is smarter than most people I know
- Deep down, doesn't everyone want to be Xena?

(http://fantasytv.about.com/tvradio/fantasytv/gi/dynamic/offsite.htm? site = http%3A%2F%2Fwww.geocities.com%2FTelevisionCity %2F5912%2Findex.html 2000).

Xena has offered rich pickings for lesbian appropriation as a number of pornographic fantasies on the Net testify (for example, *Passion Improvised* by TZ – (http://fantasytv.about.com/tvradio/fantasytv/gi/dynamic/offsite.htm?site = http%3A%2F%2Fwww.geocities. com%2FTelevisionCity%2FStage %2F6263%2Ffanfic2.html 2000).

Whilst it is fruitful to consider how sub-cultural groups can read texts, this tends to lose sight of 'everyday life'. The Centre for Contemporary Cultural Studies, at Birmingham University, attempted to

Figure 6.3 Xena – offers women a strong role model

see how particular social groups, defined by their occupation, would read *Nationwide*, a magazine news programme broadcast in the 1970s and 1980s. By showing how different occupational groups read the programme (which they did not normally watch), and questioning them about their readings, Morley and his colleagues were able to offer a chart (see Figure 6.4; Morley, 1992, p. 117) based on Hall's three types of reading, described above.

Morley *et al.*, concluded that it is necessary to look beyond the social class of a position; both apprentices and shop stewards were working class; bank managers and university students were middle class. The discourse the individual inhabited was the most influential factor; those who believed society to be racist, for example, were more likely to read texts as racist and vice versa.

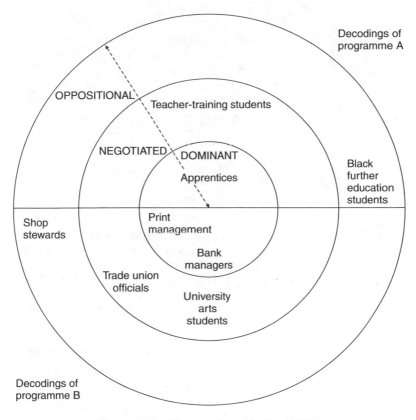

Figure 6.4   Diagram from Morley (1992)

Like texts, media analysis is inevitably a product of its time. We have seen how audience studies have developed from the 'effects' debate through 'uses and gratifications' to ethnography. It is clear from Figure 6.2 that the occupational classifications are not so obviously applicable now. For instance, the category of 'Black further education students' refers to the 1970s when further education was offering black people an opportunity for both general and political education; shop stewards wielded significant power on factory shop floors. Similarly it is arguable that trade union officials, in these days of New Labour, are far more likely to make Dominant readings than in the 1970s. (See also section 5.11 of *Image and Representation* for readings of *Oranges are Not the Only Fruit*.)

However, what the chart illustrates is how the particular group you belong to, whether sub-cultural or not, can have a strong influence on how you read a text. On a simplistic level, football fans reading a match report that is not favourable to their team are more likely to dismiss the reporter's views than those reading a neutral report.

Although ethnography appears to be the way forward in audience studies, the difficulties inherent within its methodology have meant its evolution has been rather fraught. Christine Geraghty characterises the current state as being polarised between the theories of mass audience (such as 'uses and gratifications') and the detailed accounts of the readings of particular programmes. She says the gap must be bridged:

> Audience studies more generally need to find ways in which what audiences say can not only be recorded but can find a public voice within discussions about television itself. (Geraghty, 1998, p. 155)

In 1979 Ball-Rokeach and De Fleur suggested another model that is useful at advanced level Media Studies. They offered a dialectical model of audience–media text interaction that suggested the media both activated and *de*activated audiences; Watson summarised the model as follows:

> *The resolution of ambiguity* or uncertainty – in the direction of closing down the range of interpretations of situations which audiences are able to make.
> *Attitude formation*
> *Agenda setting*
> *Expansion of people's system of beliefs*
> *Clarification of values* – but through the expression of value conflicts.
> (Watson, 1998, p. 65)

In *Image and Representation* the way news values limit what is defined as news, and how news is presented, was investigated. For example, the way in which news stories are selected and presented to confirm consensus values, has the effect of 'closing down the range of interpretations' available to audiences. Similarly, they suggested that the less diverse the sources of news, then the greater the influence of the media upon audiences' attitudes. If all news organisations are peddling the same line, then this is more likely to affect the audience's views.

6.6 Conclusion

The first audience theory considered was the 'hypodermic' theory; not because it is a particularly useful way of considering the relationship between audiences and media texts, but because it has had an immense influence upon the way 'moral panics' are engendered, usually in order to enhance censorship powers. A more useful approach, the 'uses and gratifications' theory, was investigated with particular emphasis given to entertainment, the driving force behind most media production. Two other ways of considering audiences, encoding/decoding and ethnography, were then considered.

Audience, as a key concept, remains deeply problematic as we can never really know what is going on in each individual's head when they consume media texts; we may not know how we ourselves are reacting.

7

DEFINING AND PERSUADING AUDIENCES

AIMS OF THE CHAPTER

➤ To see how audiences are classified.

➤ To examine how media texts can attempt to persuade audiences.

➤ To consider how scheduling is used to attract audiences.

➤ To consider modes of address.

➤ To consider sub-cultural groups.

7.1   Introduction

The audience has always been an essential feature of a media text. While there are examples of acclaimed works not being released in the lifetime of the creator (Schubert's Ninth Symphony and John Kennedy Toole's *The Confederacy of Dunces*, 1980), most texts do, at least initially, reach an audience. For some media, the audience is self-evident, for example, in the number of units sold for DVDs or how many seats are taken in the cinema or theatre. Broadcasters, however, do not have this luxury and terrestrial radio and television stations do not know that they are actually being listened to or watched. So when broadcasting began in the early twentieth century it became immediately necessary to find out if the audience did exist and who they were.

The need to define audiences has been driven by commercial prerogatives. As we saw in Chapter 1, many media businesses need to deliver audiences' eyeballs, or ears, to advertisers in order to be profitable and so the audience needs to be quantified. In order to be quantified, audiences need to be measured; in order to measure them, definitions are required for the various sub-groupings.

However, audiences are not simply commodities to be sold to advertisers; public service broadcasters (see Chapter 2) must address their audiences as the general public:

> The audience-as-public consists not of consumers, but of citizens who must be reformed, educated, informed as well as entertained – in short, 'served' – presumably to enable them to better perform their democratic rights and duties.   (Ang, 1991, pp. 28–9)

This conception of 'audience as citizens' has been under siege for a number of years, fuelled by the de-regulatory policies of 'free market' governments that started in the 1980s. Since then, audiences' desires have been defined as 'having a choice' of programmes. On the face of it this seems positive: if there is greater choice, then there is more likely to be something for everyone. However, as we saw in Chapter 2, this does not necessarily follow.

The conceptualisation of the 'public as consumers' is explicitly ideological, as it defines the value of existence as being determined by money. Most people, even in the West, would probably not define their individual *self* in terms of how much money they have; that is to say, when we first meet people we are more likely to state our occupation or what subjects we are studying, not the fact that our overdraft is *so* large (though this information may soon follow). Nevertheless, the notion of 'freedom of choice' has increasingly been defined in relation to markets and not the ballot box:

> the managers of the 'infotainment telesector' identify the ability to make purchases with human existence itself so as to make way for a proliferation of so-called democratic markets, as espoused by President Clinton during his visit to Europe and Russia in 1994.   (Sanjek, 1998, p. 176)

This chapter focuses on the individuals who populate these 'democratic markets'; these are audiences who are sold as commodities; Chapter 8 will consider 'audiences as citizens'.

7.2   Audience classification

Audiences are the Holy Grail of virtually all media texts; after all, if no one experiences the text then it might as well never have been created. Audiences, however, are often an elusive group of people as the title of Ien Ang's study on audience – *Desperately Seeking the Audience*

(1991) – suggests. One of the basic and most common ways of defining audiences in Britain is through social class. The Registrar General's Social Scale is the way the British Government defines the populace through their occupation.

Group A   Professional Workers (lawyers, doctors etc.), Scientists, Managers of large-scale organisations.
Group B   Shopkeepers, Farmers, Teachers, White-collar workers.
Group C1   Skilled Manual (i.e. hand) workers – high grade, e.g. master builders, carpenters, shop assistants, nurses.
Group C2   Skilled Manual – low grade, e.g. electricians, plumbers.
Group D   Semi-skilled Manual, e.g. bus drivers, lorry drivers, fitters.
Group E   Unskilled Manual, e.g. general labourers, barmen, porters.

From a media perspective, these definitions are often used as a shorthand way of defining the social class of audiences: the middle classes are called 'ABC1s' and the working classes are 'C2DEs'. This is an exceptionally crude way of defining both audiences and social class but can be useful in characterising certain media texts; for example, broadsheet newspapers usually have a predominantly ABC1 readership while 'red-top' tabloids have a C2DE audience. Some tabloid papers even signal to their readers which channels they should be watching, by giving more space and clearer type to listings for channels 1 and 3.

It is also probable that while terrestrial channels 1, 3 and 5 in Britain address a mass audience, that is, ABC1C2DE, channels 2 and 4 target ABC1s. ABC1s tend to be more attractive to advertisers because they have more disposable income.

■ Exercise 7.1 ■

Using a copy of a broadsheet newspaper and a red-top tabloid, list the first 10 advertisements and decide which social class they are aimed at.

The preponderance of adverts in broadsheet newspapers explains why they can be financially viable even though their circulations are a lot less than most 'red tops'; most of their revenue is derived from advertising.

The rigidity of the ABC1 classification has long been recognised as being too blunt an instrument to measure audiences, and various new systems have appeared in recent years. As recently as 30 years ago the social classes could be defined in terms of their environment:

the structure of the middle-class environment . . . is based on the concept of *property* and private *ownership*, on individual differences of status, wealth and so on, whereas the structure of the working-class environment is based on the concept of community or collective identity, common lack of ownership, wealth etc.   (Cohen, 1992; first published in 1972, p. 81)

However, it is doubtful now that there are many communities left that can celebrate working-class culture. During the 1980s in particular, traditional working-class communities declined along with the 'heavy' industry with which they were associated.

Possibly a better way of defining audiences is by categorising them by the values and attitudes they hold and the lifestyle they have; these are psychographic variables. For example, one of the better known systems is the Values, Attitudes and Lifestyles (VALS):

Actualisers
Actualisers are successful, wealthy, dynamic people for whom image is important as an expression of their individuality.

Fulfilleds
Fulfilleds are mature people who are well-educated professionals. This group values order, knowledge and responsibilities.

Achievers
Achievers are successful and career-orientated people. They are politically conservative and value the *status quo*. Image is important to them and they tend to buy established, well known products.

Experiencers
Experiencers are young, impulsive and rebellious. They like new products and styles but soon tire of them and search for new novelties. They spend as much as they can afford on clothing, fast food, music and films.

Believers
Believers are conservative people who believe in traditional institutions, such as the Church, and in the importance of the family and community. Their lifestyle tends to be very routine. Their income is small but sufficient.

Strivers
Strivers tend to be unsure of themselves and have a low income. They are striving for approval from others, which they feel they could gain by ownership of possessions, most of which they cannot afford.

Makers
Makers are do-it-yourself enthusiasts and tend to live a conventional, family life.

Strugglers
Strugglers are on the lowest income and tend to be loyal to their favourite brands.

■ Exercise 7.2 ■

Consider which group you and your friends belong to. If you can, compare your friends' assessment with your own.

While VALS attempts to classify everybody psychographically, there are definitions that focus on one group, for example:

Young Audiences for Advertisers

- **Trendies**: who crave the admiration of their peers
- **Egoists**: who seek pleasure
- **Puritans**: who wish to feel virtuous
- **Innovators**: who wish to make their mark
- **Rebels**: who wish to remake their world in their own image
- **Groupies**: who just want to be accepted
- **Drifters**: who are not sure what they want
- **Drop-outs**: who shun commitments of any kind
- **Traditionalists**: who want things to stay as they are
- **Utopians**: who want the world to be a better place
- **Cynics**: who have to have something to complain about
- **Cowboys**: who want easy money

(Selby and Cowdery, 1995, p. 25)

More recently, it has been suggested that people are best classified as member of tribes, who are defined by their characteristic way of consuming the media. For exampie, *Broadcast* magazine (21 April 2000) suggested:

- the couch potatoes – stay, basically, with one television programme with channel hopping only between one or two other channels;
- the specialists – devotedly watch a certain number of programmes, such as *EastEnders*, *Who Wants to Be a Millionaire* and *Friends*;

- the comedy addicts – are characterised by laddish behaviour and focus on sitcoms and satirical programmes;
- the insomniacs – watch post-prime-time TV.

Often one of the first things that students studying Media Studies learn to consider is how audiences are addressed by texts. While companies cannot possibly know their target audience as individuals, they can get a good idea of the type of people they are and so address them more effectively. However, categories like VALS can offer more than what a target audience is like. Market research companies, such as SRI Consultants, state that:

[Their] VALS team can help you apply VALS most effectively for your specific projects. Use VALS to:

- Identify **who** to target
- Uncover **what** your target group buys and does
- Locate **where** concentrations of your target group live
- Identify **how** best to communicate with your target group
- Gain insight into **why** the target group acts the way it does
  (Source: http://www.future.sri.com/vals/VALS.segs.shtml#SELF)

The location of target audiences is usually defined by post codes (zip codes in North America). Another system, ACORN, categorises post codes as one of the following:

- Agricultural areas
- Modern family housing
- Older housing of intermediate status
- Poor-quality older terraced housing
- Better-off council estates
- Less well-off council estates
- Multi-racial areas
- Higher-status non-family areas
- Affluent suburban housing
- Better-off retirement areas

These geodemographic variables can be very useful for niche distribution of texts; for example, free magazines aimed at affluent audiences can be distributed to 'rich' post codes.

185

Marketers characterise audiences for their products. While it is a truism to say that one can only drink so much alcohol (before collapsing), drinks companies successfully expanded the market in the late 1990s by focusing on females, who drank less than males. Branded spirits such as Bacardi Breezer and Vodka Source drove the expansion. The success was a tribute to the importance of branding, as these products were, basically, available before they were branded. The branding added value for the consumer and so sales rocketed.

Women's drinking patterns can be characterised in eight ways:

1. Being – vegging out, goes with gin and tonic.
2. Bonding – girlie gossip, shared wine or bottle of lager.
3. Shepherding – having to behave; half a lager.
4. Indulging – Baileys or wine.
5. Minxing – power drinking, cocktails or pints.
6. Princessing – first date, glass of wine or single spirits.
7. Bloking – acting like a bloke with draught lager or doubles.
8. Hunting – on the 'pull' with spirit mixer or cocktails.

The branded spirits, however, did not solely appeal to women; they appeared to be 'gender neutral':

> 40% of Breezer drinkers are male. That's interesting because a lot of the signals the drink sends out – the colour, the packaging – are feminine, I see it as part of a feminisation of drinking, which itself is part of a wider feminisation of society as a whole.   (Bacardi Breezer marketing controller, quoted in Benson, 2000, p. 8)

Although the last part is contentious, the fact that many men buy toiletries was almost certainly inspired by 1970s marketing that convinced males it was okay to use deodorant. The fact that this was considered feminine, as was the wearing of any body jewellery except rings, until the 1970s, shows how much, and how quickly, social conventions can change. Possibly the harbinger of this transformation was the Brut adverts that featured Henry Cooper (who would 'splash on the great smell of Brut all over'). Cooper was the heavy-weight boxing champion and so epitomised masculinity. The use of a macho role model overcame the homosexual connotations of men doing 'feminine' things. Being gay was literally a crime in Britain (for men) until the early 1960s and socially one until sometime – possibly – in the 1990s.

We can apply these categories to the analysis of media texts. Often we only have the text to deduce its target audience. However, all commercial media organisations have media packs that give statistical detail about their audience to help them sell their product to advertisers. The British newspaper that is most successful at delivering an audience to advertisers is the *Sunday Times*.

The *Sunday Times* and its advertising

The *Sunday Times* is probably the most profitable newspaper in Britain, not because it is the biggest selling but because it delivers an audience profile desired by many heavy advertisers. It was normally published in 11 sections (since increased to 13, with a Property section and an Internet guide) but our case study (30 January 2000) had an extra tabloid section previewing the Six Nations Rugby Union Championship. The analysis below focuses on how the advertising is organised in the newspaper, and does not consider the news it delivers.

The eleven sections were: the main news section, Sport, Business, Money, News Review, Travel, Appointments, Funday Times (comic), Culture, Style, the magazine, the Six Nations supplement. It takes little imagination to realise what sort of advertising ran in each section. The back of the sports section was entitled 'motoring' and the back of the news review carried classified property advertisements.

The front page, in common with most broadsheet newspapers, carries one advertisement only (a solus), usually 20 cm high and two columns across equalling 40 column centimetres (c.c.). Print advertising is sold on a single-column centimetre rate, which is determined by its position, so the front-page solus would be more expensive than a 'run of paper' advertisement that could be put anywhere. The advertisement on this edition is unusual as it is seven centimetres high and spread across the whole eight columns (equalling 56c.c.). The advertiser is Kuoni, a travel company that specialised in 'longhaul tours'; in other words, expensive holidays. We need to look no further, though we should, to determine that the *Sunday Times* delivers ABC1s to advertisers.

Most of the travel advertising is found in the Travel section; the Appointments pullout is full of jobs, three of which on the front page offer 'six-figure packages'. The magazine is printed on glossy paper and so is better able to run lifestyle advertisements that need to look good. Only the 'Funday Times' carries no advertising, but does have promotional material for bikes and roller blades.

While many companies will want to advertise in the newspaper, some will need persuading to do so; advertising sales executives attempt this persuasion.

7.3 Persuasion

As we saw in Chapter 4, it could be argued that virtually all media texts are involved in selling or promoting something. This normally takes the form of trying to influence individuals' behaviour to persuade them to purchase something or consume a media text. When markets are expanding, selling can be a relatively straightforward activity. However, once the market has matured, so demand has reached a level of saturation, and it is essential that advertisers differentiate themselves from their competitors.

The mnemonic AIDA sums up one well-known model of persuasion: awareness; interest; desire; action. Others include the 'hierarchy of effects' and the 'communications' models. The four stages of AIDA are relatively simple:

1. the audience has to be made **aware** of the product;
2. they need to have their **interest** piqued;
3. they need persuading that they **desire** this product;
4. this desire must be turned into an **action** (it is no good if the potential client says 'Yeah I love it but can't afford it').

If you have ever spoken to a professional salesperson it is likely that they tried to structure the conversation in the above fashion. However, adverts themselves also try and persuade their target audience and it is possible to see these four stages in the text.

■ Exercise 7.3 ■

Apply AIDA to 'The Dot' (Figure 4.1), reproduced on p. 96.

We have already considered this advertisement from the point of view of communication, in Chapter 4; here, we are focusing on how it is structured to persuade.

Awareness Placing the advert in an environment that is appropriate for the target audience generates awareness. Secondly, the use of the

Jaws parody, along with the deep turquoise colour (OK, you couldn't see that), grabs the reader's attention.

Interest   Having noticed the *Jaws* reference, the reader – ideally – then wishes to find out what this advertisement, in a 'digital economy' publication, has to do with the film. In addition, the suited businessman is likely to represent the reader (businesswomen will be familiar with the male address of most business adverts). The graphics of the advert, added to the *Jaws* reference, make it clear that the businessman is under threat. This stimulates a narrative interest: what is the threat and how can I avoid it? The caption, with the personal address 'your', anchors this threat as coming from the competition.

Desire   The trickiest emotion to elicit. The fact that the target audience has got this far is a triumph for the advertiser but a hollow one unless they progress through the final two stages. The technical copy beneath the dot will no doubt be understandable by the target audience; if it convinces them that the product is capable of delivering a 'powerful force' then action will probably follow.

Action   In a personal consumer environment, the action is often the sticking point because we do not have the cash to purchase all we want. Clearly businesses also operate under cash constraints; however, if the advert has convinced the audience that the product is crucial to the business then money will be found. The final line of the copy gives contact numbers and a website in order to facilitate the action.

An advert such as this is basically trying to generate leads. Anyone who contacts Sun will be interested but will not necessarily be ready to buy. It is not like impulse purchases in shops (or, even worse, on the Web where a click of a mouse heaps debt onto your credit card), this lead has to be converted, which possibly will be attempted with a different method.

A more detailed model of persuasion, one often employed in one-to-one selling whether in person or on the telephone, is summarised by DIPADA:

1.   **definition** of specific needs;
2.   **identification** of product (being sold) with need;
3.   **proof** of fulfilment of need;
4.   **acceptance** of that proof;

5. **desire** activated;
6. **action** to purchase product.

A skilled salesperson will take a customer through each of those stages by first finding out what the client wants and then asking ('test closing'): 'If it can be proved that the product in question will fulfil your needs will you buy?' Then, often using statistics, which can be manipulated to mean anything, the salesperson will attempt to show how her or his product is ideal for the client's purpose.

As new products were developed for the burgeoning consumer society of the twentieth century, advertising was required to explain how they worked and why they were useful. Similarly, in the 1920s, 'reason-why' advertisements were introduced that helped differentiate the product in the market place; this became the unique selling proposition (USP) described in Chapter 4. By focusing upon a product's USP the advertiser is modelling the audience as 'rational' beings. The advert is giving the buyer a reason to purchase this product and no other. Of course, in a crowded market place, where one successful product is bound to be followed immediately by competitors' versions, the USP may be more apparent than real.

Advertisers also use various other techniques of persuasion; outlined in detail by Brierley (1995):

- To raise awareness, many advertisements operate on the assumption that interests are gendered and so sex, sport and cars are commonplace in texts aimed at men; women are favoured with babies, weddings and fashion.
- Females are also often the target of advertisements that try to generate the 'ah' effect. Andrex's 'long toilet roll' campaign, using Labrador puppies and children, is probably intended to be cute.
- Since the 1950s, established brands have constantly attempted to renew themselves so that they do not become associated with being stale and old-fashioned. The 'new' and/or 'improved' formula has been with us since that time.
- The mode of address used is distinctive – the 'second person' you. 'You'll love the Azores like we do,' an Air Portugal ad suggests. This type of direct address personalises the message in an attempt to engage the audience.
- This direct form of address may be used to question the audience, suggesting that they have a problem. For example, an anti-virus computer company, McAfee, states: 'suddenly you're a prime target for uninvited visitors. Hackers, viruses, worms –

they're out there, ready to wreak havoc and steal your digital assets. What to do?'

A variation on this technique is the suggestion that buying this (usually financial) product will give the audience 'peace of mind'. The intention of the advert is to destroy any peace of mind the consumer has by pointing out that the lack of, say, mortgage insurance is a problem.

- The questions often attempt to stimulate a 'narrative disruption'. Apply Proppian ideas (see *Narrative and Genre*) to most ads and it is likely you will find the product in the sphere of action of a hero, helper or donor.
- A product that uses the 'At last...' prefix to the copy is suggesting that it is the culmination of a long wait; for example, DeLonghi's 'At last an oven even men can use'. A variation on 'at last' is shown in the advertisement for Faith Hill's album *Breathe*: 'The American number 1 album finally available in the UK'.
- The use of 'celebrities' (see also Chapter 4) often draws upon the established persona of the individual. For example, Gryff Rhys Jones's eccentricity is appropriate for the frustrated boffin of the Vauxhall ads that ran in 2000.
- The postmodern borrowing (or stealing) from genres has been a common device, from the Milk Tray man of the 1960s and 1970s (ref. James Bond) to the Nike 2000 ad that referenced *The Matrix*. There are a number of genres specific to advertising, such as the car advert that shows speedy driving in broodingly impressive landscapes.
- Slogans are usually built into an advertisement: a catchy phrase that tries to sum up the USP, such as the National Lottery's 'It could be you!' (it wasn't).
- Logos lurk somewhere on most advertisements and these are meant to represent the company as a whole, suggesting that even if the audience is not familiar with the particular product it does come from a reliable source.
- Jingles, particularly important on radio, can irritate the consumer to distraction but, in doing so, raise awareness.
- The use of songs, or extracts of classical music, attempts to hook the product into the consumer's mind with catchy ditties, some of which may already be familiar.
- The rise of computer-generated special effects during the 1990s found large corporations using digital effects in their advertisements; such as the National Lottery's 'hand of God' pointing at awestruck lottery participants. The effects used in Nike's 2000

Matrix ad are obviously 'state of the art', hooking audiences in to stay watching to relish the effects and so see the swoosh at the end.

- Entertainment is also invoked in advertisements that try and make us laugh. The bearded boffin, played by Gryff Rhys Jones, of the Vauxhall 2000 campaign is meant to put the audience in a position where they laugh at his idiocies (and so agree with what Vauxhall have done).

- Another way in which entertainment is invoked is through escapism (to the 'idea of utopia'). Chocolate advertising regularly uses this device, from the 1970s' Bounty 'taste of paradise' to the Galaxy 2000 campaign where a bite took the female character to a heavenly landscape characterised by high mountains and clouds.

- As advertisers perceive audiences becoming more cynical, and so resisting making the preferred reading, the ads themselves have used cynicism to sell. This drew upon the expansion of the 'alternative comedy' scene in the 1980s where comedians cast an acerbic eye on contemporary society. Getting a 'celebrity cynic' to endorse the product signifies that the product is what it says it is. Examples include Chris Tarrant and Ondigital; Jack Dee and John Smiths; Rowan Atkinson and Barclaycard.

- Not far from cynicism is the use of parody. The adverts themselves are saying 'We know you do not take us seriously, neither do we.' Heineken's 2000 campaign spoofed – as did Boddingtons before it – various advertising genres including soap powder.

With the arrival of the broadcast media, particularly television, advertisers found that it was better to appeal to the audience's emotions, rather than their intellect. While it is relatively straightforward to develop an argument with writing in a print advertisement, television's pictures are stronger at offering an emotive appeal. This, in part, explains the dominance of branding, a feature that relies upon image rather than actuality (Nike's 'swoosh' is simply a line, it only has meaning by association). Similarly, the rise in lifestyle advertising relies upon the audience accepting the premise, in a metaphorical sense, that buying a product will allow him or her to have a lifestyle similar to that shown in the advertisement.

▩ Exercise 7.4 ▩

What lifestyle does Figure 7.1 invite the target audience into?

Figure 7.1   Motorhome advertisement

The advertisement suggests that buying a motorhome can allow you to live your dream; 'you', in this instance, is a typical family. The motorhome will make it possible to have holidays more often ('when you want' states the copy) as it is expensive for families to stay in hotels or bed and breakfast. In addition, the home's mobility means, if you wish, you can go anywhere ('where you want'). While the motorhome dominates the image, and the letterbox framing emphasises the vehicle's size, we can see enough of the background to know that it is situated in a place of great beauty.

The size, and the copy, emphasise luxury; this is certainly not a case of 'roughing it'. This is reinforced by the suggestion that this product will allow you to 'live your dreams'. In addition, there is a call to 'change your life'. This assumption that the audience are dissatisfied with their lives in some way is a common advertising technique. As noted above, it is suggesting that dissatisfaction is akin to a narrative disruption that can be resolved by purchasing the product.

The lifestyle is decidedly middle class, with the emphasis on outdoor pursuits, both in the main picture and in the smaller one. The absence of price suggests the product is expensive, and the advertisement is trying to generate leads through coupon reply, phone, fax, e-mail, or via the Internet. This absence of price is not simply a ruse to encourage the reader to seek further information; if there is no price then no one can be put off by it. The omission of cost also elides the act of consumption:

> In confirmation of consumption outside economics, ads rarely exhort us to *buy* the commodities, but merely to *use* them, hence glossing over the capitalist moment of exchange – the purchase with money. (Winship, 1992, p. 217)

The ideology of the advertisement is decidedly bourgeois, with the mother providing refreshment while her family plays. Unsurprisingly, advertising tends to be conservative in nature; it draws upon conventional values in an attempt to sell the product. It should be mentioned that the manufacturers did not agree with this aspect of my analysis, feeling that the term 'bourgeois' was outdated. You should make up your own mind what you think but it is to the company's credit that they still gave me permission to use the advert and did not pressure me to alter my reading.

The advert is typical of lifestyle selling as it attempts to define people's sense of self: 'Instead of being identified by what they produce, people are made to identify themselves with what they consume' (Williamson, 1978, p. 13). As we saw in Chapter 6, media texts cannot *make* audiences do anything; that aside, Williamson's conception certainly describes what advertisers are trying to achieve. This aspirational advertising is a relatively new development:

The rise of lifestyle advertising in the UK in the 1980s was [not just] a response to the saturation of markets: it has also been attributed to the success of the account planning discipline in advertising agencies. (Brierley, 1995, p. 142)

Most advertising agencies are split between the planners and the creatives. The planners' role is to research the target market to work out what persuasive techniques will work best. The creative department's agenda, on the other hand, may conflict with this, as it tends to work with what is aesthetically pleasing. For example, in 2000 a clever cinema advertisement had a well-known magician (not well known enough for me to identify) doing a card trick: asking us, in the audience, to pick a card and then showing us the card we picked. When he got this right (for the majority anyway) the audience often gasped (the first time anyway). The advertisement was trying to sell a car; the brand name of which escapes me. This was a great ad to look at but probably very poor at selling the product. The directors of TV and cinema ads are sometimes criticised for being more concerned with forwarding their careers, into cinema, than actually selling things.

7.4 Audiences and scheduling

During the 1990s the number of channels vastly increased, primarily due to the technological developments of cable, satellite and digital television. In the twenty-first century the Internet will be a significant distribution network for television programmes; however, it will not be television as we know it.

Up until the development of satellite television in Britain in the late 1980s, the BBC and the ITV companies formed a duopoly. Indeed, the BBC had a monopoly in television until 1956 and in radio until 1974. This cartel disappeared when Sky Television became a serious competitor in 1989, though it was not until a decade later that the new competition started making significant inroads into the terrestrial broadcasters' audience share. Up until the 1990s, most broadcasters attempted to create a varied schedule that would attract an audience early, in prime time, and keep them for the rest of the evening. This audience was usually characterised as a 'family', though only a minority of households were family based. The scheduler had to take into account shifting demographics, as Todd Gitlin described television in the USA in the early 1990s:

The evening starts with an audience that averages about 17 percent children under twelve, with some 23 percent adults over fifty-five. By the ten-to-eleven time period, children are only 6.5 percent of the audience, and adults over fifty-five are now 26 percent.   (Gitlin, 1994, p. 58)

Obviously, early in the evening less adult fare was broadcast; in Britain the nine o'clock watershed signifies the time when adult-themed programmes can legitimately be broadcast. By 2000, the remote control had a massive effect on people's viewing habits; though it is difficult to believe that the two metres movement required to switch channels on the television before 'remotes' was a deterrent. However, it was not until the advent of a multi-channel environment that the remote control became a powerful piece of equipment. Flicking between three channels in the 1970s was not exactly a 'sensory overload' experience. In 2001, hundreds of channels were available: the *Radio Times* was listing 45 of them.

On 2 May 2000, the ITV network had the following prime-time schedule:

7.00	*Emmerdale* – soap opera
7.30	regional programmes
8.00	*The Bill* – soap opera/crime
9.00	*Bad Girls* – drama series set in a women's prison
10.00	*Metropolis* – comic thriller series

On the face of it, this seems a rather unbalanced schedule (two soaps and two drama series) but the art of the scheduler in the twenty-first century is not about constructing a sequence of programmes that audiences would watch all night, as there are too many competing attractions. The successful scheduler now needs to find hit programmes, like *Who Wants to Be a Millionaire?* and *Survivor* (in the USA), that can be shown as regularly as possible.

Radio, as yet, is not experiencing the same degree of fragmentation as television.

▓ Exercise 7.5 ▓

Listen to a whole day's output of BBC Radio 4 (or another radio station you do not normally listen to) and consider how it structures its schedule throughout the day. Failing that, examine the station's schedule in a 'listings' magazine.

The art of scheduling is to maximise the station's share of the target audience at any time of day, and by studying a schedule we can see who the media organisation is targeting. BBC Radio 4 has a predominantly middle-class audience and so would never attempt to address a mass audience like BBC Radio 5 Live. Indeed, most radio stations address niches: the other BBC stations focus on the young (Radio 1), the forty-pluses (Radio 2) and middle-class music lovers (Radio 3).

Schedulers, however, can never rest easy if they are to successfully deliver their audience profile. Radio 4, for example, appeals generally to the over 35s; if new 35-year-olds are not converted to the station then its audience will inexorably decline as the old listeners die.

In 2000, Radio 4's schedule was as summarised in Figure 7.2, taken from 'Listener Report'. Of the 34 'time zones', 22 are constant during the week: this includes the news programmes *Today*, *The World at One*, *PM*, *The 6 O'clock News* and *The World Tonight*. The great advantage of this stability in the schedule, to the listener, is he or she knows what to expect at certain times of day and so is not likely to miss any programmes they are likely to enjoy. The advantage to the institution is that they are maximising their audience.

This is an example of 'stripped and stranded' schedule: strips of the same programmes can be seen to run across the week at the same time as do strands of similar programmes, such as the 'documentary/debate' type at 20.00–21.00.

Michael Green, when he was the Controller of BBC Radio, described the difficulty in evolving a schedule without upsetting the audience. He characterised his audiences as being divided between: 'traditionalists' (mostly women over 55), who view the BBC as a guardian of the nation's morals; 'atheists', who are younger and hostile to the BBC; and the 'agnostics', who fall between these viewpoints. His challenge, therefore, was to 'widen the network's appeal to new audiences, whilst continuing to satisfy the demands of the loyalists' (Green, 1995, p. 138).

The mid-1990s was a traumatic time for Radio 4's traditionalists as attempts to appeal to a younger audience saw an upheaval in the scheduling. Particularly contentious was *Anderson Country*, a phone-in programme hosted by Irishman Gerry Anderson during the weekday afternoons. This was perceived by some as evidence of 'dumbing down' (see section 3.4); that is, high intellectual standards being compromised in order to garner popularity. The fact that Anderson was Irish may have been significant: he did not speak with the 'BBC voice' that many (erroneously) identify as being

🎻 The weekly schedule 🎻

	Monday	Tuesday	Wednesday	Thursday	Friday	Saturday	Sunday
5.30 – 6.00	Shipping forecast / Prayer					Leisure Report/Weather	Bells / Weather
6.00 – 7.00	Farming Today		Today			10' News Bulletin / Open Country / Weather	5' News Bulletin / Something Understood / On Your Farm / Weather / News/Papers
7.00 – 8.00	Today / Weather		Weather			Today / Thought for the Day / Weather	Sunday / Weather
8.00 – 9.00	Thought for the Day / Weather		Thought for the Day / Weather				Sunday Worship / News / Letter from America
9.00 – 10.00	Start the Week	(Interview) Feature	Midweek	In Our Time / Feature	Desert Island Discs	Home Truths	Broadcasting House
		The 9 o'clock Interviews					
		Book of the week on FM / Daily Service on LW					
		(Yesterday in Parliament on LW)					
10.00 – 11.00	Woman's Hour					Loose Ends	The Archers Omnibus
	Drama Series						
11.00 – 12.00	Features & Series (Varied formats and agendas)			FOOC / Crossing Continents	Light Features & Travel	Week in Westminster	Desert Island Discs
	Comedy / Dramatisations	Comedy / Archive	Comedy / Sitcom	Music & Literature Feature	Comedy / Light Drama	From Our Own Correspondent	
						News Summary (Shipping forecast on LW) / Money Box	News Summary (Shipping forecast on LW) / Comedy
12.00 – 13.00	4' News Summary (shipping Forecast on LW)		You and Yours			Comedy	The Food Programme
			Weather/Trails				
13.00 – 14.00	Quizzes & Games	Music conversation	Quizzes & Games	Open Country	Feedback	The One O'clock News	The World This Weekend
	The World at One		The Archers			Any Questions?	Music Entertainment
14.00 – 15.00	The Afternoon Play					Any Answers? / History	Gardeners' Question time / Leisure Feature

The weekly schedule

	Monday	Tuesday	Wednesday	Thursday	Friday	Saturday	Sunday
15.00 - 16.00	Money Box Live	The Exchange	Interaction / Gardeners' Question Time / Reading / Feature	Call You & Yours	Various	The Saturday Play	The Classic Serial
16.00 - 17.00	Magazine	Conversation	Conversation	Magazine	Magazine	Weekend woman's Hour	Open Book/Book Club / Poetry Please
17.00 - 18.00	Conversation	Magazine	Magazine	Conversation	Conversation	Saturday PM	File on Four / Letter Weather (Shipping Forecast on LW & FM)
	PM / Weather (Shipping forecast on LW)					Talking Pictures Weather (Shipping Forecast on LW & FM)	
18.00 - 19.00	The 6 o'clock News		Comedy			Live From London / The Now Show	The 6 o'clock News / Pick of the Week
19.00 - 20.00	The Archers / Front Row					Saturday Review / Letter	The Archers / Entertainment
20.00 - 21.00	(Social Documentary) / Crossing Continents	File on 4 / In Touch	Moral Maze / Debates / Political Talk	(History) / Letter from America	Any Questions? / Letter from America	The archive Hour	Feedback / Magazine
	Woman's Hour Drama Series / Documentary/Debate						
21.00 - 22.00	(Natural World)	(Health / Case Notes)	Science (Documentary) / (Technology / IT / Science Research)	(Technology / IT / Science Research)	The Friday Play	The Classic Serial	Documentary / Analysis/In Business
	The 9 o'clock Interviews						
22.00 - 23.00	The World Tonight / Book at Bedtime					Moral Maze / Debates / The 10 o'clock News	Westminster Hour / Political Talk
23.00 - 24.00	Home Truths	Comedy	Comedy / Today in Parliament	Comedy	Sport Late Tackle	Music Entertainment / Poetry Please	The Learning Curve / Something Understood
	The Midnight News / Weather / The Last Book					The Midnight News and Papers Weather / The Last Reading	The Midnight News Weather / Feature
24.00 - 1.00	'Sailing By' / Shipping Forecast / National Anthem						

Figure 7.2 Radio 4 schedule

'proper English'. Paul Gambaccini, an American, was similarly vilified on Radio 3; an ex-Radio 1 DJ, he migrated to Classic FM after being expelled from the BBC.

When we consider how a text is speaking to its audience we are engaging in analysis of its mode of address.

7.5 Modes of address

In chapter 1 of *Image and Representation* the numerous variables in communication were investigated, and we have seen, above, how persuasion is used to address audiences, particularly in advertising. All media texts address audiences in a particular way: it may be the 'tongue in cheek' mode of spoofs such as *Scary Movie* (2000), or the serious tones of a newscaster.

■ Exercise 7.6 ■

Analyse Figure 7.1 to assess how it addresses its target audience.

Decoding the mode of address tells us about the institutional voice of the text and also tells us about what assumptions the institution is making about its audience. If a text successfully addresses its audience that audience may also use it to reinforce its identity. For example, lifestyle magazines, in their preferred reading, offer a view of what is fashionable. If the audience accept this then they may use it as a guide (uses and gratifications' personal identity) for themselves; for instance, the use of the monochrome Norm character in the long-running series of Twix advertisements. Norm defines what is not cool – badly dressed and buck-teethed – and is set in opposition to the attractive individuals who eat the chocolate bar.

The *Sun* newspaper has a very emotive form of address:

NICHOLA Holt was evicted from the Big Brother house last night – outraging fans who said the vote should not have gone ahead.

Seventy-two per cent of people voted for Bolton lass Nichola, 29, to get the boot from the TV show, while 28 per cent voted for the other nominee, Scouser Craig.

But thousands flooded The Sun Online with complaints after Channel 4 bosses insisted on going ahead with the public vote a day after fellow contestant Nick was exposed as a cheat.

(http://www.the-sun.co.uk 19 August 2000)

200

The newspaper's tone is melodramatic: 'outraging' and 'flooded'. People in power are called 'bosses', and the *Sun* often claims it is representing readers against bosses' excesses. Compare the above with the *Guardian*'s coverage:

> The pantomime villain of the voyeuristic game show *Big Brother* turned out yesterday not to be so much of a scheming Machiavelli after all. (Wells, 2000c, p. 5)

Here the formality of 'big words' is evident and is speaking to an audience who have at least a passing familiarity with Machiavelli.

■ Exercise 7.7 ■

What mode of address do the Peta ads (Figures 7.3, 7.4 and 7.5) use and how are they trying to persuade you to their point of view.

Clearly one of the modes Peta (People for the Ethical Treatment of Animals) uses is 'gross out', something that usually appeals more to young people. Young people can be characterised as a sub-cultural group, albeit a very large one.

7.6 Sub-cultural groups

While we can define, say, teenagers as being members of a sub-culture this does not mean that all teenagers will share the same values. We saw in Chapter 5 how the mainstream co-opts oppositional texts by commodifying them for its own uses; sub-cultural groups can operate in the other direction. They must, by definition, define themselves against the mainstream and one of the most potent ways they do

Figure 7.3   Peta ad – 1

Figure 7.4 Peta ad – 2

Figure 7.5 Peta ad – 3

this is by appropriating 'normal' objects for their own purposes. The punks 'stole' safety pins from babies; mods 'pinched' middle-class Vespas; rappers use high fashion. Through bricolage:

> 'humble objects' can be magically appropriated; 'stolen' by subordinate groups and made to carry 'secret' meanings: meanings which express, in code, a form of resistance to the order which guarantees their continued subordination. (Hebdige, 1988, p. 18)

Some sub-cultural groups come from the 'street'; that is, a place which is not mediated and therefore has connotations of being genuine. For example:

> While the oversize parka and wool cap has been a hip hop cultural artifact for most of its history, the heavy winter boots as year-round attire flowed out of their use by crack dealers clocking on corners. (George, 1999, p. 161)

The particular style of dress was derived from the material conditions of selling drugs.

▓ Exercise 7.8 ▓

Analyse the image of the hip hop 'superstar' (then known as) Puff Daddy. What would you say is specifically 'hip-hop' about his look (see Figure 7.6) and what connotations do the signs possess?

While hip-hop came from the streets of New York, some sub-cultural groups do not spring up from the street but congregate around particular texts. As we saw in Chapter 6, Fantasy TV programmes often garner a devoted fan base, as do cult movies such as *The Rocky Horror Picture Show* (1975), and Russ Meyer's movies with big-breasted women. Barry Keith Grant has suggested that cult movies:

> present a conflict between the normal and the Other by making a clownish spectacle – of caricaturing – the normal while minimizing the threat of the Other. (Grant, 2000, p. 19)

In other words, we are urged not to take the subject matter seriously, through either camp signifying systems (*Rocky Horror*) or sheer over-the-top vulgarity (see Paul Verhoeven's films such as *Showgirls*, 1995). 'Gross out' movies often attain cult status because they disgust mainstream audiences and so help define the cult audience as those who can 'take it'; hence they are often a youth phenomenon.

Media texts that are aimed at a sub-cultural group must use that group's system of signs in order to address their target audience. Mainstream texts, if they aim at sub-cultural groups, tend to do so in a fairly broad way in order to maximise their audience. *Kerrang!*, for instance, is ostensibly a heavy metal magazine but will also cover artists who have crossed over into the mainstream. Fanzines, however, tend to be far less compromised, usually because they exist because of their producers' enthusiasm rather than a desire to make money.

> *Slimetime, Grind, Trashola, The Gore Gazette.* The titles reflect an unseemly juvenile fascination with unrespectable and illicit imagery, the domain of the horror film. For most adults horror films are the junk food of the imagination, trivially dispensable cultural artefacts undeserving of critical attention and devoid of artistic or intellectual sophistication. (Sanjek, 2000, p. 314)

For those who do take 'gross out' horror movies seriously, and usually hold Hollywood horror in contempt, the fanzine is a text where like-minded enthusiasts can 'meet'.

Figure 7.6 Puff Daddy

Sub-cultural groups, hip-hop excluded, often hold capitalism in contempt and define their pleasures as being a genuine love of the text or texts. Hence audiences co-opt texts for their own purposes. However, as we have seen in this book, business is the driving force in western society and virtually all texts are produced for profit. It is reassuring then that we, as an audience, can gain ownership of texts through making our own readings. What is missing, though, is true diversity as alternative texts are extremely rare.

7.7 Conclusion

This chapter has investigated a number of ways in which audiences are categorised. These categories are used to help institutions under-stand their target audiences, which is particularly important in selling. Two selling techniques were considered as well as numerous devices that advertising uses to try and persuade audiences to buy.

Broadcast scheduling is crucial to reaching audiences; though the number of channels available has increasingly marginalised the art of scheduling, on television at least. While schedules help institutions to reach audiences, they must also use an appropriate mode of address in order to speak to them. Certain audiences define themselves against the mainstream by inhabiting sub-cultural groups that have their own particular set of pleasures.

8

AUDIENCE AS CITIZENS

AIMS OF THE CHAPTER

➤ To consider audiences' rights as citizens in relation to the media.

➤ To examine political bias in newspapers.

➤ To investigate news sources.

➤ To consider the media as a public sphere.

➤ To investigate the gender imbalance in the media.

8.1 Introduction

Democracies often represent themselves as being 'free societies' where the electorate wields power, in contrast to totalitarian states where dictatorships rule. In order for a democracy to work properly its citizens need an unrestricted flow of information on which to base their vote. The press is seen to have an important role in this and journalists are thought to offer a check on potential abuses of power perpetrated by those in government; they act as a 'fourth estate'. However, as Graham Murdock (1994) pointed out, having access to information is only one aspect of possessing 'cultural rights', which he sees as being crucial to citizenship.

Murdock stated that while it was important that the information available to citizens should be both disinterested and comprehensive, we should also have access to 'knowledge', that is, the various ways that the information could be interpreted. In addition, we should be able to see our own social group represented in the media as well as being able to communicate through, and so have access to, the media. In this way audiences are 'providers' as well as 'consumers' of images and ideas.

8.2   Information and knowledge

As we have seen in Chapter 1, most media organisations are businesses that define audiences as consumers and not as citizens. However, as dealt with in Chapter 2, public service broadcasting (PSB) is ideally meant to operate in opposition to this conception and so could provide audiences with their 'cultural rights'.

The news, both broadcast and in print, is the most important type of media text that provides information and knowledge. However, it is worth noting that most newspapers have a political bias.

Political bias

Unlike broadcasters, who have a legal obligation to be impartial, newspapers are free to campaign on behalf of political parties, but they tend to do this in an indirect fashion and so are usually only open about their support during elections. It is important that readers are aware of any political bias in the newspaper they are reading as they can then more readily understand the bias in the information being presented to them.

Up until the late 1990s it was relatively easy to state which newspaper supported which political party (see Table 8.1). With the emergence of New Labour, a number of previously staunch Conservative publications switched allegiance. This was because New Labour was much more sympathetic toward businesses than it had been

Table 8.1

Market	Party allegiance, early 1990s
'red tops'	
Sun	Conservative (Con)
Mirror	Labour (Lab)
Daily Star	Con
'middle market' tabloids	
Daily Mail	Con
Express	Con
broadsheets	
Daily Telegraph	Con
The Times	Con
Guardian	Lab
Independent	Lab

in its original incarnation when it was the party of the working classes.

Changes in ownership can also alter political allegiance. Up until the late 1990s, the *Express* was a Conservative-supporting newspaper; however, it shifted toward Labour when Lord Hollick (a Labour peer) bought the newspaper. In late 2000 it was sold again and, at the time of writing, it is unclear whether its stance will change.

The most significant switch of party support was in the *Sun*, not only because it is the biggest selling daily newspaper. Under Rupert Murdoch's proprietorship it had usually supported the Conservative Party. However, its predominantly working-class readership would 'naturally' vote for Labour. It has been suggested that Labour lost the 1992 election because the *Sun* urged its readers not to vote for Neil Kinnock, Labour's leader, with the headline: 'If Kinnock wins today will the last person to leave Britain please turn out the lights.' Political leaders give winning the support of the *Sun* a high priority, as it is the 'floating voters' – those who do not always vote for the same party – who decide the results of elections. Because about 17% of the electorate are *Sun* readers, if the newspaper influences just 1% of the floating voter readers, this can have a significant effect on the election.

Clearly, if the *Sun* is so influential, though it is difficult to quantify its *actual* influence, then it is a very powerful publication. This power is, to an extent, transferred to its proprietor, Rupert Murdoch. (For more on political orientation, see 'News Sources', below.)

Newspapers' role in providing citizens with comprehensive and disinterested information is not only compromised by political bias, for the news agenda of many newspapers, as we noted in Chapter 3, is driven by the need to garner lifestyle advertising. In addition, tabloid newspapers in Britain emphasise the trivial above important news. For example, the biggest selling daily newspaper, the *Sun*, led (on 20 December 2000) with 'Madonna: A Song for Guy', referring to Elton John's intention of singing at Madonna's wedding. In terms of the 'uses and gratifications' theory, the *Sun* newspaper obviously places entertainment over information. Most other newspapers have a more serious agenda, though this is ideologically motivated (for example, see the case of the *Daily Mail* and *Crash* in Chapter 6).

Broadsheet newspapers are often viewed as more serious because they provide more 'hard' news. However, if the 'serious' newspapers and broadcast news do provide more information that is relevant to citizens, it is still questionable whether this is contextualised in such a way as to provide the knowledge required. For example, during Easter 2001 the story of a missing 'slave ship' off the West African coast shocked many, especially as the slaves were children. What was lacking in much of the coverage was the explanation that the reason children were sold into slavery by their parents was linked to the West's demand for cheaper chocolate to make the eggs that were consumed during the festive period.

The reason this uncomfortable link between the plight of 'slave children' and western consumers is *not* highlighted is unlikely to be an accident. Whilst it is doubtful that any formal censorship intervenes in such cases, Herman and Chomsky (1986) have argued that the structure of news organisations is such that the occurrence of this sort of censorship is institutionalised:

> [Herman and Chomsky] hold that the media maintains a corporate class bias though [*sic*] five systemic filters: Concentrated private ownership; a strict bottom-line profit orientation; over-reliance on governmental and corporate sources for news; a primary tendency to avoid offending the powerful; and an almost religious worship of the market economy, devaluing alternative beliefs. (Phillips, 1998, p. 141)

Whilst PSB can avoid the first filter, it is affected by the others as much as any commercial organisation. News sources are crucial to the way news is presented to audiences.

News sources in Britain

The news obviously does not come from nowhere and most of it is not a result of journalists' investigations. The main sources of news are split between primary and secondary sources.

Primary sources
Parliament (Westminster and Europe) and local councils
the emergency services
hospitals
industry
sports clubs
pressure groups
trade unions

Secondary sources
the armed forces
schools and colleges

local pressure groups
local businesses
geographically specific sources: for example, lifeboats on the coast

This rather traditional list misses out the media as a whole as a source; journalists can always poach stories from their competitors. It also suggests a rather benign process where news organisations receive a multitude of information and act as gatekeepers, passing the important information on to its audience. In this way they appear to be reflecting what is going on in the world. Much of this information is in the form of press releases written by a company's press office or by a public relations (PR) agency hired for the purpose.

Occasionally the press, usually local but sometimes the national press, will even run these press releases as they receive them, without accrediting their source.

■ Exercise 8.1 ■

Take a newspaper and examine the news pages. For each story try and guess what its source may be, using the above list.

The Guardian, Monday, 4 October 1999

Clearly guess work is involved in this exercise but my reading suggests that the sources of the first three pages of this issue of the *Guardian* were as follows:

Page 1

Headlines
1. Revealed: how UK's net pioneers made £1.3bn
2. Tories worse off with Portillo
3. Big vote for right in Austria
4. Former Guardian editor dies at 79

Both lead stories were derived by surveys commissioned by the *Guardian*: the newspaper itself therefore generated its own news. The second story dealt with a speech that had not yet been given, it was to be delivered by the Conservative leader, William Hague, later that day – see below. The other two stories are obviously responding to events that did happen the day before.

Page 2

Headlines
1. Interest rates are set to rise
2. Dobson will now run to stop Archer
3. Sensation seekers defy mayor as show goes on

The top story here is probably derived from the 'diary': that is, the Federal Reserve was due to make its monthly announcement on interest rates the day after this report. There is, nevertheless, a PR element to this as experts quoted have their companies named. Indeed, it is possible that financial houses may have sent out press releases that speculated that rates would rise. That finance companies are aware of the benefits of PR was evidenced when Prime Minister Blair's child Leo Blair was born in May 2000. The event prompted 'a flurry of baby-related press releases from financial services companies eager to use the occasion to promote their wares' (Jones, 2000, p. 6).

The second story (number 2), written by the Political Editor, about Frank Dobson running for the position of Mayor of London, was said to have 'emerged last night' (White, 2000, p. 2); in other words, Dobson, or an associate, told the journalist that he was going to run but this was to be 'off the record' so it could not be described as an official announcement. Such 'off the record' briefings are often used by politicians to get their views aired in such a way that they can deny having said it if necessary.

The third story (about a modern art exhibition in New York) was 'legitimate' in that it reported events from the day before.

Page 3

Headlines
1. Blair's earlier learning centres
2. If you're carrying this, you're carrying cocaine

The 'cocaine' story was based on a BBC Newsroom South-East story and the first one was so topical that it had not yet happened:

Early learning goals to be announced by the government today...
(Carvel, 1999, p. 3)

Like another story that received prominence in this edition – Opposition leader William Hague's speech on page 1 – this was not 'news' at all because it dealt with an event that *would* be happening that day. The newspapers had obviously received Hague's speech, or at least a summary, in advance; and the government press release about nurseries was part of a coordinated campaign to give the story the best 'spin'. Indeed, the *Guardian*'s sub-heading helps anchor this positive reading:

> Nursery school goals should help children from less privileged backgrounds to acquire the basic skills they need.   (Ibid.)

The Conservative leader allowed the press an advance view of his 'common sense revolution' in the hope that it would receive coverage on the day of his speech *and* the day after, when it could actually be reported as news. Whether this occurs, of course, is down to the political orientation of the newspaper. The *Guardian* did indeed feature the speech in its lead story but only in the context of its 'spoiler' feature (a survey it had commissioned): 'Tories worse off with Portillo'. In addition, we can also read the 'nursery places' story as an attempt by the government to 'steal Hague's thunder'. This could have been announced at virtually any time; the Monday of Hague's speech was specifically chosen to distract attention from his keynote speech.

The *Guardian* had commissioned an opinion poll about the Conservative Party that was anything but positive news for William Hague. This was to be expected as the *Guardian* is a slightly left-of-centre publication. The *Daily Telegraph*, a right-wing newspaper, was more positive, leading with the 'fact' that a previous prime minister, Margaret Thatcher, would be demonstrating support for Hague. The *Telegraph* was quite open about the way in which politicians attempt to use the media:

> Mr Hague's image-makers are keen to show more of the private side of the Tory leader to remove some of the negative impressions of him. The plan to highlight Mr Hague's rich family life was set out in the 'Project Hague' memo in the summer which proposed ways to show him as a well-rounded individual.   (Shrimsley, 1999)

It is interesting to note that the concern was not so much that William Hague *is* a 'well-rounded' individual but that he should be *seen* as one. In the postmodern world it is appearance that counts for more than actuality.

Clearly newspapers offer partial views of the world. However, we should not despair of ever getting at the 'truth'; if we know the political leanings of a publication, and how news sources are relatively limited, we are more able to 'read between the lines': never take news at face value until you have thought about it.

While broadcast news is meant to be balanced in its presentation of stories, and exhibit no political bias, it too relies upon the same sources as the press.

Broadcast news: *BBC One O'Clock News*, 31 May 2000

A clock is shown counting six seconds to the hour; the continuity announcer says: 'This is BBC One. Now the BBC News with Huw Edwards. It's one o'clock.'

Most television programmes do not start at the time they are scheduled but a few minutes afterwards. Audiences 'tuning in' will then get to see the various trailers for other programmes. The news, however, has a special status in its relationship with time. Its exact link to time suggests accuracy in its presentation of what is happening in the world.

The programme begins with the headlines read by Huw Edwards, who is seen briefly in a conventional framing over pictures accompanying the lead stories. The start of each headline is punctuated dramatically by drumbeats. This is followed by the actual title sequence that accompanies (brands) all BBC television news broadcasts.

Marshall Sahlins stated that the news can be seen as:

an event [that] is not just a happening in the world; it is a *relation* between a certain happening and a given symbolic system.   (Sahlins, 1985, p. 153)

A textual analysis of the news can show us how the news organisation uses, and creates, a particular symbolic system to communicate events to the audience – the 'knowledge' required by citizens. For instance, a generic characteristic of news is the dramatic fanfare-like title music. Whilst the fanfare derives from the times when such musical phrases accompanied announcements, drama belongs in the realms of fiction. How news is constructed narratively was discussed in *Narrative and Genre* (Chapter 1); *Image and Representation* (Chapter 5) looked at how the world was represented in the news, through news values, and included an analysis of a title sequence. Here we consider the presentation of information and knowledge in the news through an analysis of the programme's lead story.

After the title sequence, a brief, high-angle establishing shot of the 'anchor' (the news presenter) is shown. The studio combines elements of old and new: a pillar, with connotations of classical Greece and Rome, is juxtaposed with chrome railings that seem both old (railings) and new (chrome). The anchor sits at a circular desk, with another desk at its side, which is sometimes used for a second anchor reading the sports news. This 'old and new' emphasises the solidity of tradition (the BBC has been reporting news for many years) with the 'cutting edge' element of new technology (the BBC is totally up-to-date).

Through a window, behind the anchor, the newsroom can be seen, emphasising the amount of work that has gone into the broadcast as well as the large number of people involved. A circular carpet beneath the desks echoes the shape of both the desks and the broadcast transmission lines animated on the title sequence, giving cohesion to the design.

The day's lead was the distribution by the government of 12 million leaflets asking the public what their priorities were for the National Health Service. The story consisted of 12 segments:

1. anchor 'setting the scene', and link to
2. filmed report: image of woman reading a leaflet in a chemist's;
3. interviews with patients waiting in a surgery;
4. footage of a focus group, presumably (as we cannot hear them) discussing the NHS;
5. Liam Fox, Opposition MP, criticising the exercise; he uses a sound bite;
6. government minister talking to waiting patients, then
7. talking to camera, stating the government's position;
8. footage of new type of centre of the sort the government plans to make more of;
9. NHS Confederation spokesman speaking in favour of new centres;
10. waiting room again – bringing a sense of closure to the film report;
11. anchor, who leads into a live interview with the Social Affairs Editor;
12. BBC News Live caption: the editor answers anchor's questions – a mix of camera on editor, on anchor, and on anchor looking at editor.

■ Exercise 8.2 ■

Consider the 12 segments. How many of them do you think are necessary for audiences to understand the story?

This report is constructed in a typical fashion: the presenter anchoring the various segments, offering stability in a flux of images; this is the report's 'composition and balance' (a news value). The anchor is particularly important for foreign news stories, which can seem remote from the viewer's concerns and confusing; the audience can always rely on the anchor to explain what is going on in simple terms.

Segment 2, however, is redundant: we do not need to see what leaflets in a chemist's look like. It is an example of television's reliance on pictures; if a story cannot be accompanied by pictures it has much less chance of appearing. The anchor's segments are kept brief as contemporary television has a fear of talking heads; producers think audiences will turn to another channel unless there are a variety of images.

Segment 3 offers a 'vox pop': what we, the people, think (consensus news value). This is one way in which audiences appear to get access to the media. The footage of the focus group – segment 4 – appears out of nowhere. We cannot be sure the group was discussing the issue that morning and, as we do not hear them speak, we cannot even be certain they were discussing health. Indeed, it is only the reporter's words anchoring the image that makes it clear what we are seeing.

Segment 4 fulfils the broadcaster's obligation to be impartial. The Opposition spokesman is situated in front of the House of Commons, giving him added status and reassuring audiences that they are seeing a genuine MP. This placement in front of appropriate settings is called a 'stakeout'. He uses a sound bite, a brief summary of his party's position, which will make it more likely that his viewpoint will be shown. In the late 1960s sound bites were about 40 seconds in length; by the end of the 1990s they had become about 8 seconds. Clearly a high degree of simplification has to be introduced to explain even the simplest thing in eight seconds. The news has become a high-concept movie pitch (see Chapter 1).

That the story's reporter was at the same surgery as the government minister is obviously not a coincidence but evidence of the PR nature of the event. The minister – in segment 6 – is seen talking (consulting) with patients before he gives his sound bite to camera (segment 7). The footage of the new centre further illustrates government intentions and was probably filmed the day before. The government press release would have hit news desks at least the day before with an embargo on reporting until 31 May; it was that day's lead story in the *Guardian* too.

A further positive sound bite is followed by a return to the waiting room, which allows the reporter to sum up, being careful to offer balance in his summation. Until recently that would have concluded the story; however, the convention now is to interview someone live about the issue. This attempts to give a sense of veracity to the proceedings though it is very rare – in my experience – for anything new to be said during this link.

While we are provided with a variety of views and the issue is treated seriously, the degree to which this story offers us enough 'knowledge' with which to contextualise the information provided is debatable. One of the most influential stories of the twentieth century was a BBC news report on the Ethiopian famine in 1984. It led to mass mobilisation of western resources to save millions of people from starvation. However, it was clear that the way the event was reported only offered an incomplete picture.

The Ethiopian famine story

The story ran for several weeks and, after the initial report, focused on the relief efforts that showed a bias toward the West. Of 108 people involved in the efforts only eight were Westerners; it was these eight who were focused on. The effect of this was to make it appear that the West was saving the Ethiopians and that the locals appeared to be incapable of helping themselves.

In general, the news lacked analysis; it was as if the famine had come out of nothing. A few documentaries that were broadcast at the time showed how such direct aid as providing food for the starving is little more than useless. What is needed is long-term development aid that helps the local people regain self-sufficiency. This long-term aid lacks the drama required for news reports. The free handouts, given as part of direct aid, also have the effect of bankrupting the local markets; no one will pay when the aid gives food for free. When the aid dries up, however, the local markets no longer exist.

As the Open University programme *Using TV – How TV was used to highlight the Ethiopian famine* pointed out, in order to offer enough knowledge to understand the famine properly several issues needed to be covered:

- economics – local and global;
- politics – the cold war (still running in 1984) and issues of national identity (the post-colonial African map was drawn with little reference to indigenous cultures; look at a map of the

continent with all those straight borders, which are defined by map references and not geography);

- war – how it affected agriculture, resources and the flow of refugees;
- drought – the effect of meteorological variables;
- environment – the effect of deforestation, soil erosion and over-population (many African nations have been forced to farm commodities, in order to service foreign debt, rather than growing food for their people);
- poverty;
- history – tribal rivalries were often exacerbated by colonial rule;
- aid – often not enough and the wrong sort.

Imagine news programmes attempting to give us all this knowledge; but without it, we cannot hope to understand the situation. What we are left with is a news that:

> is at once dehistoricizing, fragmented and fragmenting. Its paradigmatic expression is the TV news and the way it sees the world – as a series of apparently absurd stories that all end up looking the same, endless parades of poverty-stricken countries, sequences of events that, having appeared with no explanation, will disappear with no solution. (Bourdieu, 1998, p. 7)

8.3   Representation and access

Jürgen Habermas (1989) argued that the public could, in the nineteenth century, help shape the direction of society through the 'public sphere':

> The economic independence provided by private property, the critical reflection fostered by letters and novels, the flowering of discussion in coffee houses and salons and, above all, the emergence of an independent, market-based press, created a new public engaged in critical political discussion.   (Curran, 1996, p. 82)

By the twentieth century, so the argument went:

> The media facilitates this process by providing an arena of public debate, and by reconstituting private citizens as a public body in the form of public opinion.   (Ibid., pp. 82–3)

217

So citizens, the argument goes, can gain access to the media and hence get themselves heard. Whilst Habermas's view is probably idealised, as it ignores amongst other things the fact that his nineteenth-century public was constituted solely of the middle class, it is apparent that the media can sometimes act as a 'public sphere'. For example, soap operas occasionally deal with contentious issues that can, as they have a mass audience, lead to a wider debate.

The 'public sphere' can operate in an oppositional sense. The Goldsmiths Media Group cite the example of hip-hop in giving black people a public voice:

> While it would be misleading to suggest that rap music has always operated as a counter-public sphere, it has clearly been productive in addressing a number of issues affecting the African-American community in the USA and elsewhere. (Goldsmiths Media Group, 2000, p. 45)

The main difficulty that the public has is in actually *accessing* this public sphere. While this is a particular problem for minority groups, who usually have less power (which is itself a reflection of their lack of access to the media), females also often have difficulty voicing their opinions and ideas.

Women: representation and access

In Britain, in recent years, exam results have been greeted with headlines expressing anxiety because females are doing better than males. For many years, when the converse was true, gender imbalance was not an issue; indeed in the old discredited 'tertiary' system, which included secondary modern and grammar schools, the 11-plus exam results were fiddled in favour of boys. During the final decades of the twentieth century women were less discriminated against, in Britain at least, than they had been for hundreds of years, but gender still remains an issue in media organisations.

In 1989 the Institute of Practitioners in Advertising published a survey into how many women were in positions of influence in the industry:

> It made for depressing reading. Women were not climbing the corporate ladder, the report said. They were noticeably absent from key senior positions.... They were almost totally unrepresented in many departments. (Archer, 1999, p. 4)

Ten years later the *Media Guardian* found progress had been minimal. Despite advances in other areas of British life, women were still a distinctly minority group in the advertising industry and, indeed, in the media in general. The consequences of this can be seen in the way women are represented in the media. Women's lack of access to positions of power means that the way they are shown in media texts is often a result of male ideas.

Rachel Abramowitz's *Is That a Gun in Your Pocket?* (2000) contained the results of 150 interviews with women who worked in Hollywood. The director Martha Coolidge describes how the head of the production company of her first film, told her that 'I want you to know that we must have naked breasts in the movie four times...' (Campbell, 2000a, p. 3). We saw in Chapter 3 how media texts are commodified; here it becomes clear how women's bodies can be part of that commodification.

■ Exercise 8.3 ■

List as many directors and film stars as you can. How many of them are female? (You can do a similar exercise listing the number of black people.)

The fact of male dominance in Hollywood, and in society generally, the way media texts are produced. In 1999, of the total number of days worked by directors only 10.2% were by women, though this was an improvement on 1985's 4%. Not all media industries, however, are so sexist. Women do better in television, in North America at least, because the:

> need to finish programmes on time [as] they had to be shown on television in a specific slot and could not be delayed meant that people behaved in a more professional and democratic fashion. (ibid.)

Research has shown that women are over-represented in administrative jobs whereas men dominate the technical area. So whilst women shuffle paper, men are the creators.

All of the above issues apply both to race and to individuals who are 'physically and/or mentally challenged'. For example, it is only very recently that black people have regularly appeared in British television advertising, and the number of non-white individuals in executive positions in the media industries is miniscule.

Audiences' access to the media is not only affected by such factors as gender and race, there is a difference between media and non-media people.

Media and non-media people

By definition, non-media people are involved in the media less than media people. We have seen in Chapter 5 how access programmes allow non-media people to use the media; this section considers other ways in which they (we?) come into contact with the media. This can be an 'eye-opening' experience. Nick Couldry wrote about two examples of what can happen when non-media people come into contact with the media.

Studio audiences obviously consist of (mostly) non-media people. They form an important part of quiz and chat shows as well as being present at the filming, on video, of some sitcoms. Many shows, particularly North American, use 'canned' laughter to highlight which bits are meant to be funny. Couldry relates an individual's experience of being a member of the audience of the National Lottery show:

> You were told to get there, 6 o'clock I think it was, but the programme doesn't go live until 7.50, so you think, Oh well, I'm going to be in the studios, it'll be nice and warm. And you get there and you stand outside on the main road, at the BBC studios, it was freezing cold . . . and it started to rain. So after about half an hour, they then let you in and you go to a Portakabin and you're searched, frisked . . . and you go through a barrier like you do at an airport. . . . I felt it was a bit like a cattle market.   (Couldry, 2000, p. 276)

The BBC, in this case, obviously does not feel obliged to look after its audience, as they do not have to pay for their tickets. This is an example of 'the reinforcement of power through the control of territory' (ibid.). Non-media people, when they come into contact with the media as a 'television audience', are treated as props. This treatment reinforces the sense that non-media people do not belong in the media, it is a place reserved for the elite.

If someone we know, or an area we are very familiar with, is represented in the media then we are likely to have a heightened interest. Appearances on television, or in newspapers, give the individual a new and elevated, if somewhat temporary, status in the eyes of her or his peers. Television celebrities, when walking on the street, are often greeted with, 'Eh, I've seen you on telly.' We would not dream of going up to a neighbour and saying, 'Eh, I saw you watching telly.'

Being in the media is glamorous; appearing in it, even if only as a member of the audience, gives the individual an iota of that glamour.

Even though our member of the National Lottery audience felt badly treated, individuals who are victims of misreporting have an even worse experience. Couldry relates how animal rights protesters, many of whom broke the stereotype by being old, were shocked at how events were reported at a protest in Brightlingsea in 1995.

> The shock of seeing the media process face to face – and realising the gap between media coverage... and their own direct experience of the protests – encouraged many to reflect on their earlier [respectful] attitudes to the media. (Ibid., p. 278)

One member of the village was so incensed to hear the local radio state that there were 26 police officers at the demo, when she could see there were more, that she rang them up to find out where they got their figure from. The answer was the police press officer; the police were trying to convince the public that they were adopting a low-key approach whereas she had seen 23 *vans*, with police wearing semi-riot gear, go past her window.

It has been suggested that the Internet will alleviate the problems of access and provide a genuine public sphere for debate. As the Net is 'naturally' interactive and does not require large media institutions to mediate access, the public can readily get information and knowledge as well as posting their own representations onto the Web. However, it is possible that the commercial nature of the Internet's development may compromise these ideals and it is unlikely that vast swathes of the Earth's population will be able to get online, even in the next 100 years.

8.4 Conclusion

One of the reasons why Media Studies is such an important subject is that it attempts to break down institutional barriers and so make us all (the audience), if only in an academic sense, media people. Yet getting access to disinterested and comprehensive information and knowledge is highly problematical. News has increasingly become public-relations based and the range of news sources is often limited to 'official' conduits. In addition, the often insidious political bias of newspapers (who pursue their own interests in the name of their readers) makes it difficult for the people to find out what is going on in the world. The notion of a 'public sphere', where exchanges of views can lead to a viable consensus, is an ideal that has not been attained, owing to the separation of the public from the media: we are conceived of more as consumers than as citizens.

However, that does not mean this will always be the case.

BIBLIOGRAPHY

Abercrombie, Nicholas and Brian Longhurst (1998) *Audiences* (London, Thousand Oaks and New Delhi: Sage).

Ahmed, Kamal (1999) 'That Friday feeling', *Media Guardian*, 27 September.

Altman, Rick (1999) *Film/Genre* (London: British Film Institute).

Anderson, Digby and Michael Mosbacher (1997) *The British Woman Today* (London: The Social Affairs Unit).

Ang, Ien (1991) *Desperately Seeking the Audience* (London and New York: Routledge).

Archer, Belinda (1997) 'Have I got ads for you?' *Media Guardian*, 21 April.

Archer, Belinda (1999) 'What's your problem?' *Media Guardian*, 13 September.

Armstrong, Stephen (1999) 'Bun fight', *Media Guardian*, 13 September.

Armstrong, Stephen (2000) 'It's a sad day for capitalism when a man can't fly a midget on a kite over Central Park', *Media Guardian*, 5 June.

Balio, Tino (ed.) (1976) *The American Film Industry* (Madison and London: University of Wisconsin Press).

Ball-Rokeach, Sandra J. and Melvyn De Fleur (1979) 'A dependency model of mass media effect', in G. Gumpert and R. Cathcart (eds), *Inter-Media*.

Barker, Martin (1997) 'The Newson Report: A case study in "common sense"' in Martin Barker and Julian Petley (eds), *Ill Effects*.

Barker, Martin and Julian Petley (eds) (1997) *Ill Effects: The Media/Violence Debate* (London and New York: Routledge).

Barnett, Steven and Ivor Gaber (2001) 'Politics under pressure', *Media Guardian*, 23 April.

Beckett, Andy (2000) 'Growing pains', *Guardian*, G2, 23 March.

Beder, Sharon (1997) *Global Spin: The Corporate Assault on Environmentalism* (Dartington: Green Books).

Benson, Richard (2000) 'Hip tipples', Guardian, G2, 12 May.

Berger, Arthur Asa (1992) *Popular Culture Genres: Theories and Texts* (London, Thousand Oaks and New Delhi: Sage).

BGH Bulletin (1999) http://www.foxbghsuit.com/index2.htm.

Bleifuss, Joel (1998) 'Personal care products may be carcinogenic', in Peter Phillips and Project Censored (eds), *Censored 1998*.

Blumler, J. G. and E. Katz (eds) (1974) *The Uses of Mass Communications* (London: Sage).

Borger, Julian (2000) 'Courage under fire', *Guardian*, 26 May.

Bourdieu, Pierre (1984) *Distinction: A Social Critique of the Judgement of Taste* (London and New York: Routledge).

Bourdieu, Pierre (1998) *On Television and Journalism* (London: Pluto Press).

Bowker, Julian (ed.) (1991) *Secondary Media Education* (London: British Film Institute).

223

rierley, Sean (1995) *The Advertising Handbook* (London and New York: Routledge).

Broadcasting Research Unit (1985) 'The public service idea in broadcasting' (London: Broadcasting Research Unit).

Buckingham, David (1998) 'Children and television: a critical overview of the research', in Roger Dickinson, Ramaswami Harindranath and Olga Linne (eds), *Approaches to Audiences*.

Campbell, Duncan (2000) *Media Guardian*, 15 May.

Campbell, Duncan (2000a) 'We must have naked breasts in this movie four times. I don't care how you do it. I just want naked breasts', *Guardian*, 'Friday Review', 30 June.

Carter, Meg (1999) 'Hey, good looking', *Media Guardian*, 29 November.

Carvel, John (1999) 'Blair's earlier learning centres', *Guardian*, 4 October.

Chambers, Iain (1990) *The Metropolitan Experience* (London: Routledge).

Chernin, Rowan (1998) 'Keep off the grass', *Loaded*, issue 45 (January).

Cohan, Steven and Ina Rae Hark (eds) (1993) *Screening the Male: Exploring Masculinities in Hollywood Cinema* (London and New York: Routledge).

Cohen, Phil (1992) 'Subcultural conflict and working-class community', in Stuart Hall, Dorothy Hobson, Andrew Lowe and Paul Willis (eds), *Culture, Media, Language*.

Conant, Michael (1976) 'The impact of the Paramount decrees', in Tino Balio (ed.), *The American Film Industry*.

Couldry, Nick (2000) 'Media organisations and non-media people', in James Curran (ed.), *Media Organisations in Society*.

Curran, James (1996) 'Mass media and democracy revisited', in James Curran and Michael Gurevitch (eds), *Mass Media and Society*.

Curran, James and Michael Gurevitch (eds) (1996, 2nd edn) *Mass Media and Society* (London: Arnold).

Curran, James and Jean Seaton (1991, 4th edn; 1997, 5th edn) *Power without Reponsibility* (London and New York: Routledge).

Curran, James (2000) *Media Organisations in Society* (London and New York: Arnold).

D. Chuck (with Yusuf Jah) (1997) *Fight the Power: Rap, Race and Reality* ((Edinburgh: Payback Press).

Darns, Tim (2001) 'Money's too tight to mention', *Screen International*, 6 March.

Davis, Jonathan (2000) 'Time to turn MEDIA digital', *Screen International*, 10 March.

de la Fuente, Anna Marie (1999) 'French kissing in the USA', *Screen International*, no. 1225 (10 September).

Dickinson, Roger, Ramaswami Harindranath and Olga Linne (eds) (1998) *Approaches to Audiences: A Reader* (London and New York: Arnold).

Diggines, Graham (2000) 'Shoppers upset by being spoilt for choice', *Guardian*, 24 April.

Dovey, Jon (1993) 'Old dogs and new tricks – access television in the UK', in Tony Dowmunt (ed.), *Channels of Resistance*.

Dowmunt, Tony (ed.) (1993) *Channels of Resistance: Global Television and Local Empowerment* (London: British Film Institute).

Drennan, Jackie (1999) 'Claims and counterclaims', *Guardian*, 17 April.

Dyer, Clair (2000) 'Four threats to the public's right to know', *Guardian*, 22 May.

Dyer, Gillian (1982) *Advertising as Communication* (London and New York: Routledge).

Dyer, Richard (1979) *Stars* (London: British Film Institute).

Dyer, Richard (1992) *Only Entertainment* (London and New York: Routledge).

Eagleton, Terry (1983) *Literary Theory: An Introduction* (Oxford: Blackwell).

Eco, Umberto (1985) 'Innovation and repetition', *Daedelus*, Fall 1985.

The Economist (1999) 'Rupert laid bare', *The Economist*, 20 March.

Elliott, P. (1974) 'Uses and gratifications research: a critique and a sociological alternative', in J. G. Blumler and E. Katz (eds), *The Uses of Mass Communications*.

Ellis, John (1982) *Visible Fictions: Cinema, Television, Video* (London, Boston, Melbourne and Henley: Routledge and Kegan Paul).

Elmer-Dewitt, Philip (1995) 'On a screen near you: Cyberporn', *Time International* vol. 146, no. 1 (3 July).

Elstein, David (2000) 'Time to end this shrill campaign', *Media Guardian*, 10 January.

Eminem (2000) *Angry Blonde* (New York: Regan Books).

Fiske, John (1996) 'Postmodernism and Television', in James Curran and Michael Gurevitch (eds), *Mass Media and Society*.

Fleetwood, Blake (1999) 'News at a price', *Guardian*, 17 September.

Fleming, Charles (1998) *High Concept: Don Simpson and the Hollywood Culture of Excess* (London: Bloomsbury).

Foot, Paul (2000) 'Betrayal of the Trust', *Guardian*, 27 June.

Fountain, Alan (1981) 'Questions of democracy and control in film culture', in Rod Stoneman and Hilary Thompson (eds), *Catalogue: British Film Institute Productions 79/80*.

Frith, Simon (1988) *Music for Pleasure* (Cambridge: Polity Press).

Frith, Simon (1993) 'Youth/Music/Television', in Simon Frith, Andrew Goodwin, and Lawrence Grossberg (eds), *Sound and Vision*.

Frith, Simon, Andrew Goodwin and Lawrence Grossberg (eds) (1993) *Sound and Vision – The Music Video Reader* (London and New York: Routledge).

Frosch, Dan (2001) 'Award Tour', *The Source*, no. 139 (April).

Gauntlett, David (1998) 'Ten things wrong with the "effects model"', in Roger Dickinson, Ramaswami Harindranath and Olga Linne (eds), *Approaches to Audiences*.

Gelder, Ken (ed.) (2000) *The Horror Reader* (London and New York: Routledge).

Gentleman, Amelia (1999) 'Horror videos inspired student killers', *Guardian*, 8 May.

Gentleman, Amelia and Duncan Campbell (1999) 'The unknown killer', *Media Guardian*, 16 June.

George, Nelson (1999) *Hip Hop America* (New York, London, Ringwood, Toronto, Auckland: Penguin Books).

Geraghty, Christine (1991) *Women and Soap Opera: A Study of Prime Time Soaps* (Cambridge: Polity Press).

Geraghty, Christine (1998) 'Audiences and "ethnography": questions of practice', in Christine Geraghty and David Lusted (eds), *The Television Studies Book*.

Geraghty, Christine and David Lusted (eds) (1998) *The Television Studies Book* (London and New York: Arnold).

Gibson, Janine (1999) 'Multicultural diversity "not shown on TV"', *Guardian*, 8 December.

Gillett, Charlie (1983, revised edn) *The Sound of the City* (London: Souvenir Press).

Gitlin, Todd (1994, revised edn) *Inside Prime Time* (London: Routledge).

Glaister, Don (1998) 'World market dances to the same pop tune', *Guardian*, 6 June.

Gledhill, Christine and Linda Williams (eds) (2000) *Reinventing Film Studies* (London and New York: Arnold).

Goldsmiths Media Group (2000) 'Media organisations in society: central issues', in James Curran (ed.), *Media Organisations in Society*.

Gomery, Douglas (1998) '"A major presence in all of the world's important markets": The globalization of Hollywood in the 1990s', in Steve Neale and Murray Smith (eds), *Contemporary Hollywood Cinema*.

Goodman, Fred (1997) *The Mansion on the Hill: Dylan, Young, Geffen, Springsteen and the Head-On Collision of Rock and Commerce* (London: Jonathan Cape).

Goodrige, Mike (1999) 'Blair Witch: the International Project', *Screen International*, 1 October.

Goodrige, Mike and Patrick Frater (2001) 'Studios stare into p&a black hole', *Screen International*, 13 April.

Goodwin, Peter (1999) 'The Role of the State', in Jane Stokes and Anna Reading (eds), *The Media in Britain*.

Grant, Barry Keith (2000) 'Second thoughts on double features: revisiting the cult film', in Xavier Mendik and Graeme Harper (eds), *Unruly Pleasures*.

Gray, Ann and Jim McGuigan (eds) (1993) *Studying Culture: An Introductory Reader* (London: Edward Arnold).

Green, Michael (1995) 'Radio 4 Scheduling', in Andrea Millwood Hargrave, *The Scheduling Game*.

Greenslade, Roy (2000) 'Do we want to go large?' *Media Guardian*, 22 May.

Gumpert, Gary and Robert Cathcart (eds) (1979) *Inter-Media: Interpersonal Communication in the Media* (New York: Oxford University Press).

Habermas, Jürgen (1989) *The Structural Transformation of the Public Sphere* (Cambridge: Polity).

Hall, John (2000) 'The 24-hour garage!' *New Musical Express*, 22 April.

Hall, Stuart (1992) 'Encoding/decoding', in Stuart Hall, Dorothy Hobson, Andrew Lowe and Paul Willis (eds), *Culture, Media, Language*.

Hall, Stuart, Dorothy Hobson, Andrew Lowe and Paul Willis (eds) (reprinted 1992) *Culture, Media, Language* (London: Routledge).

Hall, Stuart (1992) 'Encoding/decoding', in Stuart Hall, Dorothy Hobson, Andrew Lowe and Paul Willis (eds), *Culture, Media, Language* (London: Routledge).

Handy, Bruce, Georgia Harbison and Jeffrey Resner (1996) '101 Movie tie-ins: with merchandising money rivaling its box-office take, Hollywood is saying, "Attention shippers!"' *Time*, 2 December.

Hanke, Robert (1998) '"Yo quiero mi MTV!"' in Thomas Swiss, John Sloop and Andrew Herman (eds), *Mapping the Beat*.

Hardy, Phil and Dave Laing (1990) *The Faber Companion to 20th-Century Popular Music* (London: Faber and Faber).

Hazleton, John (2000) 'Drink this! It's great!!!' *Screen International*, no. 1259, 19 May.

Hebdige, Dick (reprinted 1988) *Subculture – The Meaning of Style* (London and New York: Routledge).

Herman, Edward and Noam Chomsky (1986) *Manufacturing Consent* (New York: Pantheon).

Herrnstein, Richard J. and Charles Murray (1996) *The Bell Curve* (New York: Simon and Schuster).

Holland, Patricia (1997) *The Television Handbook* (London and New York: Routledge).

Hood, Stuart (ed.) (1994) *Behind the Screens: The Structure of British Television in the Nineties* (London: Lawrence & Wishart).

Howitt, Peter (1998) 'Lose the tube train, cut the leading man – and by the way, *who wrote the script?*' *Saturday Guardian*, 2 May.

Interactive movie database   www.imdb.com.

James, Martin (1997) *State of Bass – Jungle: The Story So Far* (London and Basingstoke: Boxtree).

Jameson, Frederic (1993) 'Postmodernism and consumer society', in Ann Gray and Jim McGuigan (eds), *Studying Culture*.

Jeffries, Stuart (1998) 'Liberté, égalité, médiocrité', *Guardian*, 24 July.

Jones, Rupert (2000) 'Fill your booties with investments for baby', *Guardian* 'Jobs & Money', 27 May.

Kapuscinski, Ryszard (1999) 'We live in a global media village. So why doesn't this woman give a damn what's on the news?' *Media Guardian*, 16 August.

Kemp, Stuart (1999) 'Oh no, they've bought Kenny', *Screen International*, no. 1226 (17 September).

Kendzior, Sarah (1999) 'Every Witch way', *Guardian*, 'Friday Review', 8 October.

Kent, Nicholas (1991) *Naked Hollywood: Money, Power and the Movies* (London: BBC).

Kermode, Mark and Julian Petley (1997) 'Road rage', *Sight and Sound*, vol. 7, issue 6 (July).

Kerr, Paul (1979) 'Out of what past? Notes on the B 'film noir', in Alain Silver and James Ursini (eds), *Film Noir Reader*.

Klein, Naomi (2001) *No Logo* (London: Flamingo).

Kotler, Philip (1980) *Marketing Management: Analysis, Planning and Control* (Englewood Cliffs: Prentice-Hall International).

Kureishi, Hanif and Jon Savage (eds) (1995) *The Faber Book of Pop* (London: Faber and Faber).

Lacey, Nick (2000) *Narrative and Genre* (Basingstoke: Palgrave).

Lacey, Nick (2000a) 'Palace Pictures and Neil Jordan: not British Cinema?' (itp, 36 Hospital Road, Riddlesden, West Yorkshire: Film Reader 2).

Lall, Bhuvan (2000) 'Murdoch pumps in $100m, boosts India's bid to be high-tech centre', *Screen International*, 17 March).

Lehman, Peter (1993) '"Don't Blame this on a Girl": Female rape-revenge films' in Steven Cohan and Ina Rae Hark (eds), *Screening the Male*.

Lewis, Miles Marshall (1998) 'Bad as bad can be', Index of Censorship – *Smashed Hit*, vol. 27, no. 6.

Lukk, Tiiu (1996) *Movie Marketing: Opening the Picture and Giving it Legs* (Los Angeles: Silman-James Press).

Maltby, Richard (1995) *Hollywood Cinema* (Oxford: Blackwell).

Maltby, Richard (1998) '"Nobody knows everything": Post-classical historiographies and consolidated entertainment', in Steve Neale and Murray Smith (eds), *Contemporary Hollywood Cinema*.

Maltby, Richard (1998a) '"D" for disgusting: American culture and English criticism', in Geoffrey Nowell-Smith and Steven Ricci (eds), *Hollywood and Europe*.

Marshall, Kingsley (1997) 'Roni Size', *Eternity Magazine*, issue 17.

Martin, Gavin (2000) 'Anarchy in the UK', *Uncut*, 37 (June).

Mathews, Tom Dewe (1994) *Censored – What They Didn't Allow You to See, and Why: The Story of Film Censorship in Britain* (London: Chatto & Windus).

Mathews, Tom Dewe (1998) 'See the movie. Ogle the star. Buy the frock. (And you thought merchandising started with *Star Wars*!)', *Guardian*, 'Review', 27 November.

Mathews, Tom Dewe (1999) 'The tough gets going', *Guardian*, 'Review', 26 March.

McClellan, Jim (2000) 'Between a dot and an ad place', *Guardian Online*, 4 May.

McCrystal, Cal (1999) 'Secret stories', *Media Guardian*, 5 July.

The McLibel Trial (1999) http://www.mcspotlight.org/case/index.html.

McNair, Brian (1999, 3rd edn) *News and Journalism in the UK* (London and New York: Routledge).

Medved, Michael (1992) *Hollywood vs America: Popular Culture and the War on Traditional Values* (New York).

Mendik, Xavier and Graeme Harper (eds) (2000) *Unruly Pleasures: The Cult Film and its Critics* (Guildford: Fab Press).

Millwood Hargrave, Andrea (1995) *The Scheduling Game – Audience Attitudes to Broadcast Scheduling* (London, Paris, Rome: John Libbey).

Minns, Adam (1999) 'Four goes East', *Screen International*, no. 1233 (5 November).

Monaco, James (1979) *American Film Now: The People, the Power, the Money, the Movies* (New York, London and Scarborough, Ontario: New American Library).

Morgan, Claire (1997) 'Genre by genre', *DJ*, no. 5, vol. 2 (20 December 1997–17 January 1998).

Morley, David (1992) *Television Audiences and Cultural Studies* (London and New York: Routledge).

Murdock, Graham (1994) 'Money talks: broadcasting finance and public culture', in Stuart Hood (ed.), *Behind the Screens*.

Music Biz, The (1995) FfP for the BBC.

Myers, Greg (1999) *Ad Worlds: Brands, Media, Audiences* (London and New York: Arnold).

Nathan, Ian (1996) 'Matthew McConaughey – Unstoppable', *Empire 88*, 1996.

Neale, Steve and Murray Smith (eds) (1998) *Contemporary Hollywood Cinema* (London and New York: Routledge).

Nichols, Bill (ed.) (1986) *Movies and Methods*, vol. 2 (Berkeley and Los Angeles: University of California Press).

Nowell-Smith, Geoffrey and Steven Ricci (1998) *Hollywood and Europe: Economics, Culture, National Identity, 1945–95* (London: British Film Institute).

Nuzum, Eric (1998) 'Music Censorship: Elvis to Ice-T', *REV*, June.

Osborne, Ben (1997) 'Speed garage – is it hip or is it just hype?' *Guardian*, tabloid, 19 December.

O'Sullivan, Tim, John Hartley, Danny Saunders, Martin Montgomery and John Fiske (1994, 2nd edn) *Key Concepts in Communication and Cultural studies* (London and New York: Routledge).

Pandya, Nick (1999) 'Soft welling soap brings hard profit', *Guardian*, 2 October.

Peak, Steve and Paul Fisher (eds) (1999) *The Media Guide 2000* (London: Fourth Estate).

Perlmutter, Tom (1993) 'A Canadian story – An international lesson', in Tony Dowmunt (ed.), *Channels of Resistance*.

Petley, Julian (1989) *Landmarks* (London: British Council).

Petley, Julian (1998) 'Coverage lite for McLibel issues', *Free Press*, no. 106 (Sept.–Oct.).

Petley, Julian (1999) 'The regulation of media content', in Jane Stokes and Anna Reading (eds), *The Media in Britain*.

Phillips, Peter (1998) 'Self-censorship and the homogeneity of the media elite', in Peter Phillips and Project Censored (eds), *Censored 1998*.

Phillips, Peter and Project Censored (eds) (1998) *Censored 1998: The News that Didn't Make the News* (New York: Seven Stories Press).

Pilger, John (1999) 'Acts of murder', *Guardian*, 18 May.

Reading, Anna (1999) 'Campaigns to change the media', in Jane Stokes and Anna Reading (eds), *The Media in Britain*.

Reynolds, Simon (1995) 'Rage to live: 'ardkore techno', in Hanif Kureishi and Jon Savage (eds), *Faber Book of Pop*.

Rodley, Chris (1996) 'Crash', *Sight and Sound*, vol. 6, issue 6 (June).

Rothenberg, Randall (1998) 'Bye-Bye' (Wired website, archive).

Sahlins, Marshall (1985) *Islands of History* (Chicago: University of Chicago Press).

Sainsbury, Peter (1981) 'Production policy', in Rod Stoneman and Hilary Thompson (eds), *Catalogue: British Film Institute Productions '79/80*.

Sandall, David (1995) 'Underground rumblings', *Sunday Times*, 'Culture', 1 January.

Sanjek, David (1998) 'Popular music and the synergy of corporate culture', in Thomas Swiss, John Sloop and Andrew Herman (eds), *Mapping the Beat*.

Sanjek, David (2000) 'Fans' notes: the horror film fanzine', in Ken Gelder (ed.), *The Horror Reader*.

Sayles, John (1995) 'How to stay independent', *Index on Censorship*, vol. 24, no. 6 (1995).

Schechter, Danny (1998) 'Introduction', in Peter Phillips and Project Censored (eds), *Censored 1998*.

Selby, Keith and Ron Cowdery (1995) *How to Study Television* (Basingstoke and London: Macmillan Press).

Shamus, James (1998) 'To the rear of the back end: the economics of independent cinema', in Steve Neale and Murray Smith (eds), *Contemporary Hollywood Cinema*.

Shipman, David (1982) *The Story of Cinema*, Volume 1: *From the Beginnings to 'Gone with the Wind'* (London: Hodder and Stoughton).

Shohat, Ella and Robert Stam (1994) *Unthinking Eurocentrism: Multiculturalism and the Media* (London and New York: Routledge).

Shrimsley, Robert (1999) 'Thatcher drinks to unity as Hague invites her to meet his family', *Electronic Telegraph*, 4 October.

Silver, Alain and James Ursini (eds) (1999, 5th edn) *Film Noir Reader* (New York: Limelight Editions).

Sinclair, Iain (1999) *Crash* (London: British Film Insitute).

Smith, Giles (1994) 'Michael defeat leaves Sony's image clean', *Independent*, 22 June.

Sparks, Colin (1999) 'The Press', in Jane Stokes and Anna Reading (eds), *The Media in Britain*.

Stables, Kate (2000) 'Indie exposure', *Sight and Sound*, vol. 10, issue 4 (April).

Stokes, Jane (1999a) 'The structure of British media industries', in Jane Stokes and Anna Reading (eds), *The Media in Britain*.

Stokes, Jane (1999b) 'Use it or lose it: sex, sexuality and sexual health in magazines for girls', in Jane Stokes and Anna Reading (eds), *The Media in Britain*.

Stokes, Jane and Anna Reading (eds) (1999) *The Media in Britain: Current Debates and Developments* (Basingstoke: Macmillan).

Stone, Jennie (2000) *Global Affairs on British Terrestrial Television, 1989–1999* (Third World and Environmental Broadcasting Project).

Stoneman, Rod and Hilary Thompson (1981) *Catalogue: British Film Institute Productions '79/80 – The New Social Function of Cinema* (London: British Film Institute).

Strinati, Dominic (2000) *An Introduction to Studying Popular Culture* (London and New York: Routledge).

Swiss, Thomas, John Sloop and Andrew Herman (1998) *Mapping the Beat – Popular Music and Contemporary Theory* (Malden and Oxford: Blackwell).

Teather, David (1999) 'Unreal thing takes on the real thing', *Guardian*, 11 August.

Teather, David (2000) 'Emap launches C4 web deal', *Guardian*, 31 May.

Tookey, Christopher (1996) 'Morality dies in the twisted wreckage', *Daily Mail*, 9 November.

Toolis, Kevin (2000) 'Why Ulster got spiked', *Media Guardian*, 24 April.

Toop, David (2000, 3rd edn) *Rap Attack 3: African Rap to Global Hip Hop* (London: Serpent's Tail).

Tulloch, John and Henry Jenkins (1995) *Science Fiction Audiences: Watching Doctor Who and Star Trek* (London and New York: Routledge).

Tweney, Chris (1997) 'Boomlay-Boomlay-Boom' (Boston Phoenix website).

Vidal, John (1999) 'Monsanto – we forgot to listen', *Guardian*, 7 October.

Watney, Richard (2000) 'Thinking globally but acting locally', *Guardian*, 'Jobs and Money', 24 June.

Watson, James (1998) *Media Communication: An Introduction to Theory and Process* (Basingstoke and London: Macmillan Press).

Watson, James and Anne Hill (1993, 4th edn) *A Dictionary of Communication and Media Studies* (London and New York: Arnold).

Watt, Brigid (1994) 'TV Lies about us in our Infancy', *Media Education Journal*, issue 16 (Summer).

Watts, Jonathan (2000) 'Sony's dream weaver', *Guardian*, 26 May.

Wells, Matt (2000) 'A little local difficulty', *Media Guardian*, 1 May.

Wells, Matt (2000a) '"It's been a terrible week for newspapers"', *Media Guardian*, 15 May.

Wells, Matt (2000b) 'More Matthew, less Melvyn for ITV as public service role is questioned', *Guardian*, 1 June.

Wells, Matt (2000c) 'Naïve Nick flounders before media', *Guardian*, 19 August.

Wells, Matt (2001) 'Arts industry worth £100bn', *Guardian*, 14 March.

Wernick, Andrew (1997) *Promotional Culture: Advertising, Ideology, and Symbolic Expression* (London: Sage).

White, Jim (2000) 'BBC's sporting future riding on Rio soap opera', *Guardian* 'Sport', 8 January.

White, Michael (1999) 'Dobson will now run to stop Archer', *Guardian*, 4 October.

Whiteley, Sheila (1998) 'Repressive representations: patriarchy and femininities in rock music of the counterculture', in Thomas Swiss, John Sloop and Andrew Herman (eds), *Mapping the Beat*.

Williams, Granville (1998) 'How Monsanto is massaging its message', *Free Press*, no. 107 (Nov.–Dec.).

Williams, Raymond (1976) *Communications* (Harmondsworth: Penguin).

Williamson, Judith (1978) *Decoding Advertisements* (London: Boyars).

Winship, Janice (1992) 'Sexuality for sale', in Stuart Hall, Dorothy Hobson, Andrew Lowe and Paul Willis (eds), *Culture, Media, Language*.

Wittstock, Melinda (1998) 'For those watching in black and white . . .', *Guardian*, 2 March.

Wollen, Peter (1986) 'Godard and Counter Cinema: "Vent d'Est"', in Bill Nichols (ed.), *Movies and Methods*.

Woodward, Will (2000) 'Single-sex lessons to counter lad culture', *Guardian*, 21 August.

Wyatt, Justin (1994) *High Concept: Movies and Marketing in Hollywood* (Austin: University of Texas Press).

INDEX